ELEANOR RATHBONE

WOMEN OF IDEAS

Series Editor: Liz Stanley
Editorial Board: Cynthia Enloe and Dale Spender

This series consists of short study guides designed to introduce readers to the life, times and work of key women of ideas. The emphasis is very much on the ideas of these women and the political and intellectual circumstances in which their work has been formulated and presented.

The women featured are both contemporary and historical thinkers from a range of disciplines including sociology, economics, psychoanalysis, philosophy, anthropology, history and politics. The series aims to: provide succinct introductions to the ideas of women who have been recognised as major theorists; make the work of major women of ideas accessible to students as well as to the general reader; and appraise and reappraise the work of neglected women of ideas and give them a wider profile.

Each book provides a full bibliography of its subject's writings (where they are easily available) so that readers can continue their study using primary sources.

Books in the series include:

Eleanor Rathbone
Johanna Alberti

Simone de Beauvoir
Mary Evans

Christine Delphy
Stevi Jackson

ELEANOR RATHBONE

Johanna Alberti

SAGE Publications
London • Thousand Oaks • New Delhi

First published 1996

SAGE Publications Ltd
6 Bonhill Street
London EC2A 4PU

SAGE Publications Inc
2455 Teller Road
Thousand Oaks, CA 91320

SAGE Publications India Pvt Ltd
32, M-Block Market
Greater Kailash – I
New Delhi 110 048

British Library Cataloguing in Publication data

A catalogue record for this book is available
from the British Library.

ISBN 0 8039 8875 3
ISBN 0 8039 8876 1 (pbk)

Library of Congress catalog record available

Typeset by M Rules
Printed in Great Britain by Hartnolls Ltd, Bodmin, Cornwall

Contents

Preface

This series introduces readers to the life, times and work of key 'women of ideas' whose work has influenced people and helped change the times in which they lived. Some people might claim that there are few significant women thinkers. However, a litany of the women whose work is discussed in the first titles to be published gives the lie to this: Simone de Beauvoir, Zora Neale Hurston, Simone Weil, Olive Schreiner, Hannah Arendt, Eleanor Rathbone, Christine Delphy, Adrienne Rich, Audre Lorde, to be followed by Rosa Luxemburg, Melanie Klein, Mary Wollstonecraft, Andrea Dworkin and Catherine MacKinnon, Margaret Mead, Charlotte Perkins Gilman, Helene Cixous, Luce Irigaray and Julia Kristeva, Alexandra Kollontai, and others of a similar stature.

Every reader will want to add their own women of ideas to this list – which proves the point. There *are* major bodies of ideas and theories which women have originated; there *are* significant women thinkers; *but* women's intellectual work, like women's other work, is not taken so seriously nor evaluated so highly as men's. It may be men's perceptions of originality and importance which have shaped the definition and evaluation of women's work, but this does not constitute (nor is there any reason to regard it as) a definitive or universal standard. *Women of Ideas* exists to help change such perceptions, by taking women's past and present production of ideas seriously, and by introducing them to a wide new audience. *Women of Ideas* titles include women whose work is well-known from both the past and the present, and also those unfamiliar to modern readers although renowned among their contemporaries. The aim is to make their work accessible by drawing out of what is a frequently diverse and complex body of writing the central ideas and key themes, not least by locating these in relation to the intellectual, political and personal milieux in which this work originated.

Do women of ideas have 'another voice', one distinctive and different from that of men of ideas? or is this an essentialist claim and are ideas at basis unsexed? Certainly women's ideas are differently positioned with regard to their perception and evaluation. It is still a case of women having to be twice as good to be seen as half as good as men, for the apparatus of knowledge/power is configured in ways which do not readily accord women and their work the same status as that of men. However, this does not necessarily mean either that the ideas produced by women are significantly different in kind or, even if they presently are, that this is anything other than the product of the workings of social systems which systematically differentiate between the sexes, with such differences disappearing in an equal and just society. *Women of Ideas* is, among other things, a means of standing back and taking the longer view on such questions, with the series as a whole constituting one of the means of evaluating the 'difference debates', as its authors explore the contributions made by the particular women of ideas that individual titles focus upon.

Popularly, ideas are treated as the product of 'genius', of individual minds inventing what is startlingly original – and absolutely unique to them. However, within feminist thought a different approach is taken, seeing ideas as social products rather than uniquely individual ones, as collective thoughts albeit uttered in the distinctive voices of particular individuals. Here there is a recognition that ideas have a 'historical moment' when they assume their greatest significance – and that 'significance' is neither transhistorical nor transnational, but is rather temporally and culturally specific, so that the 'great ideas' of one time and place can seem commonplace or ridiculous in others. Here too the cyclical and social nature of the life of ideas is recognised, in which 'new' ideas may in fact be 'old' ones in up-to-date language and expression. And, perhaps most importantly for the *Women of Ideas* series, there is also a recognition of the frequently *gendered* basis of the judgements of the 'significance' and 'importance' of ideas and bodies of work.

The title of the series is taken from Dale Spender's (1982) *Women of Ideas, and What Men have Done to Them.* 'What men have done to them' is shorthand for a complex process in which bodies of ideas 'vanish', not so much by being deliberately suppressed (although this has happened) as by being trivialised, misrepresented, excluded from the canon of what is deemed good, significant, great. In addition to these gatekeeping processes, there are other broader factors at work. Times change, intellectual fashion changes also. One product of this is the often very different interpretation and understanding of bodies of ideas over time: when looked at from different – unsympathetic – viewpoints, then dramatic shifts in the representation of these can occur. Such shifts in intellectual fashion sometimes occur in their own right, while at other times they are related to wider social, economic and political changes in the world. Wars, the expansion and then contraction of colonialism, revolutions, all have had an effect on what people think, how ideas are interpreted and related to, which ideas are seen as important and which outmoded.

'Women of ideas' of course need not necessarily position themselves as feminists nor prioritise concern with gender. The terms 'feminist' and 'woman' are by no means to be collapsed, but they are not to be treated as binaries either. Some major female thinkers focus on the human condition in order to rethink the nature of reality and thus of 'knowledge'. In doing so they also re-position the nature of ideas. Each of the women featured has produced ideas towards that greater whole which is a more comprehensive rethinking of the nature of knowledge. These women have produced ideas which form bodies of systematic thought, as they have pursued trains of thought over the course of their individual lives. This is not to suggest that such ideas give expression to a 'universal essence' in the way Plato proposed. It is instead to reject rigidly dividing 'realist' from 'idealist' from 'materialist', recognising that aspects of these supposedly categorical distinctions can be brought together to illuminate the extraordinarily complex and fascinating process by which ideas are produced and reproduced in particular intellectual, cultural and historical contexts.

The *Women of Ideas* series is, then, concerned with the 'history of ideas'. It recognises the importance of the 'particular voice' as well as the shared context; it insists on the relevance of the thinker as well as that which is thought. It is concerned with individuals in their relation to wider collectivities and contexts, and it focuses upon the role of particular women of ideas without 'personifying' or individualising the processes by which ideas are shaped, produced, changed. It emphasises that there is a history of *'mentalités collectives'*, recognising the continuum between the everyday and the elite, between 'commonsense' and 'high theory'. Ideas have most meaning in their use, in the way they influence other minds and wider social processes, something which occurs by challenging and changing patterns of understanding. As well as looking at the impact of particular women of ideas, the series brings their work to a wider audience, to encourage a greater understanding of the contribution of these women to the way that we *do* think – and also the way that we perhaps *should* think – about knowledge and the human condition.

Liz Stanley

Introduction

Eleanor Rathbone (1872–1946) was a suffragist in the reign of Queen Victoria who became a Member of Parliament at the first election in which all women could vote in Britain. She is the one feminist who was active in the Victorian women's movement and then in the parliamentary political arena within which that movement had sought to give women a place and power. Her ideas therefore provide us with a way of tracing the thinking of a Victorian feminist through the Edwardian suffrage era to the period after the First World War when the women's movement seemed to disappear.

Feminist historians have devoted much attention to the Victorian women's movement. Eleanor Rathbone's life demonstrates what some of the results of that movement were. She was given the tools to move at least some distance away from the Victorian mould because she benefited from one of the earliest campaigns of the Victorian women's movement for higher education, becoming a student at Somerville College, Oxford. Her years of study provided her with intellectual confidence, but she rejected the possibility of staying in academic life, disapproving of the detachment from the world that such a life would have offered. Instead she moved into the world of social action.

Rathbone chose social and political engagement because the wrongs of the world shouted in her ears (Stocks, 1949: 53). Her aim from the first was to give herself the satisfaction of being able to achieve change in a visible and tangible way. This discourse had its roots firmly in her Victorian heritage. Her early life and thought were strongly influenced by her father, who devoted his wealth and his energies to public and political activities such as the establishment of district nursing, the foundation of Liverpool University and the relief of poverty. But Eleanor's work as a visitor for the Liverpool Central Relief Society led her to desire to change not just people's lives but the structure of the organisation. Examination of her ideas provides us with a sense of the way one feminist moved from concern with the lives of individuals to a more general political analysis of social deprivation.

The pattern of Rathbone's thinking before the First World War gives us a tool for the exploration of the interconnections between feminism and other Edwardian discourses of the public and the private. Like other Victorian feminists, her feminism was rooted in social action and the experience of living in a community of like-minded women. Through the Victoria Women's Settlement she met Elizabeth Macadam, who became her lifetime's companion. Their first public co-operation was on a scheme to enable social workers in the Liverpool area to be trained and educated at the Liverpool School of Social Studies and Training for Social Work.

Rathbone's understanding of suffrage illuminates the links between social action and feminism. She rejected the concept that women could fulfil their role as citizens without the vote, and believed that women could and should play a full role in British political democracy. She wanted women to be able to exercise political power partly because she herself desired agency. The path which she took towards political power throws light on the genesis of women's participation in political structures. Her move from Victorian social work to political action was facilitated by her work as a social investigator: her involvement in social investigation gave her a platform from which to begin to argue a political case. Her early writings are reports on the result of social investigations and the recommendations gradually move in the direction of state intervention. She became the first woman city councillor in Liverpool, seeing local politics as a place where women could prove themselves and also bring pressure to bear for the recognition of their need for the vote.

During her lifetime Rathbone was best known as a combative campaigner for family allowances. From her observations of poverty in the working-class homes she visited, she concluded that the main source of such deprivation was inadequate wages for families with children. This unsurprising analysis came together with another strand in her thinking which had begun with a theoretical survey of women's low wages she had made in 1902. Her solution to both these evils was the payment by the state of allowances to mothers and children. She argued that equal pay should follow rather than precede such payment. Her thinking as a feminist on this issue was inextricable from her determination to tackle poverty.

An examination of the continuity and change in Rathbone's ideas gives us a glimpse into the way feminism can seem to disappear in a hostile context. The dispersal of the women's movement in the interwar period has not received much attention from historians, and Rathbone's history gives us some purchase on what that dispersal meant to an active political feminist. The suffrage movement brought her in contact with the deeply ingrained misogyny of the society in which she lived. Her awareness of this hostility and of the precarious nature of women's position within the political structures puts into perspective the lack of political change in this period. Because she was desperate to ameliorate suffering, she was willing to compromise, hoping that attitudes would gradually change, but unprepared to wait for such change to take place before some action was taken. Her thinking provides us with one perspective on the way feminist power was exercised through the democratic process. She spoke as a feminist and saw herself as a representative of the interests of women, especially working-class married women. The instability of this position is documented in her speeches as an MP.

Questions of cultural identity are in the forefront of feminist ideas today, and Rathbone's ideas on citizenship were firmly embedded in a national identity. Citizens should serve their country, she asserted: this was part of a deeply felt patriotism shaped by living through two wars which she understood to have been fought in defence of democracy and liberty. Her faith in the basic goodness of the British people was the rhetorical basis from which she persistently criticised the British government. When faced with Indian women's perspective on British imperialism she was perplexed, and a study of her response is rich in information about British cultural imperialism.

Finally, Rathbone's thinking provides fascinating material on the subtlety and fluidity of feminist ideas on equality and difference. She did not put forward an essentialist case for women's influence within the political structures, but she did express a hope that women might, because of their experiences in life, have 'a specially good reception' of the 'wave-length to suffering' (Rathbone, 1929: 48). This construction released her to argue a passionate case for those she felt were suffering most in the world: child brides in India, children living in poverty, refugees from Nazism. Working within a patriarchal context, she did not doubt the validity of her own analysis and never lost her inner conviction that she spoke as a feminist.

Eleanor Rathbone: a life

A life of Eleanor Rathbone is interwoven into the exploration of her ideas in this volume: there is no way in which they could have been separated. At the end of this chapter a list of dates is intended to give a framework of reference for her life. At present there is only one extant biography of Rathbone, written by her friend Mary Stocks soon after her death and published in 1949. It is out of print. However, Susan Pedersen is working on a biography: her articles are described in the annotated key texts at the end of the book.

What is most striking about Eleanor Rathbone is the extent of her political activities. She was above all a campaigner and this makes the attempt to provide a clear summary of her ideas a frustrating task. As Antoinette Burton has pointed out, middle-class British feminists 'occupied a place at the crossroads of several interlocking identities', as feminist, British and bourgeois (Burton, 1991: 69). Rathbone's identities are blurred, and the shape of her ideas made more elusive by her insistence on remedies rather than theories. She took as a basic premise that there *are* solutions to problems, that it is possible to make the world a better place. She wrote mainly to persuade her readers to *do* something. Reading Rathbone has put me in touch with the ethical roots of my own political beliefs, and her life reminds me of my early optimism about political efficacy. These bubble dreams have been pricked by 16 years of reactionary government and international instability causing suffering to millions. This is very similar to the context in which Eleanor Rathbone lived, and her energy has been a goad, her refusal to abandon hope an inspiration.

The variety of Eleanor Rathbone's activities also makes the task of placing her ideas in relation to other political and intellectual ideas of the time a daunting task. What follows here is a brief and simplified outline of the ideological context in which she operated, together with the references to the annotated bibliography which give more detailed analysis of that context.

Chapter 1 (Heritage) looks at the ideas and values which formed Rathbone's Victorian inheritance. She did not subscribe to any one political philosophy, turning away impatiently from the 'great questions' soon after her university days to the immediacy of social work. But she held to a constant belief in the primacy of an ethical politics, and in the adaptability of human beings to control and improve their economic environment. As a student she was taught by D.G. Ritchie, whose ideas were influential in the development of what has become known as the 'new liberalism' (Freeden, 1978). The new liberals conformed to current ideas about the possibility of establishing explanations for human behaviour from empirical observation. Rathbone became a social investigator of the lives of the poor of Liverpool, and worked with organisations such as the Women's Co-operative Guild in a survey of the living standards of widows under the Poor Law. Her main motivation, however, was always one of persuasion rather than discovery. She moved into the Victorian women's movement, in particular the suffrage and settlement movements. These structures offered her 'a model of alternative political and personal behaviour which valued a pragmatic humanitarianism, whatever its limitations, over the politics of domination' (Levine, 1987: 161).

Chapter 2 (The Public and the Private, 1909–19) focuses on her ideas about the state and describes her involvement in social work up to the end of the First World War. Rathbone's acceptance of state intervention was informed by an ideology which was close to the ideas formulated by Ritchie and the 'new liberals' who were influential in giving ideological backing to the social welfare legislation of the Liberal Party in the first two decades of the twentieth century. Anna Davin has argued that, while state intervention was becoming more acceptable over this period, it was contained within an individualist ideology which stressed the mother's role in the creation of a healthy workforce (Davin, 1978).

In the period before 1914 the question of the role of the state in relieving the oppression of both class and gender was a controversial one (Thane, 1984; Lewis, 1986; Stoate, 1988; Lewis, 1991a). Crucial to this debate were understandings of the family (Dyhouse, 1989; Land, 1990; Lewis, 1991b). Feminists wanted to see change, especially in the economic deprivation which women and children suffered, and there was a wide variety of solutions offered. Philippa Levine has pointed out that feminists experienced bewilderment and contradiction in seeking solutions to such problems, and she warns us to recognise that: 'Whilst feminists at this time were clear in their articulation of the gendered ills of their society, they were still within its grasp as the constructors and consumers of their culture' (Levine, 1990: 176).

Recent studies of the women's suffrage movement have challenged Les Garner's conclusion that 'suffragism had a limited concept of equality based on entry into the male world' (Garner, 1984: 114; see also Holton, 1986; Kent, 1987; Rubinstein, 1991; Vellacott, 1993). The feminist demand for the vote contained within it an implicit and often explicit belief in the power of legislation to effect social change. Rathbone shared this faith: her understanding of suffrage was close, if not identical to, the demand for a 'feminised democracy' identified by Sandra Holton (1986). She devoted her life to achieving political change first as city councillor from 1909 to 1935, and then as an MP from 1929 until her death in 1946. She was at her most buoyant about the possibility of change through Parliamentary means in the period 1909–18 because of the strength and political influence of the suffrage movement and because of what she saw as the positive influence of the war. The way war undermined the position of women has been analysed by Lucy Bland (1985) and also by Susan Kingsley Kent (1993) who has argued that 'The Great War shattered the category of "women" in ways that may have made it impossible, before the 1960s, for feminists to effectively recover their movement, its goals and its critique of the gender system' (p. 143). Susan Pedersen has argued that the fault at the heart of Rathbone's wartime optimism was the acceptance of a construction of the family with the man as the breadwinner (Pedersen, 1990).

Chapter 3 (Equality and Difference, 1911–29) is concerned with Rathbone's ideas about gender equality and difference, and also her understanding of the differences between women. Rathbone's name is firmly associated in studies of feminism with her elaboration of what became known as the 'New Feminism'. The ideology so labelled was not in fact new (Holton, 1986; Black, 1989). The factors behind its reappearance in the interwar period and its effects have been much debated in recent years (Lewis, 1975; Fleming, 1986; Pugh, 1992). Recent assessments of the results of the challenge to male paradigms which was the professed ambition of New Feminists have concentrated on failure. Susan Pedersen has written a telling and 'cautionary tale about the dangers of the adoption of difference-based arguments in a world where women lack significant institutional or economic power' (1989: 106). Most recently, Susan Kingsley Kent has argued that the new feminism amounted to collusion with the ideology of separate spheres and the result was that 'By the end of the 1920s, "new" feminists found themselves in a conceptual bind that trapped women in "traditional" domestic and maternal roles, and limited their ability to advocate equality and justice for women' (1993: 7).

I have emphasised the hostility of the political context of the interwar period to the achievement of feminist claims. There was intense debate about the political enfranchisement of women and one that was informed by fear of women's power. Feminist responses to this hostility varied: the use of the freedom of fiction to explore possibilities was one response, another was the creation of an androgynous world (Smith-Rosenberg, 1985). The 'new feminism' was constructed at this period in opposition to a focus on equality which Rathbone felt was becoming arid, and in the context of the burgeoning of women's organisations rooted in women's private, domestic desires (Light, 1991; Giles, 1993; Morgan, 1994).

The pressure to re-orient feminist ideology – or to claim that this was happening – came from the awareness of women like Rathbone that feminist organisations were losing membership. Moreover, she consistently rejected conformity and believed that differences between feminists should be expressed openly, while at the same time calling for solidarity between women of different classes. The desire for solidarity was informed by her awareness of the resilience of misogynist attitudes, but her view of the needs and wishes of working-class or married women could only ever come from the outside (Lewis, 1986; Thane, 1991).

It is easy for historians to forget that by the late 1920s her lifetime had seen many changes in women's lives which contemporary feminists understood to be positive. Margaret, Lady Rhondda, Winifred Holtby and the contributors to *Our Freedom and its Results* (Strachey, 1936) shared Rathbone's sensitivity to the way women's achievements were undercut by an economic crisis which fed into the prevalent misogyny (Alberti, 1994a, 1994b). They were also fully aware of the extent of change, and they valued both the vote and Parliament as a source of political power (Cott, 1987; Alberti, 1989). In the interwar period feminists in Britain were faced with the challenge of how to act and speak as they moved into that space within the power structures of liberal democracy which they had demanded the right to enter.

Chapters 4, 5, 6 and 7 examine Rathbone's reactions to this experience. Her commitment to suffrage implied a belief that it was possible to operate as a feminist within the House of Commons. But the circumstances of the 1930s were not conducive to the use of that power for feminist aims. Chapter 4 (Taking the Path to Power, 1924–9) traces the roots of Rathbone's political position in the late 1920s and her understanding of what she thought was possible: to speak out as an independent representative of women, and in particular working-class women (and the validity of such a claim has been challenged by studies such as that of Ayers and Lambertz, 1986). Chapter 5 (Speaking Truth to Power, 1929–39) focuses on how she understood these three contested concepts: 'independence', 'representative' and 'women'.

One way in which she felt she spoke for women was to speak for the oppressed and the suffering, and in Chapter 6 (The Indian

Minotaur, 1927–41) I have traced how Rathbone was drawn into Indian politics by her deep-rooted concern for suffering. She spoke as a woman on child marriage in India, and the implicit base from which she acted was as a patriotic Briton. Like other feminists, she was a collaborator in 'the ideological work of empire', an aspect of British feminism which has recently received much needed attention (Forbes, 1979a, 1979b, 1981; Burton, 1990, 1991; Ramusak, 1990; Pedersen, 1991; Ware, 1992; Curthoys, 1993).

Patriotism was also the explicit ideological basis of her position on international affairs which became the main axis of her parliamentary attention in the 1930s. Chapter 7 (A Passionate Patriot Fighting Fascism, 1930–45) looks at her response to the international context of the 1930s. Rathbone shared with Winifred Holtby a view that in presenting a threat to women, Fascism was also destructive of the liberal values of an open and rationally conducted political life (Holtby, 1934). She never had any doubt where she stood on the need to resist Nazism by every means possible including, if necessary, by the use of force, and argued forcibly against pacifism. Among those she sought to convince were members of the Women's International League for Peace and Freedom whose consensus was fractured when faced with the painful dilemma Fascism posed the peace movement (Liddington, 1989: 152–71). Chapter 7 also looks at Rathbone's understanding of war as an opportunity to question again the position of women and the state. Fascism alerted Rathbone to the use of propaganda by governments, and she was aware that during wartime British women were the target of the government propaganda machine when their labour was again needed. There was a sceptical edge to her welcoming of wartime opportunities which may have further separated her from other women MPs whose increased co-operation Martin Pugh has argued met with some success from 1940 to 1945 (1992: 275–82). Hilary Land's (1975) study of the eventual introduction of family allowances just before Rathbone's death suggests that her scepticism was justified.

The Bibliography at the end of this book is divided into three sections. The first comprises an annotated list of Eleanor Rathbone's main writings and the second, an annotated list of key secondary sources for studying her ideas.

The list of Rathbone's writings is not comprehensive: some of the articles referred to in the text do not appear there, and there are references in this list to some articles and speeches which are not referred to in the text. It is arranged chronologically, and the intention is to give a sense of the overall development of her thinking. The secondary sources are listed alphabetically: there are references to the current and most significant of these books and articles in the main text.

It should be possible for readers of this book to use these sections to develop their own reading of Rathbone's ideas. My text is clearly only one interpretation of her thinking. Please note that references to Rathbone's writings in my text do not carry her name, only a date in brackets.

The third section of the Bibliography comprises a list of other useful background secondary texts, and references to contemporary books mentioned in the text. The small number of contemporary articles are referenced in brackets in the main text.

Dates

1872	(12 May) Eleanor Rathbone born in London
1893–6	Student at Somerville College, Oxford
1897	Secretary, Liverpool Society for Women's Suffrage
1900–19	Member of the Executive Committee, National Union of Women's Suffrage Societies
1909–35	Liverpool City Councillor
1913	Founded Liverpool Women's Citizens' Association
1917	Founder member, Family Endowment Committee (later Family Endowment Council and then Family Endowment Society)
1919–29	President, National Union of Societies for Equal Citizenship
1922	Stood unsuccessfully as parliamentary candidate, East Toxteth Constituency
1929–46	Member of Parliament for the English Universities
1932	Visited India
1933	Chairman, British Committee for Indian Women's Franchise
1934	Set up Children's Minimum Needs Committee
1934	Visited Palestine
1937	Visited Yugoslavia, Rumania and Czechoslovakia
1946	(2 January) Died in London

1

Heritage

In this chapter I will trace the conceptual heritage which Eleanor Rathbone took with her into her public life. From the first she sought ways to be useful, to retain her independence and to exercise power to change the world for the better. Poverty in working-class families and the powerlessness of women were the interconnected issues to which she sought solutions. Her search led her into the women's movement and then into local and central government.

Rathbone's ideas were part of a complex pattern of thinking on social questions in Edwardian England, when the Victorian heritage was changed but not abandoned. The creed of individualism which fostered social responsibility within a family framework led some Edwardian thinkers to move from ideas about participatory citizenship to the acceptance of a role for the state. Rathbone placed the responsibility for the amelioration of social poverty on the individual, but she began to move beyond the Victorian philanthropic position she learned from her father. The main Rathbone texts referred to in this chapter are *Report on the Results of a Special Inquiry into the Conditions of Labour at the Liverpool Docks* (1903), *William Rathbone: A Memoir* (1905) and articles published in *The Common Cause* (*CC*).

Family

> 'The faith I believe is the faith that whatever ought to be done can be done.' 'Success': Address by William Rathbone to the Liverpool Institute. (1905: 363)

Eleanor Rathbone's first published book was a life of her father, William Rathbone (1905). I began to read this book in the hope of discovering more about Eleanor herself, only to find that she was apparently not 'there'. Gradually I realised that reading Eleanor writing about her father was like opening a door to an essential element at the core of her ideas: the value she placed on her own heritage. She was determined that the biography should not be a eulogy, yet her admiration for her father's principles emerges as a key note for her commitment to political life. She is clearly 'an active agent in the biographical process' without apparently being there at all (Stanley, 1992: 9).

The main focus of the biography is on William Rathbone's 50 years of 'social service', which began around 1850. Eleanor added a footnote on this phrase which indicates her own view of the work which she was to engage in throughout her life:

> The phrases in common use to describe generally the pursuits which occupied much of William Rathbone's life, – 'philanthropy,' 'charitable work,' 'social reform,' even the vaguer 'public work,' – have such a ring of cant about them that I can only vacillate between them. The reader can choose whichever he finds least distasteful. (1905: 140)

For her, as for her father, there was never any doubt that she would engage in such 'pursuits', and she claimed no credit for doing so. Nor did she separate such work from her private life: as a member of William Rathbone's family she had always been aware of his public activities (1905: 417). After he became a Liberal MP in 1869 (at the age of 50; Eleanor was 57 when she was elected), the family spent half the year in London, half of it in Liverpool. Eleanor wrote that while he 'fully recognised the obligations of party . . . he held a very strong view that members of Parliament should be representatives, not delegates, and that while giving full weight to the opinions of constituents, they must in the long-run be free to vote upon their own convictions' (1905: 289). She was elected to Parliament exactly 60 years after her father as an Independent, never held office and, as I shall describe later, presented herself as representing women.

At the root of William and Eleanor Rathbone's commitment to politics lay a belief that the world could be changed, that it could be improved. In 1884 William gave an address with the title 'Success' – a title Eleanor did not like – in which he asserted that 'the goal of everyone's endeavour' was 'To leave the world something better than we find it – each of us can do that, and that is Success' (1905: 412). Responsibility for this task, in his own words, lay with 'the class of educated men above the pinch of poverty' (1905: 278). The means to achieve change lay in the wealth he and his forebears had accumulated. When he was given the honorary freedom of the city of Liverpool in 1891, he said in his speech of thanks:

> Whatever we may possess of wealth, talents, station, and opportunity are not freeholds to be selfishly enjoyed by a man and his family and friends, but sacred trusts to be employed for the welfare of the community. And of all beyond what is necessary for maintenance, education, and moderate provision for his family, an increasing proportion is due as wealth and power increase to the public service, not from generosity, but as honest payment of debt. (1905: 466)

Eleanor was probably more aware than was her father of the slipperiness of the concept of what was necessary for maintenance. In an earlier section where she had outlined his belief in the importance of limiting personal expenditure, she added a passage which exactly describes her lifelong attitude towards socialism and the redistribution of wealth:

> There are probably some people who, in reading advice like this, cannot shake off the feeling that in a country in which the great majority of families have incomes of less than £3 a week, it is an anomaly that there should be a class at all to whom six or seven hundred a year represents poverty, or at least the modest competence suitable for young people to begin life on. To these any system of giving away percentages will only seem to make the best of a state of things which has something fundamentally wrong about it. With this point of view William Rathbone had great sympathy. He sometimes said of himself that he was a Socialist in respect of ends, and would become one out and out if he could see his way clearer as to methods. For the so-called 'rights of property,' except so far as they fitted in with the interests of the community, he cared little, and his whole trend of opinion shows that he would have been willing to adopt very drastic measures for securing a

more equal distribution, if he could have convinced himself of their practicability and efficacy. (1905: 125)

A concern with poverty was a deeply personal and moral commitment which lay at the root of Eleanor Rathbone's political engagement. Her first public and political activities were within the Liverpool Central Relief Society which her father had been involved in setting up. Before his death on 6 March 1902, she had chosen a path of social action rather than academic philosophy for her life. Her choice was guided by a sense that she was one of those who could say, 'Our lot is fallen unto us in pleasant places. Yea we have a goodly heritage' (1929: 18). Her understanding was that this heritage laid on her an obligation to use the wealth inherited from her father to benefit society: that attitude itself was part of her heritage.

On a pragmatic level, Rathbone's acceptance of state intervention was also foreshadowed by her father's view of the role of the state in the relief of poverty. The control of 'charity' had been in the hands of the church: nonconformists such as William Rathbone were prepared to move to the secular administration of relief in their search for justice and efficiency. In 1889 he put forward a resolution in the House of Commons during a debate on the establishment of government grants towards Poor Law expenditure, 'conditional upon efficiency', similar to those given for education (*Hansard*, 22 June 1869: 197; cols. 430–6). He continued to press for a uniform national scheme for local government, motivated by a desire for justice to both the poor and the rate-payer (1905: 246–51). The intertwining of practical and moral considerations such as these lay behind the willingness of Victorians committed still to the ideology of self-help and moral reform to accept state intervention. It was a discourse Rathbone had available to her throughout her life.

A community of women

The discourses on the poor and on social work within which William and Eleanor Rathbone developed their ideas were gendered ones, involving different and complementary roles for men and women (Lewis, 1991a). Eleanor's sense of herself as a woman must have developed within the family framework, but the biography is not explicitly informative on this issue: William Rathbone's views on the role and position of women are almost entirely unremarked. There are one or two hints: when she acknowledged that her father had 'repaid a harvest which had been sown by at least four other men and one woman', Eleanor was including his mother, her grandmother, in her list of those who 'had done in their day good service to the city' of Liverpool (1905: 465). Elizabeth Rathbone was, according to her granddaughter, a woman of 'great insight into character, and a cool, clear judgment, upon which her husband, and later her sons and daughters, placed an almost unbounded and implicit reliance.' Eleanor added that Elizabeth's husband 'consulted her upon all his work' and on educational questions she was the one 'who initiated and suggested, though the custom of the day prevented her from coming forward openly' (1905: 40). Intriguingly, Stocks wrote that, rather than being inspired or influenced by her, Eleanor greatly disliked her grandmother (Stocks, 1949: 25). There is a hint here of the rebelliousness in Eleanor's character which forms a counterpoint to her sense of inheritance from her family.

Writing of her father's involvement in the training of nurses, Eleanor described his high expectations of them, commenting that 'There was something exhilarating and invigorating in this high standard of expectation, especially perhaps, from its unwontedness, to women' (1905: 186). Despite, or perhaps because of, the model of mutual respect within the family, the 'unwontedness' of male expectations of women was something that she seems to have been aware of from early on in her public life. It is likely that her experience within the family protected Eleanor from the misogyny which the Edwardian suffrage movement later released into the public domain (Kent, 1987). Yet there runs through her ideas a strong strain of anger at men's construction of women as inferior.

In a household such as that of the Rathbones where women were valued yet remained within a domestic space, it is likely that the view of women was contained within the ideology of separate spheres. This view was based on the expressed assumption of women's moral superiority, but placed them outside the scope of

effective agency, of power. It was more difficult for women contained within a household dominated by the father to develop a
critical analysis of this patriarchal construction of women. This
was especially true when the father was loved and admired, as was
William Rathbone. There are signs, however, that he considered
the possibility of a role for women outside the domestic. On the
issue of women's suffrage, the biography offers only this – literal –
footnote:

> He was indifferent, though not opposed, to the enfranchisement of
> women, until experience with the Registration of Midwives Bill showed
> him that women's interests were apt to be neglected because they could
> not enforce them. (1905: 448)

The representation of women's interests would be crucial to
Eleanor's understanding of her political role. A second hint of
paternal encouragement for her move beyond the domestic realm
appears at the end of the biography where Eleanor drew attention
to her father's belief that what young men and women of his class
should aim for was a 'career of public usefulness' (1905: 493). The
concept of usefulness was one which had wide currency and could
be contained within the concept of separate spheres, but it could
also lead beyond them.

   The beginnings of an awareness of patriarchy may have pre-
ceded Eleanor's years as a university student, but such awareness
needed a female world outside the domain of a man in which to
develop (Smith-Rosenberg, 1985; Holton, 1986). Her first experience of such a world came as a student at Somerville College,
Oxford. Before going there she had studied as a non-matriculated
student at Liverpool (Rathbone Papers [RP] XIV: 3.3). William
Rathbone was unsympathetic if not hostile to Oxford and
Cambridge, whose atmosphere he thought 'mentally and morally
enervating' (1905: 342), and Mary Stocks was unable to discover
how or why or by whom the decision was made that Eleanor
should be the first Rathbone to go there: Stocks believed that she
had to overcome her father's opposition. This is a scenario which
fits with the strain of independence in Eleanor's character and
thinking which were part of a family tradition, and which led her to
challenge some of the traditions in an inheritance she valued.

   There is little material available to establish any direct links which Eleanor Rathbone may have made between the philosophy she learned in Oxford and the philanthropic practice she later engaged in, but there are letters quoted in Stocks's biography which suggest that Oxford failed to produce a firm philosophical basis for her actions. Hilda Oakeley, who had been a student with Eleanor, wrote to her in about 1900 to propose that they should engage in a joint project in philosophy. Eleanor rejected the idea and in a letter to her explained:

> I have grown utilitarian, in one way. It is nearly always in connection with some practical problem that I think of the ultimate problems, and it is for their bearing on people's lives that I care for them . . . in a world where everyone was as well off as oneself, the utilitarian spirit might be a thing to fight against. But in such a world with all its wrongs shouting in one's ears and every miserable face claiming kinship, how can one be sorry that it is no longer easy to shut one's ears and revel in thought for thought's sake. (Stocks, 1949: 52–3)

She added that she doubted if 'philosophical methods . . . are the right weapons with which to accomplish any increase of knowledge at all', that she was growing 'more intolerant of half lights'. Given the absence of satisfactory proofs for philosophical questions, her position on 'metaphysical questions' was 'rational scepticism' (Stocks, 1949: 53–4). It seems that her family heritage which urged social action was stronger than the pull of academia towards contemplation. Her writing would always be designed to persuade her readers to adopt particular actions, rather than an intellectual exploration of a question.

It is unlikely, however, that her study in Oxford had no connection at all with the nature of her commitment to social action. She was taught by two followers of T.H. Green and the idealism which was influential in the period between 1880 and 1914 (Simey, 1964; Lewis, 1991a). A basic premise of Idealism was the vital importance of the individual as a means of implementing social change: this was Eleanor's starting point as a political activist. Idealism also emphasised an ethical individualism based on the moral imperative of the development of a more complete human nature: this was the starting point for her feminism. It seems that her years at Oxford fostered her feminism rather than her intellect.

In 1896 she returned from her years as a student at Oxford and lived at home with her mother and sisters: she moved back into the domestic and philanthropic world of Victorian women. According to Mary Stocks, Eleanor both loved and feared her mother; and Stocks hints that they were very different. Emily Rathbone was 'a skilled craftswoman; an adept master of materials. She worked assiduously in leather, silk, wool, wood, paint and ink – Greenbank bore traces of her handiwork at every turn' (Stocks, 1949: 56). These were the skills of the ideal Victorian lady. Eleanor, by contrast, was to become well known for her untidiness and for her lack of interest in domestic matters (Harrison, 1987: 99–100). However, she corresponded with her mother about her working life, and in her first parliamentary election leaflet she paid tribute to the 'valuable lessons in public service' she had learned from both her father and her mother (RP XIV: 3.2). There were plenty of opportunities for public service as a middle-class woman philanthropist in Liverpool in the late 1890s.

Liverpool: social action within the women's movement

On her return from Oxford Eleanor became a visitor for the Liverpool Central Relief Society, and after four months of practical relief work she sent her father an analysis of the cases in which she had been involved. Her practice and her approach, not surprisingly, were deeply imbued with the attitudes considered appropriate by the Charity Organisation Society (COS) to which the Liverpool Relief Society was linked. Relief should not be given when assistance was unlikely to lead to improvement, and the help that was given should be in a form such as to encourage self-help and thrift.

The tone of the COS with its emphasis on the moral rehabilitation of the poor is also to be heard in Eleanor Rathbone's first publication, the report of her research into the *Conditions of Labour at the Liverpool Docks* (1903). The research had been started before her father's death and on her father's initiative (1903: 18). It is a careful, detailed piece of research. She wrote as an economist but it is also gripping and personal to read: for her economics was not an impersonal subject. The study focused on the inefficiency of a casual labour system which operated more to the benefit of employer than employed, although she acknowledged that the sense of being 'their own masters' was for young men some compensation for their irregularity of earnings. But there is also a moral condemnation implicit in the description of the sudden large earnings of these young men, an argument Eleanor would use again and again in her writings. The study ended with the conclusion which was to be an even more central and dominant theme for her: 'It is by the wives and children that the hardship of irregular earnings are felt most keenly' (1903: 54). The solution to the system of casual labour at the Docks which Rathbone recommended was to change the method of payment. This was one step on a path which was to make her an advocate of extensive state intervention.

After completing the report on dock labour, Eleanor wrote the biography of her father which may well have helped her to consolidate her thinking about her own activities. At this time she was becoming increasingly socially active in a way which was to lead her away from her family home and city. It is as if her father's life and interests and her own reflections on it formed a jumping off point for her own entry into public life. Her description of her father's investigations and views on the question of poverty form a central part of her narrative of his life: by the time it was published she herself had been philanthropically involved in the lives of the poor in Liverpool for almost 10 years. The letter to Hilda Oakeley quoted above had continued with an explanation of the choice Eleanor had made as to the work she wanted to do:

> I think one of the most interesting points to consider between various professions or kinds of work lies in the consideration – whether they make a very small difference to a great many lives, or a great difference to a very few lives . . . Personally, I think the latter kind of work is quite as important, quite as interesting, and much more satisfactory to the workers, because they are so much better able to see and judge of the result. At any rate, I feel as if it were almost a necessity to have that kind of work to do. That is why I like the despised C.O.S. work so much. If one's large schemes fail, if dock labour is never properly organised, or the executive power better guided, or any other question of philosophy elucidated, it will be a satisfaction at the end of life to know that, at any rate, some poor bicycle-maker and his wife and children were set on their legs and saved from the House and made respectable citizens through my agency. (Stocks, 1949: 54–6)

Yet her involvement in social work led her quite quickly beyond the acceptance of amelioration by small degrees to look for alterations in the structure of institutions which would enable change to take place more effectively. She would always be pulled between the two axes of personal action and political change which were for her inseparable. The analysis of her work as a visitor for the COS had ended with the assertion that the society was doing 'little permanent good' and 'some positive harm'. She was severely critical of the voluntary visitors whom she found 'willing and interested, but not highly educated and quite untrained' (Stocks, 1949: 50–1). Her emphasis on training led her away from a commitment to voluntarism which was central to her father's social philosophy.

Rathbone's concern with poverty and her increasing focus on women brought her to the Liverpool Victoria Women's Settlement (VWS), and her work there was to be crucial to her thinking about women, the state and the family. The settlement had been established on a voluntary basis in 1897 with two members of the Rathbone family on the Committee. Eleanor became a voluntary visitor in 1902 and Honorary Secretary in September 1904. In 1905 she donated £45 for a scholarship which was to be used to support a worker at the Settlement for a year. After a rapid turnover of voluntary 'Heads', Elizabeth Macadam had become a paid Warden in 1903 and reorganised the work of the volunteers on a more regular and well co-ordinated footing. Macadam had worked at the Women's University Settlement in Southwark, the first women's settlement to be established. There she had taken part in the earliest training scheme for social work which was taught by Margaret Sewell, the warden of the Women's University Settlement for 10 years (Macadam, 1925: 11, 12). A process of professionalisation was taking place in social work, and Macadam was one of the rapidly growing number of women – estimated in 1893 to be 20,000 – who were 'paid officials in works of philanthropic usefulness in England' (Vicinus, 1985: 211–12). In 1905 both Rathbone and Macadam became members of a committee for the establishment of a School of Social Studies and Training for Social Work. Rathbone was a lecturer on the programme; Macadam took a half year sabbatical from the Settlement to study other institutions and then was appointed to a temporary paid lectureship at the School in

1910, partly in order to work on a Guarantee Fund to establish the school on a firm financial footing. The School clearly had similar origins and history to the School of Sociology of the COS in London: Margaret Sewell, who had taught Macadam, was 'an active COS advocate' and had run her training scheme in conjunction with the School of Sociology (Vicinus, 1985: 225).

The Victoria Settlement was a crucial part of a women's network in Liverpool in the first decade of the twentieth century. After her arrival in Liverpool, Macadam rapidly developed personal links with other voluntary organisations working with women and children, including schools, the District Nursing Association, the Charity Organisation Society, the Women's Co-operative Guild and the Women's Industrial League. This network was similar to those developed all over England and formed the structure for a thriving women's movement. The genesis was largely social but the direction was increasingly political, and those two strands in the lives of feminists active before the First World War are inseparable.

Rathbone's involvement in the Victoria Settlement is significant for two linked although separate reasons. First, her commitment to state action was fostered by the movement of which the settlement was a part. She came in contact there with like-minded social theorists such as E.J. Urwick, professor at the newly formed Department of Social Science and Administration at the London School of Economics (Harris, 1989). Urwick was prepared to be flexible on the question of the role of the state in the solution of social problems (Lewis, 1991a: 176). In his *Luxury and Waste of Life*, published in 1908, there are echoes of ideas Rathbone shared with her father: he 'set out the economic arguments for a pattern of income distribution in which no one received more than £200 per year' (Harris, 1989: 50–1). During the First World War Urwick was external examiner for the School of Social Studies at Liverpool.

Second, the process whereby a commitment to change from voluntarism to professionalism could lead to political involvement can be traced in these Liverpool beginnings of Eleanor Rathbone's career. The honorary secretary of the committee for the establishment of the Liverpool School of Social Studies was the senior resident at the Victoria Settlement, Miss S.E. Oliver, who held the same post for the Liverpool Central Relief Society (VWS Yearly

Report, 1906: 9). The work of Rathbone, Macadam and Oliver was crucial in the success of the Liverpool School and they became well-known within the broader political structures of the city. For Rathbone, like her father, concern for poverty was one impetus towards personal involvement in elected politics. The possibility for such an involvement was provided by the suffrage movement which played a counterpoint to her philanthropic activities.

For many women settlement work in the early years of the century did not satisfy their desire for social reform. Two other suffragists of Rathbone's generation, Kathleen Courtney and Maude Royden (who was a resident in 1901 at the Victoria Women's Settlement) were both unhappy as settlement workers and did not find a satisfying 'cause' for their reforming energies until they joined the suffrage movement (Fletcher, 1989).[1] Eleanor Rathbone had from the first combined her involvement in social work with secretaryship of the Liverpool Women's Suffrage Society and, from 1900, membership of the executive of the National Union of Women's Suffrage Societies. Her suffrage work combined with her settlement work to bring her into electoral politics, and during her first election campaign she said that the suffrage campaign was for her 'the greatest and dearest of all political causes' and one to which she would devote 'all the time and energy' she had to spare (*Liverpool Courier*, 5 October 1909).

A gendered citizenship

During the five years before the outbreak of the First World War Rathbone was a Liverpool councillor, a key figure in the foundation and running of the School of Social Studies and deeply involved in the suffrage movement when it was at its most visible and politically powerful. The range and extent of her activities may be one reason why she has left no writing which explains in detail her understanding of women's suffrage. Another explanation is that she wrote when she wanted to persuade others, never just to explain her own position. From what she did write on the subject, I have no doubt that enfranchisement was for her the basis from which any change in women's lives must begin. As she expressed it in 1918, it was 'the keystone of the edifice' which the National Union of Women's Suffrage Societies sought to build. She also referred to the vote as a 'symbol' (*CC*, 5 July 1917: 163), but she linked that concept specifically with citizenship (*CC*, 11 June 1915: 131–2). For her the vote was always a 'practical instrument for effecting reforms' (*CC*, 5 July 1917: 163).

Women involved in social work in the late nineteenth century firmly believed that in undertaking such work they were fulfilling their obligations as citizens. This emphasis on citizenship could be contained within a gendered view – that women's active citizenship implied a different mode of action from men – or it could lead to what Jane Rendall has identified as a demand for suffrage which was rooted in a commitment to altruism (Rendall, 1993). Rendall has pointed out that leading suffragists of the mid-century such as Barbara Bodichon and Millicent Garrett Fawcett formulated their demands in the language of 'patriotism' and 'public spirit, "an unselfish devotedness to the public service"'. For feminists in this tradition, women's 'rights were conceived in relationship to a duty or responsibility to others' (Rendall, 1993: 13, 17). Rathbone's articles in *Common Cause* express this perspective on citizenship. In the middle of the First World War she wrote that most suffragists were 'obeying a sound political instinct which tells them that the present time is more suitable for exercising such functions as are open to them than for actively pushing their demand for fuller rights'. But she went on to argue that 'there has never been a time when women were more conscious of their citizenship, or when the public were more ready to acknowledge it'. She wanted to seize this opportunity when women – she used the image of 'reclaimed land' to describe them – had 'discovered themselves to be citizens for the first time'. Her purpose was to persuade suffragists to form Women's Citizens Associations to harness this new-found consciousness into 'a permanent spring of action' which would lead to better social conditions in the towns (*CC*, 30 June 1916: 155).

Two other aspects of Rathbone's perception of the suffrage are implicit here. One is that democracy required the active social participation of 'the citizen'. For example, she placed the responsibility for the deficiencies in Poor Law administration . . . not upon officials nor Guardians, but upon the general body of citizens, who at present take so little interest in the matter, that not more than a fourth of them usually trouble to vote at the April elections, while of those who do vote many care to know nothing about the candidates except their creed and their politics. (1913b: 2)

The other point of view on both suffrage and political organisation which Rathbone held was that working-class women needed the leadership of 'the educated women' (*CC*, 30 June 1916: 155). She was to represent herself as able to speak for working-class women for the rest of her life. Her view was that 'the average working woman (of course there are exceptions), . . . is inevitably so much absorbed with her own struggle for existence that you cannot expect her to become a keen politician until you have made her realise the bearing of politics upon her own problems' (*CC*, 30 June 1916: 156). Her own experience of making working-class women realise the relevance of politics is implied in a later article where she urged suffragists to 'try the experiment' (*CC*, 5 July 1917: 164).

Her experience of the suffrage movement shaped Rathbone's perspectives on class. Coming from social work where she was a visitor, and as such an outsider and observer, she found herself in a movement where class differences appeared to have dissolved. The most active suffragists at the turn of the century were the Lancashire radical suffragists, a mass movement of working-class women initiated by the secretary of the Manchester Suffrage Society, but then operating independently of the more staid and middle-class North of England Society. Millicent Garrett Fawcett, the President of the National Union of Women's Suffrage Societies (NUWSS) to which the Liverpool Society was affiliated, had formed links with the Radical Suffragists when their petition was presented in London in 1901. It was from this source that paid workers were recruited to the NUWSS in the autumn of 1906. During the campaigns which resulted Eleanor Rathbone sometimes accompanied one of the workers, Selina Cooper, for meetings, canvassing and the distribution of leaflets.

This experience may have been partly responsible for her commitment to the idea that women's interests were the same across class barriers. Rathbone's definition of 'working class' included both women who earned their own living and women who were 'without wage-earning occupations but keeping no servant' (*The Times*, 12 July 1910). She did not share with colleagues such as Catherine Marshall and her own cousin Margaret Ashton, the 'conviction of the interrelatedness of feminist and class politics' (Holton, 1986).[2] She worked hard to persuade politicians of any party to support suffrage, helping with the plan of giving dinner parties for leading conservatives and donating money for work among the miners (Vellacott, 1993: 151–2, 300). In 1913 she played a crucial, and for her a painful part in opposing a proposed change in policy which was to have the effect of withholding the NUWSS Election Fighting Fund from Liberal candidates in by-elections (1913b; NUWSS EC Minutes 6 March 1913; Vellacott, 1993: 168, 212–13). She was not motivated by any devotion to the Liberal Party, but was concerned that the new policy would take the NUWSS on to a 'path of *constitutional coercion*, as opposed to its previous record of what may be called constitutional persuasion'. She did not express any theoretical objection to this method, but she did argue that 'if it does not succeed, then we shall be worse off than before', and that the policy was in fact likely to antagonise Liberals without converting Conservatives (1913b). Rathbone's concerns in this controversy were that any policy adopted should be as practically effective as possible, and that minority opinions should not be suppressed. When Rathbone acted independently of the executive in expressing her views on this subject, she was shocked to discover that her colleagues found her behaviour unacceptable. They were then shocked in their turn when she resigned (NUWSS EC Minutes 20 June 1912, 15 Jan. 5, 19 March 1914).

Sandra Holton sees this controversy as an organisational and tactical one: she has argued that within the suffragist movement there was a spectrum of thinking contained within one ideological framework. Within this framework there was a largely unexamined spectrum of claims for the vote ranging from those based on essentialist views of women, to those which were deliberately humanist (Holton, 1986: 28). At this stage in her life Rathbone did not argue that women's 'skills, attributes, and forms of knowledge' were 'particularly relevant to social reform' (Holton, 1986: 7), although she would later develop her own version of this point of view in the

'New Feminism'. She did not claim the vote in terms of women's essential qualities as did Millicent Garrett Fawcett, who declared in 1889: 'We do not want women to be bad imitations of men; we neither deny nor minimize the differences between men and women. The claim of women to representation depends to a large extent on these differences' (Holton, 1986: 12).

Rathbone and Fawcett were committed to emphasising the common ground between suffragists and to presenting a solid front. Neither of them condemned outright the methods of the militants in the Women's Social and Political Union (WSPU). In 1912 Rathbone wrote approvingly of the recognition by the militants of the 'psychological value of mere repetition' (*CC*, 5 September 1912: 373). Jo Vellacott has challenged Holton's assertion of ideological homogeneity in the suffrage movement, arguing that as far as the WSPU was concerned 'one cannot divorce method from ideology'. Vellacott associates the rationale of militancy with the 'argument of the antisuffragists that since physical force was the basis of the state, and women did not fight, therefore they should not vote' (1993: 131–2). If this is the case, then there were ideological differences within the NUWSS: Rathbone's wartime arguments about women and 'national service' which are described in the next chapter, make it clear that she was not fundamentally opposed to the use of force. Her argument against its use by the WSPU was that it was counterproductive (n.d. *c*.1913). Twenty years later she advocated the use of WSPU methods to Indian women (1934a: 107, 111–12).

Rathbone's emphasis during the suffrage struggle was always on the most effective way of achieving her purpose. Moreover, she saw the vote itself in terms of purpose: she saw it as a way of giving women the power to legislate. In her view it was working-class women who most lacked and most needed power. The method of payment of seamen through which their wives suffered went unaltered, she argued, because those women did not have the vote (1911b). She understood the activities of the Radical Suffragists in terms of their need to have some control over 'the increasing flood of industrial legislation' (1912a: 19). And she declared that both 'the capitalist class' and the trade unions had exploited and excluded women, and that this situation would continue for as long as such women did not have the protection of the vote (*CC*, 18 August 1916). But she did not rest her case only on the representation of interests, asserting that:

> Nor is it only upon questions specially affecting their sex that women have a right to be heard. Are they not as deeply concerned as men in securing the conditions of a stable peace? Have they no interest in the future economic and fiscal system of the country, in its relations with its colonies, with those who are not its allies, and, not least, with those who are now its enemies? (*CC*, 18 August 1916: 238)

Rathbone believed that 'democracy and feminism are the twin children of liberty' (*CC*, 26 April 1918). She did not share the doubts about the British political process inherent in Millicent Garrett Fawcett's statement that it was 'not so much that women were not good enough for votes as that votes were not good enough for women' (*The Woman's Leader and Common Cause*, 6 February 1920: 1). Rathbone had an enduring faith in the power of 'legislation and public action':

> if we think far enough into the particular matter (whatever it might may happen to be), we shall generally find that had public action or the laws of the country been different, we might not have been distressed by some special exhibition of cruelty or injustice . . . Distribute political power, education and the nation's wealth more evenly . . . and, at once, we shall find an improvement in the conduct of individuals among themselves. (*CC*, 25 October 1918: 322)

This conception of the vote is similar to the 'orientation' identified by Sandra Holton as 'democratic suffragism'. The phrase 'democratic suffragist' was coined by Margaret Llewelyn Davies in 1909 to describe those who believed that 'the fighting force of the women's suffrage movement will be greatly strengthened by showing that it is in harmony with democratic sentiment' (Holton, 1986: 65).[3] Holton points out that Davies's aim was to find a 'unifying idea' for suffragists with different class and party loyalties. Rathbone both responded to and resisted such an appeal. She did not value harmony and never fitted easily into the structure of institutions, but she did favour joining hands with other women across barriers of race, class and party.

Rathbone's sense of gender solidarity was rooted in the personal experience of the suffrage movement in that intense period before 1914. Difference was tolerated within an agreed feminist framework provided by an overall focus on the vote. Suffragists were able to assume and act on the assumption of ideological homogeneity because the size, strength and ethos of the prewar suffrage movement allowed them the space to do so. Significantly, the controversy over which she resigned from the NUWSS executive occurred at a time of uncertainty when the need to maintain a solid front was imperative.

Her involvement in the suffrage and settlement movements had provided Eleanor with a 'female world' where her feminism could be nurtured. Although she only briefly experienced again the communal living which had fostered her appreciation of female companionship at Oxford, she was for the rest of her life to belong to women's organisations and to spend her leisure time with other women. In particular, her friendship with Elizabeth Macadam was central to her life and after the First World War when they moved to London they lived together. Eleanor wrote to Elizabeth during one long separation: 'I am not really good at any form of social intercourse and nothing can cure that. And except when I am with you I am always alone to all intents and purposes' (Stocks, 1949: 181).

Conclusion

In 1909 the strands in Eleanor Rathbone's public life – her commitment to women's political role and her concern with social reform – had come together when she was elected as the first woman to sit on Liverpool City Council. She was to hold an elected position as an Independent for the rest of her life at the local or parliamentary level, or both. She had moved some distance from her desire to be an instrument of change for the 'poor bicycle-maker', but she had not lost the determination to be effective, to be an agent. Her early awareness of the 'cant' which could so easily become part of social work, drew her away from philanthropy and towards institutional politics. She took with her a passion for activity combined with a sense that it was the needs of the individual which mattered.

In 1938 Eleanor Rathbone wrote: 'To anyone with the temperament and experience of a pre-war Victorian, the readiness with which the post-war generation, or most of it, throws up the sponge must be for ever incomprehensible and baffling' (1938: 111). Eleanor's Victorian heritage provided her with underlying principles which shaped her actions: a faith in humanity, an optimism about change and an obligation to act. She inherited a confidence which meant that she could accept differences of opinion, and wealth which allowed her to enjoy a sense of independence. She experienced the ability to choose and understood her choices as moral ones. Her primary political aim was to try to alleviate suffering, above all the suffering which arises from poverty. The professionalisation of social work in which she was involved moved her towards an acceptance of the need for structural change. The world of social action in which Rathbone began her public life was a gendered one. Victorian feminists both accepted and challenged this construction: Rathbone was among those who resisted it.

The suffrage movement brought together her sense of solidarity among women and the exhilaration she experienced in exercising the power of persuasion. She sought to represent women within a parliamentary democracy to which she was strongly committed. She took with her into her political life a sense of difference on which she laid emphasis at certain periods of her life. But her central commitment was to the moral possibilities of all human beings, and she saw citizenship within the existing political structures as a site for their attainment. Eleanor's faith in the potential of the individual as an agent of power led her to an advocacy of female suffrage. Strengthened by a sense of connection with other women in the social work and suffrage circles of the time, and by one friendship in particular, Eleanor Rathbone would publicly assert the capabilities of her own sex, as a sex, for the rest of her life. After the war she took another step into the world of patriarchal power with the support of women, in order to represent women and to offer particular skills and perspectives as a woman (RP XIV: 3.2 (2)).

Notes

1 During the war both these women were active in the peace movement, and peace became the focus of Courtney's activity for the rest of her long life (1878–1974). Maude Royden (1876–1956) continued to work for peace in the inter-war period, but her main activities were connected with her demand that women be accepted as preachers and priests within the Anglican Church.

2 Catherine Marshall (1880–1964) was the immensely hardworking and effective Parliamentary Secretary of the NUWSS until she left the Union in 1915 over the policy towards the war. She then transferred her immense energies to the No Conscription Fellowship. From 1917 she suffered from bouts of ill health but continued to be politically active, especially in the Women's International League for Peace and Freedom (WILPF). Margaret Ashton (1856–1930) came from Manchester where she was active in the Liberal Party, resigning over suffrage in 1906. In 1908 she was elected as the first woman member of Manchester City Council and she was an active member of the executive of the NUWSS. Like Marshall, she resigned over the refusal of the Union to oppose the war and joined the WILPF. In 1926 Manchester City Art Gallery refused to hang her portrait because of her pacifist activities.

3 Margaret Llewelyn Davies (1861–1944) was general secretary of the Women's Co-operative Guild from 1889 to 1921. She was influential in making the Guild an effective pressure group for suffrage and for the needs of working women. During the war the Guild clashed with male co-operators when it took a stance against the war.

2

The Public and the Private, 1909–19

The first chapter of this book traced the movement of Eleanor Rathbone's activities from the private world of her family home into the public realm. Victorian feminist demands entailed a challenge to the restriction of women to the private sphere: the struggle to achieve the vote and to take part in the parliamentary process was the most obvious challenge, but the commitment to social action inherent in the development of Victorian philanthropy also involved women in a transgression of the division between the spheres. What constituted the dividing line was contested, and Eleanor Rathbone participated in the debate about how to delineate the boundary. The controversy was enmeshed in a linked debate about state intervention, about how far the public role of the state should be allowed to encroach on the private life of the individual. Rathbone's thinking on state intervention was influenced both by the pragmatic, nonconformist approach of philanthropists like her father, and by New Liberalism which wrapped new practices round in an ideological advocacy of state intervention as enabling the citizen to fulfil his or her potential (Freeden, 1978; Lewis, 1991a). Philosophical approaches to the state and the individual were influenced by, and in turn influenced, the growth of the social sciences.

This chapter will introduce Rathbone as an economist and social scientist. Her university education together with her practical experience gave her the confidence to use the concepts of the social sciences – and to challenge them. Her motive was political: social investigation and the demonstration of need was a first step necessary in a process which could lead to change. Apart from the biography of her father, as noted earlier, Rathbone's first substantial writings were the investigation of dock labour (1903) which she did by herself, a paper on women's wages (1912a), and two reports of work done by the voluntary organisations with which she was involved (1909, 1913a). The first and the last two of these were surveys following the tradition initiated by Booth in the late 1880s. In this chapter I will look at *The Problem of Women's Wages* (1912a), *How the Casual Labourer Lives* (1909), *Widows under the Poor Law* (1913a), together with some of her articles in the NUWSS journal, *The Common Cause*. I will also refer to her article 'The Remuneration of Women's Services' (1917), and to the Family Endowment Committee book *Equal Pay and the Family* (1918) which she co-authored: these will also be used in the next chapter. This chapter will investigate Rathbone's ideas on the public and the private, the relationship between the individual and the state, and her understanding of how women fitted into those constructions.

The needs of women

Rathbone's focus on women's needs emerged strongly during the years 1909–12 when she became more intensely involved with suffrage. Her increasing stress on the need for a public and political response to these needs was the motive behind, and stimulated by, her election as a representative for Granby Ward to Liverpool City Council as an Independent and the first woman councillor on 7 October 1909. Her experience and activities as a councillor are a foretaste of her role as an MP: she was an independent critic of those in power, especially in the area of equal opportunities for women. She became a councillor in the same year as the publication of *How the Casual Labourer Lives* (1909). The focus of this study was on the economy of the family, and women are portrayed as the managers of this economy. It was also women who were the money-lenders. They did not become rich and were possibly 'agents for others', running the 'money-clubs' which made it possible for families to survive the fluctuations of their income (1909: xxviii). There are parallels between Rathbone's conclusions and the retrospective study by Ayers and Lambertz (1986) of the inter-war period: Liverpool women appear in both studies as the hard-pressed survivors of an unsatisfactory system. For Rathbone, writing in an attempt to change the situation, there were 'remedies': 'devices' such as compulsory saving, the teaching of arithmetic, free adult cookery classes. But her main recommendation was for the reorganisation of dock labour. She recognised that this would require state intervention because of the conservatism and self-interest of the employers (1909: xxxii).

The premise of *How the Casual Labourer Lives* was that there was a basic level of need for human beings. Rathbone's paper on *The Problem of Women's Wages* (1912a) worked from the same assumption and concluded that the system of wages which was in place failed to do this. 'Payment of motherhood' was Rathbone's solution to the problem of poverty and it entailed state intervention, however vaguely expressed. Her argument contained the premise that wages were based on the needs of the workers, and in support of this she asserted that:

> Much as the theory of wages has varied in the course of the past hundred years, the importance as a factor in determining wages of the standard of living of the worker has always been recognised, in one form or another, by economists from Adam Smith onwards. (1912a: 7)

This assertion was highly debatable: for Rathbone it was part of an argument about the responsibility of society for the well-being of the citizen. Wages for workers were paid by employers: society was employing women to ensure its continuity and it was the duty of society to fulfil the needs of mothers. It was all too apparent to her that these needs were not being met, and one of the most needy groups were widows: *Widows under the Poor Law* (1913a) was designed to demonstrate this. In this report, Rathbone accepted the ideological categorisation made in the Poor Law Report of the characters of 'out-relief mothers' in the Parish of Liverpool (1913a: 21), and then turned it upside down. Some women, she accepted, were '"really bad mothers", in which we include the grossly negligent and slatternly, as well as the chronic drinkers and the loose livers' (1913a: 24). But she then went on to make it apparent that these women were precisely those whose children had been handed over to state control in the workhouse. The vast majority of mothers were '"good in intention," but of varying degrees of inefficiency in execution' (1913a: 24). What they needed and invariably responded to was a steady and adequate income. Her political purpose was to put pressure on the government to introduce widow's pensions.

In adopting the methods of social science, Rathbone did not want to lose the concept of personal responsibility in social action as a response to the problems she described. There are suggestions in such a construction of the practice of 'mothering' the poor which has been identified by Eileen Yeo (Yeo, 1992). But in Rathbone's writing there is a political element which goes beyond this. She wanted to change the situation, and not just by the improvement of the moral behaviour of the poor which McKibbin (1977) has identified as the ideology of the surveys he analysed. Rathbone wanted to engage the emotions of her readers for a political purpose, and she was critical of the limitations of the ideology of what Yeo has termed 'social motherhood':

> If the well-to-do people who enlarge on the incompetence of the English workingwoman and undertake to teach her 'Mothercraft' had to lead her life under her conditions, how many of them could stand the strain for a week? (1913a: 29)

Rathbone's main motivation in her writings was to persuade, and it is therefore necessary to bear in mind whom she was addressing, and in what political context. *Widows under the Poor Law*, for example, was written at a time when the suffrage movement had established itself as a force in British politics (Vellacott, 1993). She was putting forward arguments intended to influence both the government and her fellow suffragists. I will look again at the ideological debates within the suffrage movement in the next chapter: part of that disagreement was focused on Rathbone's arguments concerning the economic position of married women. An article by her on that issue was published in *The Common Cause* early in 1912, and the editor, Helena Swanwick,[1] added a footnote describing it as a 'clear and reasoned statement of a view generally very ill-expressed and more usual perhaps among anti-suffragists than suffragists'. The 'anti-suffragist' component of Rathbone's argument was concerned with her views on equal pay which I will also look at in more detail in the next chapter. But the central aim of her article was to persuade her fellow suffragists of the fact that the wage system was both unstable and designed in the interests of men. Should it break down, then 'the community would have to take upon itself the cost of rearing future generations'. The article also made apparent the nature of some contemporary criticism of 'the payment of motherhood', and gave a presage of Rathbone's later extended feminist analysis of such criticism. She wrote that mention of such 'direct payment to the mother during the years of childbearing . . . generally means pulling the cord of a showerbath of sentiment about the outrage on the sacredness of motherhood'. The present system which operated was, she suggested, satisfactory 'to masculine sentiment and to masculine love of power' (*CC*, 4 January 1912: 674–5).

The role of the state

Rathbone's observation that the wage system did not satisfy the needs of either married or single women had led her at the start of her public life to consider the intervention of the state in an economic system based on private enterprise and a family wage system. In the gap between the first reading (1902) of *The Problem of Women's Wages* and its publication (1912a), the Liberal Government had introduced a measure of state intervention, and in her subsequent writing Rathbone referred to these measures to give her ideas political legitimacy. In 1917 she wrote:

> the State has taken directly upon itself the cost of the school education of its young, and it is gradually in a hesitating and half-hearted way taking over the cost of some of the minor provisions necessary for child-nurture. (1917: 113)

This reference suggests that for her the legitimacy of state intervention was partly rooted in practice, in what had proved politically possible. The extension of the state had taken place as the result of political pressure, and in response to perceived social need.

Rathbone did not argue that state intervention was necessarily the right choice nor that it was morally better than private practice. In arguing for widow's pensions she started from the premise that the state had already accepted responsibility for widows when out-relief was given, and she asserted that 'No-one can seriously maintain that the "children of the state" ought to be driven to live by cadging on their neighbours' (1913a: 13). Once aid was given, she could see no reason for giving an inadequate amount. She then returned to the source of funding and argued that widows should not continue to be given assistance through the Poor Law but by some form of state financed support. She pointed out that it was neither humanly likely nor actuarially possible for 'a thrifty young workman to provide, not only for unemployment sickness and old age, but also for the contingency of his own premature death' (1913a: 31). The implication was that there should be some form of insurance, although she wrote that it was not within the scope of her report to suggest whether provision should be through con-tributory insurance or by 'State grant' (1913a: 32).

There is already a significant element of concern for national efficiency in Rathbone's ideas before the war. She supported her argument that the widow should be on a higher plane than that of a 'pensioner upon the bounty of the State', by pointing out that she was 'earning the money which she draws from it by . . . services to the community . . . not much less valuable than those of the Relieving Officer or Poor Law Guardian who now browbeats or patronises her' (1913a: 16–17). The nation required efficient house-wives and parents, and it was 'hard for a woman to be an efficient housewife and parent while she is living under conditions of extreme penury' (1913a: 29). She concluded her argument with the idea that the Widow's pension should be seen as a 'contract of ser-vice, binding the mother in exchange to bring up her children in such an environment as would make it likely that they should grow up into normally healthy and useful citizens' (1913a: 32–3). This concept of the mother as a 'useful citizen' would become a central part of the debate over state intervention during the war.

Women, war and national interest

The high-watermark of Rathbone's hopes of state intervention occurred at the end of the war which had seen a marked increase in government control and an unequalled intervention in the economic position of mothers. The war, she argued, 'taught us that, where national interests are at stake, go-as-you-please methods may be too dearly paid for' (1917: 121). Wartime experience demonstrated that by 'doing just enough to keep slum babies alive, but not enough to keep them healthy . . . we are as a nation recruiting the national stock in increasing proportion from those who have sunk into the lowest strata because they are physically, mentally and morally degenerate' (1917: 123). Rathbone's patriotism drew her into a eugenist discourse in wartime, as I shall suggest again in a later chapter.

The 'most fundamental necessity of the State' was, she argued, 'its own reproduction'; which was 'left to haphazard individual effort', and child-rearing was 'the most essential of all the services to the state' (1917: 116). The proposal drawn up by the Family Endowment Committee in 1918 referred in Rathbone's phrase to 'The Provision made by Society for its own Continuation' (1918: 14), and described its proposal as 'State endowment of families' (1918: 34). The discussion of whether to endow the unmarried mother and her child was partly conducted in that proposal in terms of 'considerations of the general well-being of the State' (1918: 51, 54). Susan Pedersen has pointed out that when feminists such as Rathbone argued that 'motherhood was a citizenship "function" equivalent to that of soldiering', they were allowing 'a dangerous analogy between the national obligations of the soldier and those of the fertile woman'. But their intention, as Pedersen admits, was to produce 'a rhetoric capable of sustaining demands for independent social rights for mothers' (1990: 1004).

The other side of the coin of Rathbone's demand that the work of mothers deserved financial recognition by the state was her perception that women owed service to the nation. She saw the war as a crisis for the nation and one that required self-sacrifice and discipline from all citizens (*The Times*, 6 April 1918: 9a). She was one of those within the NUWSS willing to abandon the struggle for the suffrage when it broke out (*CC*, 11 June 1915: 131). In the debates within the NUWSS in the spring of 1915, she was associated with suffragists such as Millicent Garrett Fawcett and Ray Strachey, whose patriotism was the strongest force in their emotional response to the war. Her articles in *The Common Cause* around this time were focused on how women could serve their country best in time of war (*CC*, 4 January 1915: 631; 11 June 1915: 131). During the German offensive on the Western Front in the spring of 1918, she asserted that in time of war 'the nation's cause was indeed "our common cause"', and that: 'Of feminism, more perhaps than any other cause in the world with the possible exception of democracy, it can be said that its fate stands or falls with the fate of our nation and its Allies' (*CC*, 26 April 1918: 15). However, Rathbone was always anxious to keep communication open between feminists who disagreed, and she did try to keep in touch when Catherine Marshall resigned from her post with the NUWSS in the spring of 1915 (Alberti, 1989: 18 and Ch. 3). In this spirit, Rathbone supported the discussion of 'what is to be done after the war is won, in order to prevent the recurrence of such a disaster in future' (*CC*, 28 April 1916: 39).

Rathbone did not lose sight of the misogyny which prevented women's desire to serve their country in wartime from being used to the full (*CC*, 11 June 1915: 131). She exposed the inconsistencies in certain patriotic arguments:

> It is difficult to understand the attitude of those Labour members and trade union leaders who were so clamorous recently in asserting the right of 'the widows of our dead heroes' to a minimum pension of at least £1 a week, but who, during all the years that are past, have never made an effort worth the name to secure for the widows of their fellow-workmen anything better than the bitter bread of pauperism. (*CC*, 17 March 1916: 648–9)

Her main hopes were pinned on the change in attitude of women: 'experiences during the war will have given them greater confidence in themselves, and a taste for the satisfaction that is to be found in skilled, responsible, well-paid work' (1917: 118).

It is clear that Rathbone's ideas on the potential of state action to remedy cruelty or injustice pre-date the war, but the war in her view shifted attitudes and thus made change possible. There is no sign in her writings of the 'defensive posture' which Susan Kingsley Kent sees in the 'feminist movement during and after the war' (1993: 114). In 1917 Rathbone wrote of married and unmarried women that 'The war has brought about a marked change in the position of both these bodies of women'. She believed that the change for married women had occurred through the system of separation allowances which had 'transformed' working-class women 'into an army of State servants' (1917: 100–1).

In the first month of the war, the Prime Minister announced that separation allowances would be paid to the wives and dependants of officers and men in both the army and the navy. At this stage there existed no machinery for the administration of the allowances other than that of voluntary organisations. Especially important in this early work was the Soldiers' and Sailors' Family Association (SSFA). Eleanor Rathbone and the network of women involved in suffrage and social work took over the Liverpool Branch of the SSFA, which acted as an administrative agent of the War Office as did other branches elsewhere. Rathbone did not doubt that the effects of the payment of separation allowances were positive for the women recipients. Direct and regular payment of these allowances meant that such women 'tasted for the first time the sense of security, of ease and dignity that comes from the enjoyment of a settled income' (1917: 125). But the administration of the scheme made her more aware of the complexity of state administration: she described the system as 'the greatest experiment that the world has ever seen in the State endowment of maternity' (*CC*, 25 February 1916: 611–12). She quickly became aware of the problems associated with any scheme which was based on an assessment of need. Allowances were paid to wives at uniform rates, but payment to mothers and 'dependants other than wives' was made after examination of their needs and former contributions of the soldiers or sailors. Rathbone criticised the use of Customs and Excise officers in making these assessments, arguing that women social workers would do the job more thoroughly and appropriately (*CC*, 22 January 1915: 663–4). She feared that the assessment of pensions for widows would be made by a similarly unsatisfactory method. It appears that she saw the question of administration of a system to be something which could and should be struggled with in a flexible way, rather than laid down in concrete. The combination of voluntary and paid social work which she had favoured foreshadowed the 'new philanthropy' advocated by Elizabeth Macadam (1934).

Susan Pedersen (1990) has analysed the pressure from feminist organisations between 1916 and 1918 for the endowment of motherhood together with the response of the male politicians. She argues that feminists failed in their attempt to 'speak for' working-class women and to challenge the right of the husbands to dictate what was in their wives' interests. At the time there was little sense of such a failure. The tone of Rathbone's writings in the period 1912–20 reflects the political context of intense feminist political activity and is significantly different from that of the later periods. One of her repeated themes in this period is that patience is a 'misnamed virtue' (*CC*, 27 March 1914: 977–8). Her faith in the power of the vote to transform women's personal and political lives is central to the optimism of those years.

When women's suffrage appeared on the political agenda again in the summer of 1916 Rathbone was wary of the intentions of Asquith's government (*CC*, 18 August 1916: 238–9). But as enfranchisement, albeit limited, became a reality, she was confident that the political system was about to be transformed. Just before the election when women voted legally for the first time, Rathbone wrote a jubilant article in *The Common Cause* which began:

> Suffragists within the next few weeks or months will probably discover that they accomplished even more than they foresaw when they won political citizenship for women. Whenever the General Election comes, we shall discover that a subtle but great change has already taken place in the position of married women. Thousands of married women will suddenly recognise that they have become persons – wholly, and not fractionally, as before. It will matter what they think, and it will matter enormously what they should think. (*CC*, 25 October 1918: 322)

Looking back, it is all too easy to read this as wishful thinking. For contemporary feminists the years 1917–20 were a time of hope, as a degree of women's suffrage was at last achieved. The limitations of the suffrage were less important to some suffragists, including Rathbone, than the achievement of the principle. Many of the women whom she was most anxious to empower through enfranchisement – married women with children – were granted the vote. In her writing on the economic position of widows, Rathbone linked their treatment as paupers with the weakness of their political voice and presented the vote as a method of empowering them (*CC*, 3 April 1914: 1021–2). Moreover – and increasingly in later years – her confidence was tempered by her understanding that the workings of the British democracy required active engagement. In her first speech as the president of the reconstituted NUWSS in 1920, she recommended the 'Kantian maxim of statesmanship: "Act so that the maxim of thy action might become law universal"' (1929: 2). From the time of her engagement in the suffrage movement she advocated constant political activity such as she was able and willing to practise herself, but others were rarely in a position to achieve (*CC*, 5 September 1912: 373–4; 30 June 1916: 155–6; 22 November 1918: 371–2).

The war had shifted both the political context of state intervention and also Rathbone's personal position within the suffrage movement. The tone of an article on 'The Endowment of Motherhood' which appeared in the spring of 1918 was combative towards the views of the 'Fabian Research Department to the effect that over 50% of the women wage-earners investigated were wholly or partially supporting others beside themselves. This, though true, is so obviously an inadequate answer that I never hear it used by women without a qualm of shame for the users.' In her view, few of such women had 'responsibilities that were really equivalent to that of a married man with the average-sized family of three children' (*CC*, 1 March 1918: 600–1).

Keeping women within the family

Rathbone had developed her ideas within the context of the family, and although she had learned a good deal more of the reality of family life in the war, her faith in it had not been destroyed. In her paper on women's wages, she had made ironic comments about the idea that a working-class woman requires very little, and she was ambivalent about the possibilities for women within marriage. Her references to marriage suggest that it was an institution which cramped girls who had been in paid work, but for whom 'matrimony – whether desired or not – must be present as a possibility, always threatening to baffle schemes and extinguish ambitions that would take more than a year or two to realise' (1912a: 15). Her wartime experience with the SSFA gave her more knowledge of the oppression of women within marriage. In 1917 she wrote:

> for married women of the working class . . . friction about money and bitter resentment, when they are unable to satisfy the needs of their children, because of the selfishness or thoughtlessness of their husbands, have in many of them effectually destroyed affection very early in their married lives. (1917: 125)

She believed that dependency lay at the root of this resentment:

> I have often wished that the numerous men who seem to think that the sanctity of the marriage tie would be broken down if wives were no longer economically dependent on their husbands could know a little of the real feelings of many of these dependent wives – the depth of inarticulate bitterness, which only finds broken utterance when they are talking 'as woman to woman'. (*CC*, 17 March 1916: 648)

The result of this bitterness was not only the corrosion of affection between married couples, but also the destruction of the wife's sense of self. In putting forward a 'Proposal for the National Endowment of Motherhood' in 1918, Rathbone and the members of the Family Endowment Committee asserted that:

> There can be no real independence, whether for men or for women, without economic independence. Few of us can realise how constantly and subtly this half-conscious, but ever-present sense of the economic dependence of the woman upon the man corrodes her personality, checks her development, and stunts her mind. (1918: 10)

Rathbone was hopeful that women's wartime experience of gaining economic independence through separation allowances would shift the balance within marriages: 'I confess to hoping that the seeds of a "divine discontent" will have been implanted in them too deeply to be eradicated, and that we feminists will then find our opportunity' (*CC*, 17 March 1916: 648). This transformation, combined with enfranchisement, would provide the impetus for political change.

The war had strengthened Rathbone's faith in the ethical basis of British political institutions, and led her to hope that it would respond to the needs and demands of newly enfranchised women. Her starting point was a moral one rooted in her Victorian heritage. She knew that to be human a certain material level of comfort was imperative: she pointed out that members of a family expected to live on the minimum income which lifted it above the poverty line assumed by investigators must, in order just to survive, 'practise the virtues of saints while living the lives of ill-housed animals' (1927: 28). Her determination to grapple with poverty led her to take an interventionist stance on the role of the state.

Understanding the state

Rathbone's ideas about the state have been called naive (Pedersen, 1990: 1004). Her language suggests an uncertainty about how she understood the concept: she refers indiscriminately to 'the community' or 'society' and 'the state'. In *The Problem of Women's Wages* she refers to the loss to 'the community' of women's absence from home, and to the advantage of 'Society' substituting a 'system of more direct payment for the cost of its own renewal' (1912a: 22–3). In 1917 she was still referring to 'the community' paying through the 'channel' of men's wages, 'indirectly and only half-consciously . . . for the continuance of its own existence and the rearing of fresh generations' (1917: 114). But just before this passage she argued that 'the most important function which any State has to perform . . . is to secure its own periodic renewal by providing for the rearing of fresh generations' (1917: 112). In an article in *The Common Cause* in 1919, she asserted that the 'underlying theory of the English Poor Law . . . had always been that the State recognises its obligation for the livelihood of the individual citizen to the extent of ensuring that no one shall be condemned by poverty to deal by starvation' (*CC*, 7 February 1919: 514). But she also understood the duty of the state to go beyond this, since she was consistently critical of 'the spirit of poor relief' (1918: 34).

Rathbone shared with other feminists of her time an over-optimistic faith in the state's nurturing functions, and a belief that the gaining of political freedom and power by women would lead to solutions to other social evils (Holton, 1986: 14–15). Denise Riley has argued that concepts of society became feminised in the nineteenth century, that women 'formed . . . a kind of continuum of sociality against which the political was set' (1988: 15). This insight throws light on the difficulties encountered by Rathbone: she was motivated by a radical desire to collapse the boundaries between private and public, but there was no understanding available of the position of women in the political arena. Later she sought for such an understanding in her challenge to the idea that the feminist demand for equality necessarily meant that women had to fit into an 'administrative and economic structure' which had been designed by men, an understanding of equality rooted in the 'serf mentality which we have inherited from generations of subjection' (1929: 47).

Conclusion

I have argued in this chapter that Rathbone's understanding of the state was rooted in her heritage of ideas concerning the obligations of the rich and the needs of the poor. Awareness of her own wealth was part of the emotional and intellectual landscape of her childhood. She carried her father's view that wealth was a trust, rather than a possession, into her observation of the very different lives led by the vast majority of the inhabitants of Liverpool and London. Behind William Rathbone's desire for redistribution of wealth lay a deep Christian faith. Rathbone's religious position is not clear, but her sense of obligation, and the moral nature of her commitment to social change, were deeply rooted in Christian values. Her acceptance of state intervention was based on her sense of individual responsibility for others.

Giving a lecture in 1927, Rathbone confessed to a 'very inferior equipment of economic knowledge', and said she would base her arguments on the 'facts and figures' used by the distinguished economist who had given the same lecture the year before (1927: 8). She then went on to demolish his pessimistic argument in presenting her own case for the redistribution of wealth. She believed that the needs of everyone should be met, and that wages should be based on the needs of each individual, and for her needs went beyond the basic need for food and shelter to the capacity for self-determination. Although she could and did speak the language of economists she never lost – nor in her perception was there any imperative to lose – her own moral focus. She believed that economic forces should be 'bridled and guided by ethical considerations' (1924: 242). Her compassion and her anger were roused by her observations of the poverty of working-class women. From the beginning her sympathies were more with the wife and mother than the wage-earner.

Rathbone believed that votes for women would begin the process of rectifying the faults in a political and social system in whose potential she had confidence. She did not challenge the institution of the family and thought that it would be possible by argument and persuasion to initiate direct payment to wives and mothers by the state. The war provided both a model for such a system, and the political opportunity to establish it: women had demonstrated the baselessness of anti-suffragist arguments and had gained the necessary confidence to insist that their demands be heard. Another part of her heritage which she did not abandon was a faith in the British: the constitution, the nation. She wrote the concept of the state into a long and comfortable tradition of English history, one that had the capacity for continued development. This construction fitted in with her sense of the superiority of English culture which was itself stimulated by the experience of the First World War. The optimism and confidence which lay behind this view concerning the potential of human beings is one that Rathbone seems never to have lost, despite living through two World Wars, the Slump and the rise of Fascism.

Note

1 Helena Swanwick (1864–1939) was editor of *The Common Cause* until the summer of 1912, when she resigned because the NUWSS executive repudiated her attacks on the militant suffragettes. She resigned from the NUWSS in 1915 over its policy on the war, and then became Chairman of the British branch of what was later named the Women's International League for Peace and Freedom. She continued to work for peace until her death.

3

Equality and Difference, 1912–29

The focus of this chapter will be on Eleanor Rathbone's ideas on gender equality and difference. The aim will be to discover where she stood in the feminist debate on whether sexual difference ought to be an irrelevant consideration, or whether the emphasis should be placed on women's difference from men. I will also look at the connected question of what her views were on differences between women. The main Rathbone texts referred to will be *The Problem of Women's Wages* (1912a), articles in *The Common Cause* and *The Woman's Leader* (*WL*), 'The Remuneration of Women's Services' (1917), *Equal Pay and the Family* (1918), *The Disinherited Family* (1924) and her speeches as President of the National Union of Societies for Equal Citizenship, published as *Milestones* (1929).

Acknowledging difference; seeking solidarity

As I suggested in Chapter 1, Rathbone assumed that there was an underlying common bond between women despite organisational and class differences. This assumption was at the core of Rathbone's theory and practice as a political feminist throughout her life, and its durability had its basis in her experience as a suffragist before the war. Yet Rathbone was always aware of and prepared to acknowledge differences between women. She was at the centre of a controversy within the NUWSS between 1912 and 1914 over the Election Fighting Fund which had been established to give financial aid to sympathetic parliamentary candidates. Rathbone felt that the executive of the NUWSS was developing a policy so weighted towards Labour that the result might be the defeat of the Liberals and the return of a Conservative majority in a General Election. She believed that the best hope for suffrage still lay with the Liberals, but her primary concern in this controversy was that members of the executive should be allowed to give open expression to different views. Her eventual resignation from the executive in April 1914, was over the question of loyalty and discipline within the executive. At first Rathbone had accepted the majority decision of the executive, and chastised herself for not asking for more time to develop an argument against a policy to which she was opposed. But later she acted independently, while still arguing that she had not broken any pledges or commitments (Vellacott, 1993: 479 n.45; NUWSS EC minutes 20 June 1912, Jan. 15, Feb. 5, March 5, 19 1914). She explained to Catherine Marshall that one aspect of 'English political life' which she hoped 'women will keep unchanged' was:

> the tradition which makes it possible for political opponents who quarrel on platforms . . . to maintain their personal friendly relations unchanged – always provided of course, that they do not doubt each other's honesty and good faith. (CEMP 3/48: 30 October 1915)

Nevertheless she found this conflict painful: in the same letter she described the time of her resignation from the NUWSS executive as 'one of the unhappiest times of my life' (CEMP 3/48: 30 October 1915). Differences between feminists then, as now, were not easily accommodated. Rathbone continued to define a willingness to look at and discuss questions on which there were divisions of opinion as a strength (*WL*, 3 September 1920: 677). In 1923 she challenged the Union to elect another president if they disagreed with such a practice (1929: 15). One of the difficulties for others was that her tolerance was sometimes hard to detect beneath her forceful manner of expressing her opinions (RP XIV 3.88d).

Rathbone's forcefulness was directed in the 1920s towards

maintaining the political momentum of the suffrage movement. She argued for the continued existence of the National Union of Women's Suffrage Societies for this purpose, denying that this was a narrow and selfish aim since women constituted 'half the human race' (*CC*, 15 February 1918: 573). During the most active years of the movement just before the 1914–18 war, suffragists experienced the power of numbers and money and became more confident that women could influence political structures and programmes. At that time the women's suffrage movement played a crucial part in the realignment of party politics (Holton, 1986; Vellacott, 1993). Rathbone remained confident that the suffrage struggle had 'built up a sense of solidarity among women of all classes which will never, if we handle our opportunities rightly, be broken down' (*CC*, 15 February 1918: 373).

Rathbone hoped and believed that the NUWSS – which was renamed the National Union of Societies for Equal Citizenship in 1919 – would provide organisational continuity for suffragists and feminists. In 1918 the NUWSS enlarged its aims to include the attainment of 'a real equality of status, liberties, and opportunities as between men and women'. This construction was intended to keep those feminists who sought for equality and those who emphasised difference within one ideological framework. Rathbone replied to those who might argue that 'equality' was 'too narrow a thing to aim at', that ' "Equality" is not a synonym for "identity". . . . It should be possible to make the status and oppor- tunities of women "equal to" those of men, without making them in the least the same.' She wanted the motto of the NUWSS to be: 'I am a woman, and nothing that concerns that status of women is indifferent to me'. Her understanding of feminism was that it meant the 'selection and concentration of work' on women's interests and needs (*CC*, 15 February 1918: 373).

Other suffragists did not agree always that the influence of women, now that suffrage was partially achieved, should remain outside the existing structures, and they chose to work within the existing mainstream political parties. The organisational divisions which had existed before the war were masked by the sheer num- bers of women involved: after the war different tactical and organisational choices were more obvious and seemed more crucial as the membership of the National Union of Societies for Equal Citizenship (NUSEC) declined. Rathbone's concern about this issue is apparent from soon after the end of the war. She was afraid that women, particularly of the younger generation, have 'been inclined to doubt the necessity for having a woman's movement at all' (1929: 8).

Throughout her life Rathbone asserted the need for solidarity among women and deplored its absence, but she never understood it to be necessary to deny that women held different views. She called for 'free trade in truth!' and wanted women in political parties to be exposed to the ideas of non-party organisations in order that their opinions could be given 'the test of opposition and friction with other minds' (1929: 5). She was especially concerned to criticise women of her own class for their failure to understand the position of working-class women. Her paper on wages, first written in 1902, opened boldly with the claim that 'everybody seems to acquiesce' in the view that women were underpaid, 'except when he or she is engaging the services of a woman' (1912a: 3). In 1917 she wrote again that she had 'not yet met the feminist whose principles compel her to pay her waitress the wages that would be demanded by her butler' (1917: 106). She wished the 'satisfied and prosperous individuals' who found the newly drawn up 'objects' of the NUSEC to be boring, 'could be brought up against the facts of life as they affect the poor section of working and married women' (*CC*, 28 November 1919: 432). Women with 'some money and leisure', she asserted, had 'got all they wanted for themselves out of the women's movement when it gave them the vote' (1929: 8).

In *The Disinherited Family* (1924), Rathbone attacked the wealthy and the professional who failed to understand the needs, as she perceived them, of working-class married women. In reply to the argument – put forward by Millicent Garrett Fawcett, among others – that family allowances would lead to a 'weakening of parental responsibility' she argued:

> Most well-to-do parents indeed would be aghast at the idea of a cherished daughter running such a risk as is undertaken by nearly every working woman who married within her own class. Such a woman knows that her future and that of her babies will depend absolutely on her husband's life and on his continued good health, good character,

and success in finding and keeping employment, and that if any one of these factors fails for more than a few weeks or months it means for the whole family destitution, mitigated only by such earnings as are possible to a woman cumbered with young children, or by the dire humiliation of poor-relief or charity. (1924: 325)

The nature of the short-sightedness of middle-class women was their failure to comprehend the mutual interests between women: Rathbone deplored the 'unnatural and involuntary warfare' which existed between the women 'who perform remunerated services of hand and brain in the labour market and those who perform unremunerated services in the home' (1924: 216–17).

On behalf of others

While she argued for solidarity between women, Rathbone still saw the political action she undertook as being on behalf of others. She was 'haunted' by the plight of the widow (1913a: 30), as she was later to be haunted by the evils of child marriage in India (1934a). Her tone here as elsewhere is of 'one who knows' what the needs of working-class women are, who can see the objective situation clearly and present a case on their behalf. She visualised the working-class woman as resigned to her lot, rather than tormented, 'occupied with what is immediately present to her in place and time' and unilluminated 'by the rays of imagination and hope' (1924: 186). She clearly wanted such women to be interested in what she saw as something better than 'the study of fashions and the handling of flowers, silks, muslins, etc' (1912a: 9–10). She described industrial workers as 'docile' and willing to do routine work (1917: 103, 109). She realised that women's characteristics as workers in industry were to a large extent socially constructed (1924: 246, 252), but she was writing from the outside, she was 'seeking to liberate' others (1929: 18). Her active participation was needed because 'The majority of mankind, including womankind, have lazy, unimaginative, preoccupied minds and to such our work makes little appeal' (1929: 32).

Rathbone believed the primary commitment of working-class women was to the needs of their families, and this view made for an

uneasiness or a lack of coherence in her presentation of the opposing pulls of 'sex' and 'class solidarity'. She recognised the common
interests and culture of working-class men (1929: 30). She understood why groups of newly unionised women would not wish to
challenge male trade union leaders (*WL*, 18 February 1921: 39).
But she also saw working-class women as outside working-class
culture, as sharing a more crucial need for loyalty to their own
sex. She had her own vision of how working-class married women
operated within their own sphere: 'Her success in her particular
job depends largely on humouring her household, especially its
male members, and getting her own way while seeming to give
them theirs.' As a result new ideas were 'passed from one woman
to another in confidential talk instead of being at once rushed into
print and on to the platform and the movement of opinion is con-
sequently slow' (1924: 194–5). Her favourite example of this was
the spread of information about birth control which she described
in 1927 as passing 'the torch from hand to hand' (1927: 114).

Rathbone thought that working-class women should work
alongside feminists outside the party because it was in their interests so to do. She was aware that working-class women did not
want to compete for wages with their husbands or future husbands,
that 'the interests of women as members of families were always in
conflict with their interests as industrial workers' (1912a: 20). She
argued that the position of the working-class married woman could
be transformed by the introduction of family endowment which
would in turn allow industrial workers to have equal pay with men.
Rathbone understood that low wages prevented women with skill
and ambition from appropriate rewards (1912a: 13), but she tended
increasingly to associate the demand for equal pay with middle-
class women.

Before the war Rathbone had referred to demands for 'equal
wages for equal work' as 'anti-feminist in its tendency' (*CC*, 4
January 1912: 675). This fits into her understanding of feminism as
acting in the interests of women. At that time she had also accused
those who claimed that 'men and women ought to receive equal
pay for equal work' of failing to 'examine whether the show of
authority about the "ought" is justified by any law, moral or economic' (1912a: 3). In 1917 she acknowledged that it was 'feminists'

who were demanding equal pay, but argued that they were denying the difficulties inherent in the claim (1917: 106). Her argument in 'The Remuneration of Women's Services' was that in order to achieve equal pay it was necessary to allow for the disadvantages of employing women workers, or the result would be their total exclusion (1917:108). At this time two of Rathbone's closest colleagues, Millicent Garrett Fawcett and Mary Stocks,[1] were in debate with her view on equal pay. Mary Stocks did not accept that women's low pay was related in any way to need, and therefore did not agree that endowment was the only way of achieving equal pay (*CC*, 5 April 1918: 630). The difference between Fawcett's view – as expressed in an article in *The Economic Journal* (Fawcett, 1918: 1–6) – and that of Rathbone's was a very narrow one focusing on the potential impact of the war and the reasons for women's low pay.

New Feminism in context: a period of reaction

It is important to be aware of the history of the development of Rathbone's views on equal pay when examining the debates in the 1920s in the NUSEC over the meaning of equality and the priorities for feminism. Her assertion in the NUSEC annual meeting in 1925 that she, like her audience, felt 'baffled and rather helpless in the face of the forces which tend to limit women's opportunities in the professions and to keep them to a definitely inferior status in industry', was disingenuous (1929: 27). The controversy focused on what became known as 'New Feminism'. What this formulation contained was neither as new nor as deeply divisive as it was once understood to be: nevertheless, at the time the division was felt as a painful one (Alberti, 1989: 170–80). In order to understand Rathbone's development of the New Feminism, I want to examine the political context in which the discussions about the future of the NUWSS during which she put forward these views were conducted, so that we can get some sense of both the emotional weight put on particular words, and the level of anxiety engendered by these debates.

Rathbone's optimism, her sense that the war had led to positive change for women, was common among her contemporaries. This hopefulness is apparent in *Equal Pay and the Family* with its 'ringing call to the ambition and vision of both men and women voters' (1918: 12). With hindsight, seeing what happened to feminist discourses, it is hard for us to give full credit to that sense of optimism, and we are apt to condemn too easily the contemporary feminists for not realising what was happening to their demands and hopes. Rathbone had been involved in social action for too long to be a naive optimist. In 1916 she wanted to transform the 'newly aroused consciousness' of the suffrage movement into 'immediately useful work' and warned of the dangers of losing, in periods of reaction, what had been gained in a 'period of enthusiasm' (*CC*, 30 June 1916: 155). The change in political atmosphere in the immediate postwar period was rapid (Alberti, 1989: Ch. 3). The achievement of the limited franchise and of the right to be elected as an MP, and the relief at the end of the war combined to give a huge surge of a sense of power. Then in December 1918 the election brought a victory for the coalition of Lloyd George Liberals and Conservatives, and the defeat of all the women candidates except Constance Gore-Booth, Countess Markevitz, who was a member of Sinn Fein and had no intention of taking her seat. The dominant feeling among contemporaries was of political volatility: the reporter for *The Common Cause* on the 1919 NUSEC Council wrote that the 'great convulsions of war have shaken and changed every political organisation' (*CC*, 14 March 1919: 584).

Beneath her determined optimism, Rathbone was aware that a continued political exploitation of women's solidarity was necessary precisely because of the ability of men to undermine the achievements of the women's movement (1929: 3). She was aware that the reaction to women's suffrage meant that feminists had to defend what had already been gained. Viewing the demands of those who were known as 'equalitarians' as defensive, she saw in the reaction to women's wartime gains one strong reason for that need to defend. Feminists must, she argued, struggle to 'keep the ground they have won and occasionally gain a fresh foothold here and there . . . there are many ways in which privileges already granted can be filched away and opportunities withdrawn and rights fall into disuetude' (1929: 17). The need to defend a woman's right to work she clearly saw as a restriction which was 'all the more irritating' because it was camouflaged as protection (1929: 6). She pointed out that the industrial women whose interests were under attack were precisely those who had not been enfranchised in 1918 (1929: 7).

Rathbone rapidly concluded that in the early 1920s feminists were, as she put it 'living through a period of reaction' (1929: 16). In 1921 her title for her presidential address was 'The Uses of Unpopularity', and she asserted, bracingly, that there was 'no better fertilizer for any cause than a good dose of unpopularity' (1929: 7). *The Disinherited Family* needs to be read within the framework in which Rathbone placed it, when

> four years of depressed trade and unprecedented unemployment have made the question of the exact terms on which women should take their proper place in industry seem nearly as unreal as arrangements for the coronation of a prince who has become a hunted fugitive. The women who are lurking in the corners of the disputed industries are, with very few exceptions, not anxious to call attention to themselves by demands for equal pay, and the men workers – except when they are also politicians – no longer feel it necessary to disguise the formula of exclusion under a euphemism. (1924: 234)

Rathbone had concluded before the war that the political parties exploited class differences between women, and her experience of the early 1920s confirmed this view. She placed responsibility for the failure of working-class women to realise their gender solidarity on the efforts of the political parties – and she had the Labour Party particularly in mind – 'to marshall the women voters behind the party banner and to prevent their energies being "dissipated" or their minds "confused" by mingling with women of other parties than their own and so discovering the bond between them' (1924: 194). What she did not recognise was that women in the Labour Party were developing their own critique of gender in the labour market and their own strategies to promote women's economic independence. Their efforts were unsuccessful in that they only made a limited impact on a male-dominated party (Thane, 1991). The Labour activists Rathbone was aware of were the visible middle-class members, and it was the leaders of 'the professional and trade organizations of women and most of those who speak for the political side of the movement' whom she accused of a failure to understand the needs of 'industrial women', because of their class biased perceptions of the equal pay issue (1924: 230).

With hindsight it is possible to understand the weakening of feminist confidence in the period 1919–25 as a result of a combination of cultural and political factors: the economic depression; the defensive reaction against women as they moved into the parliamentary political arena; and the need for the Labour party to consolidate its support as it came to power for the first time. It was in these contexts as well as in the light of the longstanding ideology of the suffrage movement that we need to read Rathbone's much quoted outlining of the 'New Feminism' in 1925:

> Now the legal barriers are down; there is still some debris left which we must clear away. But we need not give ourselves entirely up to that, for women are virtually free. At last we have done with the boring business of measuring everything that women want, or that is offered them by men's standards, to see if it is exactly up to sample. At last we can demand what we want for women, not because it is what men have got, but because it is what women need to fulfil the potentialities of their own natures and to adjust themselves to the circumstances of their own lives. (1929: 28)

The meanings of equality

Within the NUSEC itself the equalitarians did not accept that what was left was nothing but 'debris'. Elizabeth Abbott was the most articulate of those who opposed the direction in which Rathbone was guiding the energies of the organisation.[2] She was afraid that the NUSEC was turning away from a commitment to the 'demand for the removal of every arbitrary impediment that hinders the progress, in any realm of life and work, of women' (*WL*, 11 February 1927: 12). The equalitarians were in a majority on the executive of the NUSEC throughout this period, but they came under pressure from the time that Rathbone became President.

I have argued that Rathbone had long ago made up her mind that the two issues were inextricably entwined, and that endowment must precede equal pay. In her paper on women's wages she had made her position clear and she never shifted from it. She had refused to enter into debate over gender difference:

> I have indeed no wish to deny the existence or importance of differences of sex character . . . and I suppose it would be possible to contend that physical and mental defects would prevent them (women) from succeeding in the trade of the steel engraver or the glass blower . . . But the contention would be a futile one, impossible to prove and leading to nothing if proved. (1912a: 4)

She believed that women's low wages were the result of the expectation both of the women themselves, and of their employers, that they would marry. Differences in wages were not the result of the 'unalterable circumstances of sex', but of 'the arrangement' which led the 'male parent' to bear 'the cost of raising future generations' (1912a: 23). This argument was repeated in 'The Remuneration of Women's Services' (1917).

Rathbone knew that her views were opposed by other feminists. Millicent Garrett Fawcett accused Rathbone – I would judge unfairly – of disregarding 'the tremendously depressing effect on women's wages of the pre-war trade union rules', and asserted that she had not given sufficient weight to the destruction of the myth that women were incapable of skilled work, and that she 'assumes too much that women are always less industrially advantageous to their employers than men' (Fawcett, 1918: Vol. 28, 2–3). Jane Lewis has interpreted this disagreement as an objection by Fawcett to Rathbone's acceptance of the claim 'that women workers were inherently less valuable than men' (Lewis, 1991b: 83). Rathbone, in fact, did not say this: she repeated her argument that 'in the eyes of most employers' there were 'certain disadvantages of women's labour which have to be reckoned with', and she pointed out that at the root of this prejudice was the male '"club" instinct which makes them feel more at ease with an undiluted male staff' (1917: 108). And it is worth noting that Fawcett wrote that she 'had endeavoured to show that such differences as exist between Miss Rathbone and myself upon this principle are very much a question of words and not of facts' (Fawcett, 1918: 4). Rathbone was characteristically combative in defence of her position, describing the 'demand of "equal pay for equal work"' as 'irresistible', but its achievement as a potential 'empty victory', one that might 'rivet more firmly the fetters which bound them in the past to low-paid, unskilled trades', and one by which women 'may check the course of their own social emancipation' (1918: 10).

Debates between feminists in the organisation took place within the 'Economic Independence of Women Committee', which was set up by the executive of the NUSEC in 1920 to examine both equal pay and the 'Endowment of Motherhood'. The minutes hint at the struggle which went on in those meetings. To the equalitarians, it was the demand for endowment that was likely to 'take many years to accomplish'. Rathbone believed there was no likelihood that 'public opinion' would shift in its view that there should be no difference between the pay of married and single men, and argued that it was unwise to base demands on the need for such a shift (NUSEC EC Minutes 11 November 1920). While feminists struggled with priorities in private, Rathbone took the argument again into the public domain with *The Disinherited Family* (1924). There her tone is less sharp but the message is the same. Her examination of the question of equal pay led to the conclusion that without compulsion equal pay was not likely 'to make much headway, so long as the forces which have led in the past to unequal pay remained unchanged'. If there was compulsion, then she argued that there would be an intensification of 'the existing tendency of the two sexes to become segregated in different occupations and to give women even less equality of opportunity than they have at present'. She pointed out that such equality of opportunity as did exist had been gained so far by the acceptance of unequal pay (1924: 234). In *The Disinherited Family* Rathbone also explored the wider issue of equal pay for equivalent work:

> Why, merely because there are men as well as women in the tailoring trade and the teaching profession, pay the tailoress more than the dressmaker? Why should the scavenger who cleans our streets get more than the charwoman who cleans our houses? (1924: 251)

She then pointed out that the result of job segregation with women getting lower rates of pay had led to 'quite the wrong estimate of the relative difficulty and importance of "men's jobs" and "women's jobs"' (1924: 252).

Rathbone was, as always, concerned to demonstrate the gap between 'what is desirable' and 'what is practicable', 'so long as the causes which have brought about the double standard of pay for the two sexes remain untouched' (1924: 252). One practical problem was financial: she was anxious about a situation where feminists were also faced with the 'old difficulty that the wealth of the country is insufficient to pay really adequate family wages' (1924: 253). Yet her own solution was an expensive one. She was also well aware of the fear and 'sex antagonism' which moulded public policy on equal pay, but in acknowledging male prejudice Rathbone was in danger of consolidating it. Her conclusion on pay was that 'Nothing can really redress the balance except to remove the weight that is pulling it down against the women', and that this could only be achieved if 'wives and mothers' were paid for their performance of 'that special task', the reproduction of society (1924: 252–3). This solution sought economic equality for women, but also involved a recognition of the status quo as far as women's dependency was concerned.

At the time when Rathbone was writing *The Disinherited Family* she openly alluded to the stresses in the executive committee in her presidential address to the NUSEC. She referred to 'two kinds of feminism', and asserted that the Union did not 'seek to bind all its members to a pedantic adhesion to every cast-iron creed, but welcomes, or at least tolerates, differences of opinion' (1929: 15). At this stage a variety of different positions were taken and openly expressed in the NUSEC. Elizabeth Macadam,[3] as honorary secretary of the NUSEC, invited Millicent Garrett Fawcett to put her case against endowment in an article in *The Woman's Leader* (30 January 1925: 4). Part of Fawcett's argument was a moral one about the relationship between parents and children, but her argument was also based on gender difference. Although she believed that women should have equal pay, and that they were not inferior workers, she had always believed that women's contribution to political life was different from men's and she now asserted that: 'The predominance of the wife and mother in the home has been a source of strength and vitality which counts enormously for good in our type of civilisation' (*WL*, 30 January 1925: 4). This was a view which Rathbone shared, but she argued that the 'wife and mother in the home' had not been able fully to realise her 'strength and vitality' (*Time & Tide* [*TT*] 25 May 1923: 537).

The two schools of thought were polarising over the question of the urgency of getting family endowment adopted as NUSEC policy. Feminists began to adopt entrenched and defensive positions as they increasingly felt the need to choose priorities. Those who resigned from the executive of the NUSEC wanted to concentrate work on the removal of protective legislation. That issue was not in itself a crucial point of division between feminists; the NUSEC continued to support the line taken by the Open Door Council which was set up by Abbott and others for this purpose. Protective legislation was a complex and emotive issue, and part of the problem lay, ironically, in the unwillingness of the NUSEC to take a line in opposition to women's industrial organisations. It had become entangled with the question of equal pay, and with the more critical and emotional issue of what was meant by 'real equality'. Members of the NUSEC found themselves unwillingly having to vote about whether family endowment, the availability of birth control information and international peace were to be defined as social reform, or as questions involving the 'real equality of liberties, status and opportunity between men and women' (Alberti, 1989: Ch. 7). There was considerable doubt expressed by members as to whether there was indeed any need to make this choice. As Rathbone pointed out, 'no two members of the NUSEC or of other women's societies working for equal citizenship, would put exactly the same interpretation' on the 'formula' to which the Union was committed (*WL*, 11 February 1927: 12). But the final division was the result of the build up of stress within the organisation.

Womanhood and citizenship

I have argued that Rathbone was never ideologically opposed to equalitarian demands. In 1923 when she had identified the two 'schools of thought', she had given a sympathetic construction to the motives of those whom she called 'identity' feminists (1929: 15). She was aware of the resistance to the achievement of equality, which she sometimes seemed to have believed could only be shifted by cataclysmic outside events, in particular by war. In 1917 she had written of how the 'barriers' to women's employment in 'ill-paid and unskilled occupations' had been broken down by 'the necessities of war' in two years, after the 'women's movement' had 'beaten itself for half a century in vain' against them (1917: 101–2). At first she was hopeful that 'possession of the vote' would give 'force to a movement that will not stop before it has swept away the barriers of the past and won for women their right place in the social as well as the industrial organisation of society' (1918: 9). A more cautious image of the power of the vote used in that same year – 1918 – was of the keystone to a building: now that this stone was in place, the work could begin. The work to be done was within the 'sphere of feminism', and this concept should not be seen as a 'limitation of purpose' but as 'merely the best and only effective way of getting the world's work done' (*CC*, 15 February 1918: 373). Two years later Rathbone was concerned that women should not throw away 'the first and greatest opportunity that has been given to them to justify at once their womanhood and their citizenship'. She was distressed by the perception of the opponents of women's suffrage that the vote had become acceptable 'because it is possible to say of it that it has made no perceptive difference to politics' (1929: 5).

The pages of *The Woman's Leader* testify to the way the question of whether there was such a thing as 'A Woman's Point of View' was openly debated by feminists (*WL*, 25 February 1921: 52; 4 March 1921: 68). Rathbone does not seem to have had a clear sense of what women's distinctive contributions would be, a result, I would argue, of her genuine open-mindedness about the question. She was later to develop the idea that there was 'a wavelength set up by human suffering, to which the minds of women give a specially good reception' (1929: 48). In 1921, referring to the 'immediate programme' of the NUSEC, she asserted that each reform stood 'for an effort to relieve a mass of human suffering' (1929: 9). She claimed that women had 'practical minds', and an inclination to 'interest themselves less in lofty generalisations than in the practical application of those generalisations to existing facts' (1929: 14). But she also wanted women to be recognised as initiators (1929: 28–9). She groped towards the sense that women might be able to cross the boundaries of the public and the private, that they could throw on the world's problems a 'light that shines from within' (1929: 28).

Behind Rathbone's thinking in the mid-1920s is an increasingly urgent desire to prevent feminism from stagnating. She could see no point in trying to achieve particular forms of equality when the resistance to it appeared to be – at least temporarily – immovable. In 1925, she belittled the idea of pressing on with the demand for equal pay by describing that path as chanting 'the gospel of sex equality to the inattentive ears of employers and Trade Unionists, comforting ourselves that the fault is theirs if they fail to listen' (1929: 28). She wanted to press on with what might be possible and what women at the time seemed to want: 'not equality but self-determination' (1929: 33). Her willingness to compromise is also apparent in her understanding of the achievements of the NUSEC in the early 1920s. The Acts which were passed felt like achievements to feminists at the time, although they were recognised as being only partial. For example, Rathbone argued that it was pointless and cruel to those who would benefit from a reform to refuse to support a 'smaller measure', and that there was no reason why the defeat of such a measure would 'hasten the coming of the wider one' (*The Times*, 14 April 1923: 8, col. a).

Susan Pedersen has persuasively argued that during and after the war there were powerful political forces operating to ensure that welfare legislation was 'profoundly gendered, filtering women's livelihood through the hands of men'. Pedersen understands the 'feminist vision of state-guaranteed economic independence for mothers' as having 'almost completely evaporated'. She suggests that Ellen Wilkinson 'was perhaps the only politician to notice the distance that the "mothers pensions" demand had travelled by 1925, and to challenge their new identification as a male right' (Pedersen, 1990: 104, 92, 104–5). My sense is that feminists were aware of what was happening, although they did not draw the links between their own demands and what Pedersen has called their 'unintended consequences' (Pedersen, 1990: 105). It was difficult for them to gain the sort of perspective which would have made such an analysis possible. Feminists realised that the Widows', Orphans' and Old Age Contributory Pensions Bill did not satisfy the demands of any of the women's organisations pressing for pensions for civilian widows, because it was limited to the widows of national insurance contributors, and thus based on the man's insurance, not the woman's need (*WL*, 21 November 1924: 343; 10 July 1925: 188; *TT*, 30 July 1926: 687). Rathbone's particular dilemma lay in her emphasis on need: it was on woman's need that she had based her arguments for widows' pensions since 1913. The fact that some women's poverty would be ameliorated by the Act led her to celebrate the numbers covered by the new Act, rather than to worry about its limitations. Her comments on the new Labour Government's Widows' Pensions Bill in 1929 suggest that she had few hopes of full coverage for widows, and that her growing concern was to ensure the well-being of children. She referred to the 1925 Act as providing the 'dubious example of granting pensions to the young childless widow' (*WL*, 8 November 1929: 303).

The new focus on cost also lay behind this acceptance of compromise. The wave of reaction took place at the end of the 1920s when rising unemployment, Rathbone noted, 'intensified masculine jealousy' within the trade unions and the professions (1929: 45). It was a reaction of which feminists were only too well aware.

Conclusion

Rathbone based her demand for suffrage neither on a claim of essential difference nor on absolute equality. She believed that human institutions were malleable, arguing that 'the circumstances of sex are not unalterable, although the fact of sex is' (1912a: 21), and her understanding of the significance of equality or difference was therefore embedded in the historical and political context. She became a suffragist in order to change the political 'circumstances of sex', and to claim a position for women within the power structures so that they could alter those circumstances. The suffrage movement led her to respect the ability of women to transform their own lives and thus change the world. Changes in the status of women during the war, which she constructed positively, confirmed her sense of optimism. Indeed, I will argue that she never abandoned her passionate belief that enfranchisement would give a voice to women, nor her hope that the political influence and presence of women would lead to social reform. With hindsight, her optimism about the impact of the war on women appears mis-placed: it was hard for feminists to adjust to the backlash of the early 1920s. Rathbone was determined not to lose the impetus of the suffrage movement, but she did recognise the necessity for entrenchment in this period of reaction. Her writing and thinking in this period is also informed by an acknowledgement of the differences between women. But her confident assertion that difference was a strength was undermined by the painful organisational division in the NUSEC.

Rathbone's impetus towards agency led her to make compromises which with hindsight appear to have blunted the feminist edge to her ideas. Joan Scott has suggested that the effect of assuming equality and difference are opposite and mutually exclusive categories has been to undercut the ends which feminists seek to obtain: they are presented with an impossible choice between seeking for equality and asserting gender difference (Scott, 1988). An analysis of Rathbone's writing demonstrates the practical and organisational problems of refusing to place equality and difference in opposition to one another. While she does not appear to have felt any less confident that she was a feminist and could continue to act as one, at the end of the decade she moved into a male-dominated arena (and one where her father's ghost must have haunted her), and this weakened her identification with women as far as organisational and practical links were concerned. It did not weaken her sense that she could and should speak and act for women wherever they lived, and particularly if they were victims of the patriarchy.

Notes

1 Millicent Garrett Fawcett (1847–1929) first spoke at a suffrage meeting in July 1869: she remained an active suffragist for the rest of her life, holding the position of President of the NUWSS between 1906 and 1918. Mary Stocks (1891–1975) carried a banner in a suffrage march in 1907, and became a member of the NUWSS executive during the First World War. She was a close colleague and friend of Rathbone's in the interwar period.

2 Elizabeth Abbott (d. 1957) was a Scottish suffragist who was involved for 40 years in the Association for Moral and Social Hygiene. In 1936 she helped to found

the Open Door Council in defence of women's right to work on equal terms with men.

3 Elizabeth Macadam (1881–1948) did settlement work in London before being appointed the Warden of the Victoria Women's Settlement in 1903. It was there she met Rathbone. They worked together to set up the Liverpool School of Social Science and Training for Social Work, of which Macadam became the Director in 1917. She was given leave of absence to join the staff of the Welfare Department in the Ministry of Munitions in 1916. After the war she moved to London with Rathbone. She was active in the NUSEC and wrote books on social work training (e.g. Macadam, 1925).

4

Taking the Path to Power, 1924–9

In July 1928 all women in Britain were finally enfranchised; in June 1929 Eleanor Rathbone was elected as a Member of Parliament to represent the English Universities and moved into a male-dominated political arena for the first time. By the late 1920s Rathbone had been involved in the women's movement for 30 years, but she was far from exhausted either as a feminist or a political activist. Before the war, she had encouraged her fellow-suffragists to remember 'the psychological value of mere repetition', asserting that 'If a new idea is to be got into the head of the man in the street, it has to be hammered in by repeated blows'. To those who protested that it ought not to be necessary to adopt the methods which she then recommended, she replied that 'It ought not to be necessary to carry on the struggle at all. It should have been terminated successfully long ago' (*CC*, 5 September 1912: 373–4). She knew that the struggle did not terminate with the vote, and in the 1920s the core of her activity was with the National Union of Societies for Equal Citizenship (NUSEC). But she spoke to much wider audiences, and was said to have been 'equally at home' talking to the people of a South Wales Mining area as to the members of the Eugenics Society (Macnicol, 1980: 20). She needed to be active, wanted to find new ways to approach complex problems.

This can be interpreted as an urge towards agency, towards power, and it was this impetus which was to take her into parliament.

I want to track down the way she responded to what she understood to be the political possibilities of the late 1920s. This was a time of volatility in political, including feminist, ideas and practices and it is therefore worth a detailed examination. Rathbone's ideas in this period were expressed in her speeches as the President of the NUSEC, in a long paper entitled *The Ethics and Economics of Family Endowment* (1927) and in two short pieces written for the NUSEC: *Why Women's Societies should work for Family Endowment* (n.d., *c*.1920) and *The Poor Law Proposals and Women Guardians* (December 1928). I shall also refer to relevant passages in *Equal Pay and the Family* (1918) and in *The Disinherited Family* (1924), and to letters published in *Time & Tide* (*TT*).

'The wind of the spirit'

Eleanor Rathbone's view of history was rooted in her faith in human agency: she believed that change could be accomplished by human actions. The choices people made were shaped by attitudes and prejudices which were hard to shift but this was never an excuse for inaction. Citizenship demanded participation and enfranchised women must not relax their efforts, nor accept complacently that progress was inevitable. They must be impatient on behalf of those who were 'suffering from . . . intolerable social conditions' (1929: 18). She used the model of the suffrage movement to exhort the societies of the Union to maintain their faith and act 'like a small electric power station in a large centre of population' (1929: 36). Rathbone was determined that feminists should not slacken their efforts, or become narrow in their demands. She was anxious that a programme based on demands for equality would not be 'likely to arouse much enthusiasm or attract new recruits' with the result that feminists would see 'the once broad river of the N.U.S.E.C. dwindle till it becomes a trickle and loses itself in the sands' (1929: 28).

I suggested in the last chapter that her sense that she understood what women wanted and needed was so firm that she felt she could be critical of other feminists. This confidence combined with her commitment to action led her to welcome all manifestations of women's organisations, without feeling the need to judge the nature of their activities. It was this willingness to include a wide range of activity under the umbrella of feminism which exacerbated the split within the executive of the NUSEC. In 1927, the year of the split, her speech to the societies paid tribute to the 'devoted work' done by the active few. But she also reproached other societies for their lack of activity and, as she saw it, their resultant 'lamentably small membership' (1929: 36). Her view was that the NUSEC was losing some of its energy and impetus towards the end of the 1920s. In a 'critical review' of the union's activities, she asked the NUSEC delegates: 'how much has been accomplished by the year's work?' (1929: 34). Her answer provided some comfort and a good deal of exhortation. Towards the end of this speech, she made a direct reference to the equalitarians who split off from the NUSEC at that meeting. She spoke of the need to 'get things done not merely to relieve our own souls by talking about equality', and asserted that 'the first essential is that our Societies must have life and have it abundantly. There must be no stagnation in the waters. They must be kept in constant motion by the inflow of currents' (1929: 37–8).

Rathbone was responsible for both the original compilation of the words of the object of the union, and the additional words which caused offence to the resigning executive members (*TT*, 25 March 1927: 292). As I indicated in the last chapter, the split was focused on ideology, on definitions of what was meant by 'real' equality. In a letter to *Time & Tide* about the 'clash' within the NUSEC, Rathbone wrote that 'if the word "real" meant the same thing to everybody' then it would not have occurred (*TT*, 25 March 1927: 292). But the division in the society happened at that time because of the decline in membership of the NUSEC, and Rathbone's speech the year before had made it quite clear that part at least of her motivation in constructing a 'new' feminism was to build up the membership. In *The Disinherited Family* Rathbone had paid tribute to women in other organisations, specifying the Women's Co-operative Guild, the Women Citizens' Associations and the Women's Institutes. Her tribute to what was offered by these organisations does suggest that she was not simply anxious about numbers, but had a broad understanding of feminism as autonomy for women. She asserted that it was not only within the overtly feminist NUSEC that women were able to express their 'revolt' against their subordination and lack of status, their 'uneasy desire for control over their own destinies' (1924: 192). In her view, 'the women's movement comprises a large number of reforms, all of which are "feminism", but only some of them "equality".' Feminism had the 'aim of enabling women to be and do their best', a goal which 'will not have been accomplished even when every sex barrier has fallen' (*TT*, 12 March 1926: 254).

I described in the last chapter how her anger was always directed towards the complacent, whether feminist or otherwise, both psychologically and materially: 'indolence and self-satisfaction' she hated (1929: 34). She was frustrated and often impatient with those who did not try to change themselves or the world. But she was also well aware of the practical problems facing women who wanted to be involved in public action. In her response to the proposal of the Minister of Health, Neville Chamberlain, to abolish Poor Law Boards of Guardians, and transfer their powers to committees of the county councils, she pointed out that women would be excluded because of the distances to be travelled because they were less likely to have 'abundant leisure or a motor car' (1928). Moreover, beneath her expression of the need for urgency and action, she did not lose touch with the underlying complexity of the causes of poverty or misogyny, and reminded members of the NUSEC that 'the forces which are opposing us, are invisible and intangible' (1929: 38).

Women's political activities were spread among different organisations in the interwar period with the resulting dispersal of energy. Rathbone herself acted within feminist organisations and outside them. For her, the landscape had changed from the prewar image she used when looking back on the suffrage movement in 1928. She referred then to 'the volcanic upheaval' which had exposed 'the oppressions, restrictions, disabilities that weighed upon women . . . the barren tracks, the sharp rocks, the creeping ugliness' (1929: 39). In the late 1920s she used natural imagery again to express her hope that there would be 'no stagnation in the waters' of the movement, so that it could be 'kept in constant motion by the inflow of fresh currents' (1929: 28). She used yet another natural image in the same year, this time perhaps to justify the dispersal which she both participated in and feared. Speaking to a non-feminist audience she lifted herself metaphorically off the surface of the women's movement to join 'the wind of the spirit that . . . can be in two or indeed a million places at once' (1927: 101).

The language of ethical socialism

In *The Ethics and Economics of Family Endowment* (1927), Rathbone balanced an appeal to conscience with an awareness of the problem of resourcing welfare and challenged the complacency of those in power, especially with regard to the well-being of children. She based her argument on an understanding of 'economic forces' which she had expressed in *The Disinherited Family*: that they should be 'bridled and guided by ethical considerations' (1924: 242). She wanted to rouse her listeners and readers to a realisation that 'present method of providing for children is fundamentally unjust' (1927: 52). This growing emphasis on children was a response to what Rathbone believed would appeal to her audience at a time when welfare reforms were focusing attention on them (1927: 51). She also sought to expose to analysis the current 'truisms' about 'the value of the family as an institution, the dangers of a C3 population, the importance of the functions of motherhood' (1927: 52). Her position was an ethical one, but she also wanted to be realistic about money, and to make the most efficient use of resources. She accepted that the difficulty of cost for family endowment was 'formidable', and suggested a gradual approach (1927: 100–2). She was also concerned to demonstrate the false savings which the opposition to allowances faced from those concerned with financial stringency. 'Society', she pointed out, 'is perpetually rushing in to avert the harshest consequences of its failure to make systematic provision in its structure for children, by doing just enough to enable them to grow up and perpetuate their kind, not enough to secure them the chance to be well born and well reared' (1927: 53–4).

Rathbone's ethical position meant that her thinking was close to the reformist, middle-class elements of the Labour Party in the interwar period. Rathbone refused to stand against Labour and it is clear that aspects of socialist ideology appealed to her, as they had to her father (Lewis, 1991a: 293). She was willing to speak the language of ethical socialism, and her advocacy of family endowment was understood in those terms by others (*WL*, 30 January 1925: 3). She saw herself as close to Labour in that she was 'utterly convinced that the rich are too rich and the poor too poor' (1927: 101). And she was prepared to use the threat of socialist revolution when making appeals to the right. Writing just after the General Strike of 1926, she asserted of 'the manual workers', that 'Never again – at least while the contrasts of wealth and luxuries are before their eyes – will they be satisfied with the conditions which kept them acquiescent if not content before.' Referring directly to the strike in the coal fields, she added: 'The forms in which discontent manifests itself, the remedies it asks for, may be unjustified, but the discontent itself is seldom unjustified' (1927: 29–30).

But Rathbone could never have worked closely with the Labour Party. The Labour Party had been succoured in the early twentieth century by suffragism, but it was an uncomfortable place for feminists whenever it became an issue whether class or gender was the priority. Her consistent line or argument was that if 'the doctrine of the "living wage"' was left untouched, then a decent standard of living could not be achieved 'out of existing resources even if they were redistributed as between classes more drastically the most extreme Socialists think practical' (1927: 26). This cut directly across Labour thinking which was based on demands for increasing wages – with the wage-earner understood to be male – and feared the effect of endowment on wage levels. Moreover, as I suggested in the last chapter, her perspective on working-class life and culture was indelibly that of an outsider. She was also resistant to the collectivist element in socialism: 'every human being, while in one sense a part of the organic whole, is in another sense an inevitably separate and even lonely individuality, to be counted as an end in itself and not merely as a means to the ends of others' (1927: 8).

Slipped into a passage on the conditions still prevailing in the mid-1920s is a phrase which demonstrates Rathbone's sense of the worst of the politics of left and right in that period:

> The ordinary child fares best, for it can enjoy the communist training of the streets and public playgrounds, where the staking out of private property claims and the kind of individualism that requires to send down its roots are discouraged by representatives of Sir. W. Joynson-Hicks. (1927: 46–7)

She wanted children who were 'scientifically-minded' or 'studious' to have opportunities which were denied to them by collectivism or by the blind selfishness of conservatism. She was an individualist, and her intention was to expose the false individualism of the right. Her final position was ethical and patriotic, retaining a faith and optimism that 'the minds of British men and women, helped by their innate sense of justice and fair play, can be trusted "to get there in the end"' (1927: 106).

Independence and the family

Rathbone was elected to Parliament as an Independent. This was totally in keeping with all she had written and said about women needing to beware of the loyalty of party cutting across their loyalty to their sex. In common with many, although not all, suffragists who had been active in the period before the great surge of the years 1906–14, her inclination was to take a non-party political stance. When political activity by the NUWSS was at its most intense in the three years before the outbreak of war, she had worked hard to persuade politicians of any party to support suffrage, helping with the plan of giving dinner parties for leading conservatives, and donating money for work among the miners (Vellacott, 1993: 151–2, 300). Her criticisms of the policy of the Election Fighting Fund Committee before the war came from a non-party position. She was afraid that the NUWSS policy was moving away from her ideal of the democratic political process (n.d., *c.* 1913b). She also disliked the class rhetoric of the Labour Party and was more wary of it than other members of the NUWSS who were moving 'From Liberal to Labour with Women's Suffrage' (NUWSS EC 6 March 1913; Vellacott, 1993). The minutes of the NUWSS give the impression that Rathbone felt she was in an increasingly beleaguered minority, and that her greatest concern was that as a minority she should not be muzzled. She argued strongly for feminists to influence political parties from within (*CC*, 8 February 1912: 752; 30 May 1912: 119–20), but she was also involved at this time in the establishment of two non-party political organisations aimed at mobilising and educating women municipal and potential parliamentary voters: the Women's Municipal Party (Hollis, 1987: 410), and the first Women's Citizens Association (*CC*, 30 June 1916: 156). I believe that she was personally happiest as an independent, and when in opposition to power.

The ideal of independence lay at the core of Rathbone's thinking, and she applied it to both public and to private life. Her explanation for the persistence of the 'monstrous injustice and criminal folly of society's whole attitude towards mothers and children', and for the 'unexplained anomaly of the acquiescence even of married men in this attitude' was 'the fact that the economic dependence of mothers and children is the best and far far the greatest weapon of masculine dominance' (1927: 61–2). She condemned the effects of this dependency on the ordinary woman 'who married in her youth the man of her choice and has found in him a partner neither better nor worse than the average run of men', but 'is to be chafed and irked by her dependency and the consequences – the expanding family and unexpanding income . . . In her sore mind there forms a little festering pool against her husband' (1924: 328). The aim of the Family Endowment Committee in 1918 was to strengthen the hand of the woman who 'by reason of complete economic dependence and life of unbroken drudgery, is at present powerless and inarticulate' (1918: 33). Rathbone later suggested that young women might be hoping for more in the 1920s because of 'post-war ideas of what the comradeship of married life should be', and yet still find that marriage and poverty made her 'a nag or scold', or, more likely, 'devitalised and rather silent and listless' (1924: 328). This image of the physical and mental deterioration of working-class women recurs throughout her writing on marriage. She emphasised that the misery was the consequence of an attitude which did not take marriage seriously, but regarded the choice of 'marrying and having children' as 'merely one of a number of alternative amenities on which the worker is free, if he chooses, to spend part of the remuneration earned by his hand or brain in the labour market' (1927: 52).

Rathbone believed that women 'should not be regarded merely as an appendage to another human being, and an incentive to that other's industry (Rathbone and Stocks, n.d., *c.* 1920: 4). She constructed an image of an ideal marriage, a close 'physical, moral and economic union' with a 'moral right to share'. This partnership was made impossible because according to 'the theory of marriage embodied in the law and marriage services . . . of this country', the wife had 'functions implicitly assigned to her in the contract', which were 'such as to impede her from contributing' (1924: 206). Her desire for more equality in marriage was not merely theoretical: she supported Maude Royden's efforts to open up discussion in the NUSEC of revision of the marriage service so as to remove the clauses which placed the wife in subordination (Fletcher, 1989: 236). A resolution supporting such revision was moved in the Annual Council Meeting in 1925, to which 'there was no opposition, but enthusiastic affirmation' (*WL*, 10 July 1925: 189). Rathbone did not view marriage as indissoluble and favoured divorce law reform (*The Times*, 14 April 1923: 8, col. a).

The description of the family which recurs in Rathbone's writings was that it was the site of 'the strongest emotions, the most enduring motives, the most universally accessible sources of happiness' (1924: 123; 1927: 12). But she was also aware of the dangers of women's containment within the family and within marriage. In particular she warned against the effect on the husband, in that 'the device of the uniform family income – ministers to the desire for self-importance by giving to the man a kind of multiple personality . . . so that he stands out like the central figure in an Italian picture against a dim richness of angel and Cupid faces' (1924: 343). She argued that it was this 'Turk Complex' which prevented change, because it gave men a power they enjoyed. The result of this attitude was that men denigrated women's contribution both inside and outside the home. Resistance to the employment of women in male dominated areas was 'intensified . . . by a feeling among the members of the dominant sex that it is belittling their own strength and skill to admit that any woman can attain to the like' (1924: 217). She gave a telling glimpse of her view of male work cultures when she described how the idea that the work of wives 'in bearing and rearing children give her any claim of her own on the community is either ignored or met with the academic equivalent of a wink and dig in the ribs of the nearest male with which the hundred-per-cent. he-man of the lower orders habitually greets every allusion to sex or maternity' (1927: 53). The determination of 'the leaders of working men . . . to cling persistently to the ideal of a uniform adequate family wage' was, she argued, 'influenced by a secret reluctance to see their wives and children recognized as separate personalities' (1924: 155). However, she was consistent in acknowledging the part played by what we would call conditioning, what she referred to as 'circumstances', in moulding male attitudes (1924: 197).

Rathbone's views on illegitimacy were also informed by her belief in the family, her wish to give it 'a fuller recognition and a more assured and honourable status' (1924: 369). In 1918, the majority of the Family Endowment Committee favoured giving an allowance to the unmarried mother, but they did so on the grounds that such an allowance would not encourage illegitimacy, and might indeed decrease it (1918: 52–3). Rathbone rejected the idea of paying family allowances to unmarried mothers in 1924, not on the basis of sexual morality, but because 'the conditions generally recognized as essential to secure (a child's) well-being . . . include a stable home and two parents – a father as well as a mother' (1924: 369). Her expressed concern is thus with the child; she did not want to benefit those who 'have chosen to bring a child into the world, regardless of whether they have fulfilled the conditions generally recognized as essential to secure its well-being' (1924: 369). And she disagreed with others on the Family Endowment Committee, asserting that girls 'who dislike industrial employment, or are mentally or physically incompetent, and who are of lowest calibre and least fit for motherhood' would be tempted to have illegitimate children if they were offered an allowance (1918: 58). She did welcome the change in attitude towards illegitimacy (1924: 371), and the legislation which introduced affiliation orders, and assisted 'in lifting the stigma' attached to the birth of an illegitimate child. But she later used an odd phrase in approving 'the change in outlook', which she described as altered 'from the days . . . when a woman raped even against her will felt there was no escape from disgrace but in death' (1936: 50).

Rathbone was well aware of how the power of men in the home could be abused at its worst. Before the war she had pointed out that 'the law, as usually interpreted, regards wife-beating and even worse assaults upon women as venial and imposes the most trivial penalties' (1912b: p.2). Her experience of working with the Soldiers' and Sailors' Family Association had extended her awareness of the fate of 'broken-spirited wives of brutal or drunken husbands' (1924: 196). She offered readers of *The Disinherited Family* an imaginative re-creation of the household 'where the husband drinks, gives his wife as little as possible of his earnings, and ill-treats her'. The description ends, cryptically: 'Then the nights!' (1924: 196). Rathbone did not avoid writing about sexuality, but her references are usually brief and often reveal her distaste. She described the crowded conditions of poor working-class homes where children 'grow up huddled together, their bodies, minds, and characters jostling each other like young chickens in an overstocked poultry farm' (1927: 46). During the Second World War she advocated the use of women police near military camps 'as a protection against the nuisance caused by loose women and silly girls who infect the neighbourhood of the camps' (*Hansard*, 24 October 1940: 365, col. 1138).

Motherhood and domesticity

Rathbone's awareness of the abuse of men's power within marriages fed into her critique of the sentimentalisation with which ideas about women and motherhood were masked. Before the war she had expressed the hope that Almroth Wright's attack on women would 'serve as sort of moral emetic to those women whose minds have been cloyed with the sentimental conception of women' (1912b: 2). Later she coined an epigram to summarise the construction of 'the wife and mother': 'Popular sentiment places her a little lower than the angels; the law a little higher than a serf.' And she referred to the wartime 'institution of Baby Week' as an 'annual festival . . . for a collective effort to glorify the functions of motherhood and impress on those who discharge it the truth that theirs is indeed "work of national importance"' (1924: 180, 177).

Rathbone's own descriptions of the domestic work done by women was determinedly unsentimental, asserting that motherhood was a craft, and presenting a stark view of the conditions under which women were forced to work (1924: 178, 180–7). She calculated the value of the work done by women in the home by estimating what each man would need to employ someone to do the work of his wife. The woman herself, in Rathbone's view, failed to value the work that she did when she 'gave up moulding cigarettes in a factory and turned instead to moulding the bodies and minds of future men and women' (1927: 58). Part of her case in feminist circles was always that women's work as mothers was undervalued. She put a resolution before the International Women's Suffrage Alliance in 1923 asserting that 'married women bringing up children . . . are doing work of as great importance to the community as those men and women who are producing material wealth or performing remunerated service of hand or brain' (*TT*, 25 May 1923: 537). The result of the undervaluing of 'the work that a woman does in her own home in bearing and rearing children', was that it was 'made to seem more distasteful than tending a loom or punching a tram ticket', while it was in fact 'much more skilled, varied and interesting than nine out of ten of the jobs done by working women, or for that matter working men' (1924: 322–3). She also pointed out when addressing the Royal Commission on the Coal Mining Industry, that childbirth was four times as dangerous as coalmining (1925: 867). Rathbone was fully aware that the pressures on women had become greater with the introduction of social welfare legislation which raised the 'standard of educational and social requirements', and reduced women's ability to supplement the household income, while failing to set any price on her labour (1924: 181). Moreover, she recognised that domestic work was not suited to or desired by all women (1929: 7).

In parallel with her avoidance of the sentimentalisation of motherhood, Rathbone referred regularly to the role of 'parents' in the bringing up of children. Nevertheless, her understanding of the difference between the genders was based on ideas about maternity: 'It is futile to shut our eyes to the fact that the difference between the functions of paternity and maternity is a far-reaching fact which has its reactions on the whole sphere of economic activity' (1929: 47). One of the aims of her recognition of that difference was to achieve a status for women which would be acknowledged outside the family: 'to enable both men and women to do the work they are individually fitted for under conditions which meet the needs of both' (1929: 47). As an MP she claimed and exercised that status for herself in a very public arena, while at the same time arguing for particular recognition of women in the home.

'The special aptitudes' of women

Rathbone believed that she spoke for the ordinary woman in the home whose main interests were private and domestic. It is possible to read the organisations which large numbers of women did join – the Women's Institutes, the Townswomen's Guilds and the Labour Party – as creating new languages of feminity which were both restrictive *and* liberating. Using the work of Alison Light as a way of approaching the 'relationship . . . to the private and domestic' of working-class women she has interviewed, Judy Giles has suggested that 'a space was created in which women of the working classes could adopt and appropriate the self-definition "house-wife" as a way of asserting their own relationship to a changing feminity' (Giles, 1993: 245). Alison Light has identified a 'resistance to "feminine" as it had been thought of in late-Victorian or Edwardian times', and she argues for a 'need to review these years as marking for many women their entry into modernity' (Light, 1991: 10). These readings challenge Susan Kingsley Kent's categorisation of the 'images of masculinity and feminity' in the interwar years as reactionary (Kent, 1993: 141). Rathbone's writings suggest that while she was aware of the continued restrictions on women's lives, she was confident that women were not contained within prewar ideologies.

The new women's organisations, although they gave women

self-respect and at times campaigned for political change, were not seeking power. Rathbone was interested in wielding power. She had commended NUSEC's activists for developing the necessary skills to operate the parliamentary system, and it was these skills which she carried with her on her chosen path into parliament (1929: 32). The question of how and what women could contribute to politics was one which Rathbone would wrestle with throughout her parliamentary career. Her perspective on the importance of circumstances in the moulding of gender meant that she was never categorical about the particular contribution which women could make. Yet she does seem to have felt impelled – perhaps as a way of encouraging other women to view themselves with respect – to assign particular qualities to women. In 1928 she criticised the removal of Guardians under the New Poor Law proposals. Many of these had been women who, she asserted, have 'a special aptitude' for the meticulous case work and supervision required by such work (1928). She asked the delegates to the NUSEC annual meeting in 1929 whether there might be 'a wave-length set up by human suffering, to which the minds of women give a specially good reception' (1929: 48).

Rathbone knew she was moving into a deeply patriarchal institution. In 1923 she commented that after experience of men's politics and administration: 'The more I see of some men, especially politicians, the less I want women to adopt all their methods and standards of value' (1929: 16). She entered it fully aware of misogyny, seeing herself as an independent outsider, in the Quaker phrase, speaking truth to power. And she took with her a faith in 'British men and women' whom she trusted to recognise 'the rights of their own children as separate personalities, each with its feet on the economic floor of the world and its head in the sunshine' (1927: 106).

Conclusion

Eleanor Rathbone was concerned in the mid-1920s with the relationship between independence of mind and independence of means. She was determined that a focus on equality should not drive away potential recruits to the NUSEC, and it was her understanding of self-determination as the core of feminism which underpinned her resistance to exclusiveness. Her political position was an ethical one which brought her close to socialism in her support for redistribution of wealth. But she was too much of an individualist to become a socialist. The value she placed on independence provided a cutting edge to her analysis of the family. She condemned the way the family operated under the 'family wage' system, but she retained a faith in its beneficial possibilities should that system change. She was critical of male behaviour within the family, but again found the explanation for it in the wage system. She refused to sentimentalise motherhood or domesticity, but she argued that women's maternal 'function' contributed to their particular skills and insights. In the late 1920s she began to focus on the needs of children, partly in response to resistance to the cost of family endowment.

It is important to bear in mind that there was always in her much of the politician, and her ability to mould her thinking to fit her audience became more pronounced as she spoke to more varied audiences. It seems to me that her reading of the late 1920s was that it was a time when feminists needed to adjust to what she saw as the political realities of the period. It is in this light that one should read her anxiety about the future of the NUSEC, her perception of other women's organisations, and her increasing emphasis on the needs of children. These shifts of emphasis did not mean that she had forgotten the way in which women's experience within marriage led to their oppression and a false sense of superiority in men. She wanted other women to share her own sense of individuality and independence.

Eleanor Rathbone may have been disappointed in women's performance as citizens in the 1920s, but she was also aware of two explanations for their limited impact on political life. One was the continuing misogyny which faced the enfranchised woman. The other was the fact that women's political activities were spread among different organisations aiming at different aspects of liberation for women. The suffrage movement had provided feminists with a language, with inspiration from contacts with other women, with the sheer excitement and emotional intensity which numbers fire and with friendship networks. These were not entirely lost to Rathbone: occasionally women MPs worked closely enough together to provide that inspiration and collective excitement and she kept a few close friendships with women outside parliament.

5

Speaking Truth to Power, 1929–39

Rathbone's thinking on domestic issues in the 1930s will be the focus of this chapter, leaving her international concerns – other than India – to the next chapter. Her parliamentary speeches provide the main source: they throw light on the way an individual feminist in this period understood and struggled to express and to change the political position of women both inside and outside the formal structures of power. Rathbone was an energetic and conscientious Member of Parliament. She attended the Commons regularly, spoke often and worked hard on the content of her speeches, adopting a meticulous approach to gathering factual information to support her arguments. There is no sign that she slackened the pace of her political efforts or the passion of her commitment: she was 57 when she first entered parliament and she was still a member when she died, very suddenly, at the age of 73.

In the 1930s feminism seemed to be in decline: there was no visible and overtly feminist women's movement. Yet in the middle of the decade there was a resurgence of interest in feminist ideas, and Rathbone's writings in this period demonstrate her awareness of how unresolved were the problems which feminists had been identifying all her active life. She wrote an introduction to a book on the changes in the law as they affected women (1934b), a lecture under the title *The Harvest of the Women's Movement* (1935), and a contribution to essays edited by Ray Strachey, *Our Freedom and Its Results* (1936). Reference will also be made to her *Memorandum on the Scale of Needs suitable for adoption by the Unemployment Assistance Board in Assessing Assistance to Applicants* (1934c).

An 'inarticulate and unorganised class'?

The debates in the House of Commons on the changes proposed to married women's right to insurance benefits offer a case study of Rathbone's approach to speaking as a feminist in parliament, and of her relationship to that institution of power, with its small number of women MPs and its genteel hostility to women. From these debates it is possible to identify the main strands of Rathbone's approach, her understanding of how best she could act within parliament. She pressed for equal treatment for women; she claimed to speak as a representative of an oppressed and undervalued group of women; she felt that she was speaking to those who represented the hostile environment in which the oppressed lived. She spoke in the belief that those in power were open to persuasion, basing her arguments on ethical grounds. She sought to work with the small band of women beside her, but she did not find that comfortable or easy. As an independent MP she saw herself as freer from restrictions than other women MPs and therefore more able to speak openly for women voters.

In the summer of 1931 an Unemployment Insurance Bill (which became the Anomalies Act) was introduced, proposing that married women's contributions before marriage should not count when they made claims for benefit. Rathbone's indignation at the weakness of women's position was intensified by the fact that it was the first woman Cabinet Minister, Margaret Bondfield, who introduced the Bill. In her first speech on the Bill, Rathbone professed to having a great respect for Bondfield, who knew better than 'anyone in the House . . . the uphill fight women have had to secure their present precarious footing on the slope of industry', but she criticised Bondfield for failing to place any women on the Advisory Committee established under the Act (*Hansard*, 8 July 1931: 255, col. 2193). The following week Rathbone moved an amendment to delete the paragraph in the Bill specifying that a woman needed to have paid contributions after marriage to qualify, thus discounting her payments before marriage. The amendment was seconded by Lady Cynthia Moseley, a member of the Labour Party, but from an even higher social strata than Rathbone herself. Speeches in support of Rathbone's position were also made by two young and radical Labour women MPs, Ellen Wilkinson and Jenny Lee. In doing so they were directly challenging Margaret Bondfield and Dr Marion Phillips, the Labour Party's Women's Officer. Towards the end of her speech proposing the amendment, Rathbone pointed out that if Margaret Bondfield and Marion Phillips (Labour Party Woman's Secretary) had been in opposition they would have made a strong case against Labour's proposals (*Hansard*, 15 July 1931: 255, cols. 668–71).

By the autumn of 1931 Margaret Bondfield was no longer in power, having become ill with what *The Woman's Leader* described as 'fatigue poisoning' even before the fall of the Labour Government (*WL*, 2 October 1931: 225). Marion Phillips was diagnosed as having stomach cancer in December 1931, and died early in 1932. No woman was returned for Labour in the November election. In their absence, Rathbone felt liberated to speak more freely in her self-chosen position as the representative of the interests of the working-class married woman. The collapse of the Labour Government was followed by the introduction of further regulations under the Unemployment Insurance Act concerning the payment of benefit to married women workers. It was alleged that married women who were not seriously intending to work after marriage were drawing benefit, and it was now proposed that a married woman prove that she was normally employed in insurable employment, that she would normally seek to obtain her livelihood by means of insurable employment, and that she could reasonably be expected to obtain insurable employment. Women claiming insurance had to put their case before a court of referees, and Rathbone had been told that the average time taken in dealing with each case was two minutes. She asked:

> How can a court in two minutes find out whether a woman is genuinely seeking employment and is normally insurable, whether she has a

reasonable chance of obtaining work because of her industrial experience and the custom of the district and the trade with regard to the
employment of married women, and whether she has a reasonable
chance of obtaining it in view of the industrial depression. (*Hansard*, 27
November 1931: 260, col. 702)

Rathbone combined this reasonable approach with a fierce condemnation of the attitude of society towards married working
women:

the married woman is liable to injustice because nobody particularly
loves her. She is liable to jealously all round. When has the Trades
Union Congress ever shown itself the friend of the married woman
worker? The traditional opinion of the Congress is that their proper
place is in the home: and many would like to sweep them out of industry altogether if they had the chance. (27 November 1931: 260, col. 703)

In the summer of 1932 legislation was introduced which led to
the cutting back of health insurance benefits paid to married
women to a lower rate than those of single women (both were paid
out, and contributed to, at a lower rate than men). Rathbone again
used two different approaches to oppose this legislation. She questioned the justice of a proposal which segregated married women
'when the cost of their insurance is heavier than that incurred for
men, while continuing to pool the two sexes together whenever
that pooling' – as in the case of unemployment insurance – 'is for
the benefit of men or alternatively to save State funds' (11 May
1932: 265, cols. 1973–8). Then she passionately defended the married working woman from the charge of malingering which lay
behind the restrictions in their rights to claim benefit, asking –
rhetorically – whether 'the Government thinks that married
women are fair game and an easy prey because they are inarticulate and an unorganised class?' (14 June 1932: 267, col. 292).

She argued that all the evidence suggested that the married
woman was 'one of the most self-sacrificing, devoted, unselfish,
and fundamentally honest human beings in the community'; and as
a group married women were more likely to suffer from ill health
than any other group of workers precisely because of these characteristics which led them to put every other member of their
family first (14 June 1932: 267, cols. 290–3). Insofar as their claims
were due to 'their motherhood' she argued that this was not a charge

which should solely be borne by the women themselves. And in the middle of a passionate speech, packed with actuarial and social survey material, she made this splendid and boldly feminist statement:

> in the economic structure the married woman inhabits a No Man's Land. The economists used to talk of the Economic Man, who responded solely to economic considerations. If there is an Economic Woman, she must be a spinster because no Economic Woman of the working class would be such a fool as to get married. The married woman of the working class gets the worst of it every way. If she decides when she marries to give up her job and look after her home and children, she is entering one of the most dangerous occupations in the world. (11 May 1932, 265: col. 1978)

Rathbone was still alert to the problem in 1934, when she argued that 'regulations made . . . by a committee who are under no obligation to get the sanction of Parliament', had transformed a married woman into 'a person who has the privilege of contributing towards insurance but very little chance indeed of receiving any benefit' (1 February 1934: 285, cols. 616–17). Later that year she raised the question of the treatment of married women under the Anomalies Act again (24 April 1934: 288, cols. 1609–10). In subsequent years she often took the opportunity of raising the unequal treatment of women under the contributions and benefits system (for example, 22 July 1935: 304, col. 1469; 4 March 1937: 321, cols. 408–10).

Representing women

In 1936 Rathbone declared: 'I am a woman and I belonged, for the greater part of my life, to a grade that had not at that time either votes or anything except its influence to depend on' (26 February 1936: 307, cols. 507–9). She was determined that women's presence in parliament should make a difference, and one way to do this was to call attention to such inequalities as the lack of provision for postgraduate women medical students; the lack of remunerative posts for women in post offices, and the treatment of women civil servants who did not get the same privileges as men because such privileges were triggered by pay levels (6 April 1930: 237, col. 2170; 3 February 1941: 368, col. 927).

She was also aware of the precarious nature of women's position within the power structures in the interwar period. In *The Harvest of the Women's Movement* (1935) and in her contribution to *Our Freedom* (1936) she examined the slow movement of women into politics with a shrewd awareness of the tenacity of resistance to women's entry into politics. In particular she identified 'men's prejudices'; women's lack of the necessary financial resources 'to spend lavishly on nursing or fighting a constituency', and the fact that women did not fit easily into the '"come and have a drink"' political culture as explanations for the small number of successful women. The exceptions were those who had 'managed to find a professional career in party or trade union politics' (1936: 29–32). Rathbone's comments on Bondfield and Phillips referred to above make it clear that she was also fully aware of the pressures such women were under to support the party line. Speculating on whether Bondfield thought that her own gender was a safeguard for the interests of women in industry, Rathbone pointed out that 'ministers are here to-day and gone to-morrow, and she may be succeeded by someone with less knowledge than herself of the case of the working woman' (*Hansard*, 8 July 1831: 255, col. 2193).

In these circumstances Rathbone declared that she could speak for those without a voice in the power structures, that she was representative of women, reminding MPs that they too easily ignored the voices of women. She consistently accused the House of having no interest in any 'question that affects nothing more important than the life and the health of women and young girls'. That question was always raised by women members and 'they rarely had any opportunity of ventilating it except . . . at the fag-end and in the tired moments of a long Debate' (2 June 1937: 324, col. 1100). Speaking on the Nationality of Married Women Bill she 'entreated the Government not to let women feel that this is one more of those questions in regard to which Governments, and political parties, are willing to pay lip service to their cause . . . so long as they are sure that the subsequent proceedings shall be purely academic' (28 November 1930: 245, col. 1753).

Rathbone used her perspective on representation to press for the placing of women on government bodies: she did this at every possible opportunity from the first session she was there. With her long perspective on the women's movement she was not insensitive to the problems of tokenism. Writing of the 'now common form' of MPs asking if there will be a woman member of any 'fresh governmental body . . . which even remotely concerns a question which either specially concerns women or excites much interest among them', she commented that the choice seemed to be

> women who have either been tried and found useful on previous commissions, or are personally known to those in high places through ties of friendship, or are fairly prominent members of one of the political parties to which it is felt necessary to accord some representation. (1936: 39)

It seemed that 'neither expert knowledge of the subject in hand, nor possession of the qualities of brain' were considered necessary in the women nominees (1936: 39).

This passage rejects the idea that any one woman could represent all women's interests. Rathbone remained committed to the idea that gender difference was largely socially constructed, and that it was the experiences of men and women which made them different. In 1936 she commented on the contribution of women to politics:

> One thing may perhaps be safely prophesied: that those who expect women's contribution to be something completely *sui generis*, utterly different from the contribution of men, will be disappointed. Perhaps five-sixths or nine-tenths of that contribution will be a fair example of the whole mixed bag of parliamentary effort. Its quantity and quality will depend on interacting forces of heredity, education, social environment, party politics, the nature of the constituency and its interests, and in all these respects women differ less from men than men from men and women from women possessing different heredity, education, etc. (1936: 34)

A gender difference of one-sixth or one-tenth meant that women had already contributed by the mid-1930s to the 'far readier and more abundant attention given to questions of housing, of public health, of every aspect of child welfare, even of international peace' (1936: 74). And she again asked the rhetorical question posed in 1929 to the NUSEC – quoted in Chapter 4 – both in *The Harvest of the Women's Movement* and in her contribution to *Our Freedom and its Results*: 'is there a wave-length set up by human suffering, to which the minds of women give a specially good reception?' (1929: 16; 1935: 17; 1936: 75).

There was still one certainty in her mind:

> We are citizens as well as women, and whatever may be the truth about the innate differences between the sexes, it is unquestionable that their differences in function, especially the difference between the paternal and the maternal function and all its results upon social life and occupational groupings, do bring it about that each sex tends to develop its own forms of *expertise*. (1936: 74, emphasis in original)

She had already used this construction in her speech to the NUSEC in 1929 (see Chapter 4), arguing then that 'much of the difficulty of getting rid of sex barriers arises from the fact that women really do not always fit well into the administrative and economic structure of society as we find it' (1929: 47). She seems to have felt that women were constrained but not limited by the domestic, and her hopes for the political contribution women could make suggest that she did not see their expertise as solely domestic and maternal. However, the use of the concept 'function' suggests a purposeful and, by implication, biological division between the genders. Yet she also used the word function with a clearly non-essentialist meaning to describe class differences:

> It is rather unfashionable, it is invidious, nowadays to talk in terms of class and class phraseology does not really express what I mean. It is not so much a question of class as of function. The point I want to make is that Parliament today interferes so extensively and intensively with the whole life of the people . . . that it is mere cant to say that representation of sectional interests is not necessary. (*Hansard*, 6 December 1933: 283, cols. 1759–60)

Her recognition of the need for the 'representation of sectional interests' did sometimes cut across Rathbone's sense of gender solidarity. When referring in 1936 to protective legislation, she argued that feminists accepted it because it was supported by 'all the great Labour organizations, of women as well as men' and 'the usual principle of collective representation of interests must be respected' (1936: 59).

Rathbone also used the concept of 'collective representation of interests' to defend her particular position as an MP for the English Universities, arguing that the representation of the interests of 'the middle and upper classes and the learned professions' could not be guaranteed by the system of voting which operated a simple majority (*Hansard*, 6 December 1933: 283, cols. 1759–60). Her sense of being in a minority was tempered by some awareness of the way political power was linked to money. Responding to the assertion of an Independent Labour Party member that he was looking forward to the time when 'the proletarians' would have elected 'a Parliament composed almost exclusively of members of their own status', she pointed to the fact that 'the proletariat . . . form the majority of voters . . . in every constituency of the country', and asked: 'Why has it not happened already?' Part of her own answer was that:

> proletarians, from no fault of their own, are so imperfectly educated they are easily bamboozled by candidates who can give them motor-cars and subscribe handsomely to football clubs, and are swayed by any cry which the opposite party machine can manage to get across the footlights. (26 February 1936: 307, cols. 507–9)

Propaganda, persuasion and conscience

Although Rathbone argued for the representation of interests in parliament, she clearly believed that voters' behaviour could be influenced and moulded by political literature. Rathbone had adopted a purist approach in the 1920s when she abandoned canvassing in local elections because 'many electors regard the usual form of canvass as an intrusion on their privacy and a violation of the secrecy of the ballot', and despite warning from her friends that she was throwing away the election 'by this innovation' (RP XIV: 3.3). Yet in the 1930s she wrote favourably of the way the 'women's movement taught women . . . much that they might never have learned if success had come more easily . . . of the arts and crafts of organization and propaganda' (1934b: vii). The meaning of 'propaganda' was especially contested at a time when the fascist parties in Italy and Germany were demonstrating its efficacy. After visiting Palestine and Egypt, and then Czechoslovakia, Yugoslavia and Romania, Rathbone became intensely concerned about the persuasiveness of fascist propaganda. This awareness made her more determined to counteract what she confidently described as 'misrepresentation' of Britain by 'an extensive and carefully planned campaign of educational work' (*Hansard*, 16 February 1938: 331, cols. 1963–8; RP XIV: 2.9). This experience made her more aware of the problems with the use of the concept of propaganda, and when interrupted in the House of Commons for using the word in a debate on the activities of the British Council during the war, she responded:

> I do not use the word 'propaganda' as though it were something nasty. There is hardly any information which is not, in a sense, propaganda. If you feel things, and believe they are true, you try to spread information. (18 February 1941: 369, col. 74)

All her life she had written to persuade, and *Child Marriage* (1934a) contained an open appeal for a crusade against suffering. Her activities as an independent MP were largely based on the assumption that words and arguments could influence voters. She did not always feel confident about whether this process actually worked, writing to her constituents in 1935:

> I do not know whether other back-bench Members share the same feeling which sometimes oppresses me – that one's work often resembles a random scattering of seeds, without feeling sure whether any of it has taken root and borne fruit. One makes speeches, puts questions, moves amendments, takes part in committees and deputations; but asks oneself afterwards whether any of it has made any real difference to the events one has sought to influence. (RP XIV, February 1935: 3.4)

But there are no signs that she ever quite lost faith in this process. Provided she achieved something of what she aimed for, she accepted that and pressed on: '"Not the optimum, but the achievable optimum" has always been my maxim' (RP XIV, 28 August 1941: 4.21). One achievement in the 1930s was the successful end of her efforts since she was first elected on behalf of literally 'disinherited' wife and children; those whose husbands or fathers had left them without financial support. The Inheritance (Family Provision) Act passed in 1938 was in the name of another MP and was not as generous as she would have liked, but she welcomed it nonetheless (*Hansard*, 28 April 1938: 335, cols. 465–6, 482–4).

The number of committees or action groups which she was involved in increased steadily throughout the decade and suggest frenetic activity. In March 1939 she wrote to her constituents that she assumed they would rather she 'did things than wrote about them' (RP XIV: 4.21). There is a hint in this letter of a problem which she faced in the spring of 1939: the opposition of many of her constituents to her actions, in particular her support of conscription in April 1939. Her plea to them was that they would not, she felt sure 'wish me to vote against my conscience on a question of such importance' (RP XIV, 11 May 1939: 4.21). This plea fits uneasily with her repeated apologies for the 'unavoidable egotism' which permeate these 'personal account(s) of her stewardship' (RP XIV, 1933: 3.4).

Minimum needs

Rathbone's claim to the overriding place of conscience refers back to the ethical roots of her political choices. Her basic commitment was still to the redistribution of wealth for the purposes of the relief of suffering, her plea was for 'The poor in this community' who 'do not get the chance to rise to the full stature intended for them, either physically or mentally' (*Hansard*, 10 April 1930: 237, col. 2987). She made no distinction between the public and the private when it came to the personal conduct of life and the position from which it was possible to make political judgements. She never abandoned the belief, shared with her father, that everyone should live on no more than they needed. Her puritanical life-style seems to have led her to see herself as quite distinct from the leisured class of which she was in fact a member, or at least as having the right to criticise that class. She objected to the cut in civil service salaries in the crisis of September 1931, and suggested it would be better to 'increase the tax on higher incomes – tax one of the most widely spread luxuries, and most prolific in its yield – the nation's sugar and sweets Bill' (18 September 1931: 256, cols. 1196–7). She believed that in this dislike of luxuries she spoke for women (10 April 1930: 237, col. 2987). Nor were her criticisms of what she saw as unnecessary expenditure limited to high earners. She was opposed to the indiscriminate apportionment of subsidised housing, complaining that 'large numbers of persons' were 'taking advantage of subsidised houses and asking leave to build a motor garage' (1 April 1930: 387, cols. 3079–80). In 1935 she proposed an amendment designed to ensure that only tenants 'who need it' would receive an 'exchequer contribution' to the Housing Bill

(20 May 1935: 302, col. 138). Her opposition to means testing, because of her own experience of such tests during the administration of separation allowances in the First World War, fits uneasily with this precept. When attacking the National Government for withdrawing subsidy and thus limiting the building of local authority housing, she professed to a hatred for the phrase 'deserving' which, like her objection to means testing, was part of her reaction against the Charity Organisation Society approach of her father's generation (20 June 1934: 291, col. 446).

Rathbone continued to subscribe to the concept that there was a basic level of need, and her assertion of its relevance to public policy was honed by time and effort into a carefully developed claim, 'a scientifically determined (physiological) minimum'. In the House of Commons she argued that unemployment benefit should allow for 'a standard of maintenance based on the physiological needs of healthy citizens' (19 February 1934: 286, col. 94). She believed that this standard was the 'only reasonable scientific basis on which needs can be assessed' and that there would be no difficulty 'in finding a formula to express those needs' (26 February 1934: 286, col. 769). The argument with its reference to the 'devitalisation which results from prolonged underfeeding and despair' was never totally factual and clinical. She combined her emphasis on science with an imaginative use of public appeals such as 'Fivepenny lunches' where the menu was based on the British Medical Association's minimum diet. The aim of the lunches was 'to demonstrate how far the comparatively modest standard of the BMA minimum was beyond the reach of the unemployed, and secondly to raise money'. Speakers at the lunches included the wife of an unemployed labourer (RP XIV: 2.7/5). Rathbone was aware that it was not only the unemployed who were poor. Referring to the assurances of the Government that the new unemployment benefit scales 'would keep a family . . . from destitution', she asked: 'What does it mean keeping a family from destitution if it does not mean keeping the family in ordinary good health?' And she prophesied that 'the scale that will be adopted will be considerably in excess of the wages for unskilled labour' (*Hansard*, 9 May 1934: 290, col. 1219). In a pamphlet for the Children's Minimum Council, she combined the threat of disturbance with humanitarian concern and economics:

But one thing is certain; that the paradox visible to all – of great numbers living in acute and undeserved poverty while Parliament and industry are creating a rising tide of dissatisfaction with the Government and with the economic structure of society. A more generous level of assistance to the unemployed, especially to those with children, would commend itself to public opinion not merely on grounds of humanity, but as a means of increasing spending power among the masses. (1934c: 14)

Rathbone's focus on poverty in the 1930s continued to shift from women to children. This was apparent in her passionate revolt against child marriage in India, and it may have resulted from her watching the children of her friends Eva Hubback[1] and Mary Stocks grow up. In part the shift in focus was one of political pragmatism, an attempt to exploit a situation where it seemed that 'Parliament was peculiarly sensitive to the needs of children', where pressure for their needs met a 'point of least resistance' (RP XIV, February 1935: 3.4). Working closely with her feminist friend and colleague Eva Hubback, she set up the Children's Minimum Campaign Committee (RP XIV: 2.7). The aim of the committee was to persuade the government that 'no child should go short of the necessaries of healthy upbringing merely because of its parents' poverty, and that the scale providing for these necessaries should be based on scientific data'. The methods the Committee used were deputations and 'memoranda summarising the relevant facts'. The effect was nevertheless to take her time and efforts away from activities which were directly related to women's needs and interests.

An ethical individualist

Rathbone's ethical politics meant that in the 1930s the positions she took remained closest to those of the left. In her earlier writings she had used the fear of revolution to press her point home (see Chapter 4). In the House of Commons she professed on several occasions to understand why working-class people would want to start one, and she was prepared again to quote Marx's maxim '"From each according to ability, and to each according to need"' (*Hansard*, 6 February 1931: 247, col. 2316; 6 December 1933: 283, col. 1762). But she did not accept the links drawn by socialists between capitalism and power: for her the purposes of collective action through democratic process was social reform, not structural change (RP XIV, February 1935: 3.4). Nor did she challenge the idea of inherited wealth – a practice which had, after all, made her whole pattern of political behaviour possible. In a discussion on housing rents in 1931 she was concerned about the possible threat to 'a number of persons in a very small way of business who, before the war, used to invest their savings in working-class property, with the idea that they were making a safe provision for their widows and children' (*Hansard*, 23 November 1931: 260, cols. 142–4). Her experience in the 1930s led Rathbone to become increasingly hostile to 'official' Labour (RP XIV, March 1939: 3.4). On the other hand she was critical of behaviour which was informed by a respect for class hierarchy: the 'snobbery' of others – local billetting officers during the war, for instance, who had 'not the courage to stand up against local grandees who refuse to take any children' (*Hansard*, 10 October 1940: 365, col. 365). During the debates on the registration of women for war work, she attacked those who were keeping on their domestic staff (20 March 1941: 370, col. 370).

Rathbone's individualism continued to make it difficult for her to work within a group, including with her women colleagues. She advocated collective action when she thought it was appropriate, for instance in the debate on the Nationality of Married Women Bill in 1930, when she put in a plea for women MPs to achieve some common agreement on the question. There was more solidarity shown in the debate on equal pay when Nancy Astor, after interrupting the male speakers, made a sparkling and at times startling speech, expressing her fervent hope that men would be mothers in the 'next' world, which might lead them to take a more reasonable view. Following her, Rathbone said she would like to bring 'the House back to a few jog-trot facts' (7 June 1935: 302, cols. 2235–40). Her facts in this speech and in the one she made a year later on a motion by Ellen Wilkinson for equal pay in the civil service, led to the familiar conclusion that only with the introduction of family allowances would equal pay achieve the effect desired by feminists (1 April 1936: 310, cols. 2030–5). Rathbone's desire for solidarity among women also conflicted at times with her strong conviction that because she was a feminist and had the interests of other women at heart, she was free to criticise other women.

Nevertheless, a glimpse of the bonds between the women MPs and a suggestion of Rathbone's stature among them was given by Ellen Wilkinson in 1937:

> When people wonder whether women have 'earned the right' (what cheek) to sit in the House of Commons, I first gulp with egalitarian rage, and second think of Eleanor Rathbone. She is a member cast in a big mould . . . she lectures the house rather, oddly enough, all we women do. Every woman member, with apologies, I include myself, always speaks to the House as one who simply cannot get accustomed to the collective stupidity of so many men.

She then went on to describe how the solution suggested in the Women's Tea Room to this 'common failing' by Mavis Tate – that they should face their own party when speaking, was greeted by total agreement that this would be worse (*TT*, 8 May 1937: 601–3).

Rathbone's confidence in her own judgement made her at times a difficult and irritating colleague, often in trouble from the speaker (for example, *Hansard*, 16 February 1938: 331, cols. 1965–6). She was always a sharp critic of those in power, often using irony to Ministers: 'I had hoped up to the last minutes that the right. hon. Gentleman would convert me to a belief in that complex subsection' (7 June 1932: 266, col. 1829). And again, nearly ten years later: 'I do not often find myself making excuses for Ministers and Under-Secretaries. They are exceedingly good at doing that sort of thing for themselves' (20 March 1941: 370, col. 368). She was also quick off the mark when her own arguments were challenged, leaping to her feet to correct Aneurin Bevan's interpretation of a book on the effects of family allowances on the birth rate in 1940 (8 February 1940: 357, col. 524).

'The patience and perseverance of Bruce's spider'

Her identity as an outsider 'telling truth to power' had its foundations in Rathbone's position in the House as an Independent, and also in her perception of herself as someone of a generation which provided her with a long-range perspective. Her assessment in 1936 of the contribution of the suffrage movement, of the impact of women's voting and of women MPs, is informed by her sense of herself as someone whose long involvement in the women's movement within the political context gave her a balanced view (1936: 15–56). 'My recollections', she reminisced in 1943, 'go back to when the mere announcement in this House that any women's question was to be discussed was the signal for a kind of humour to make itself manifest' (*Hansard*, 3 August 1943: 39, col. 2129). She was making a general comment about women's advancement and not a personal statement, when she wrote to her constituents that had she been told when she was a student that she would 'become successively a City Councillor, a Magistrate, a Member of Parliament, an LL.D of Liverpool University and a D.C.L. of Oxford, it would have seemed the most fantastic of prophesies' (RP XIV, March 1939: 3.4). This perspective lay behind what may otherwise be read as an over-optimistic assessment in the mid-1930s of the 'results of women's enfranchisement', that they 'exceed expectations'. Her view was that 'progress has been rapid when it depended on political action and slow when it depended on changes in hearts and habits. What else could you expect when the instrument was the vote?' (1936: 16). Read in the light of this perspective, her activities in the 1930s can be seen as focusing on political action, while not forgetting the need for change in 'hearts and habits'.

The emphasis in both *The Harvest of the Women's Movement* (1935) and in Rathbone's chapter in *Our Freedom and Its Results* (1936), was on the long history of the women's movement and on the scale of the task which faced feminists. Now she advocated patience, which she had earlier termed a 'misnamed virtue' (*CC*, 3 April 1914: 1022). This quality was one she approved and understood as peculiarly British: 'It is our way in this country to proceed by way of homeopathic doses of reform' (*Hansard*, 5 November 1937: 335, col. 483). She may have wondered whether such faith was that of her generation, one that had found 'it easier than we find it to-day to live by faith, believing that success must come as part of the steady and ordered progress of society' (1934b: viii).

The most intractable of 'habits and hearts' were attitudes to the payment of wages, and Rathbone continued to remind members of the House of Commons of the problems of the existing system and to press for the payment of allowances for children. Rathbone's perspective on arguing such a case over a long period, together with her experience on India, contributed to her perception that the process of change was slow, irregular and complex. She recalled in 1942 that Beatrice Webb had told her that it took nineteen years for 'a new idea to germinate and take fruit': on that basis the concept was overdue. She was prepared to acknowledge that 'to bring about any social reform are needed the patience and perseverance of Bruce's spider, the importunate widow, the Ancient Mariner, and the giant Sisyphus rolled into one', but she asserted that patience 'could be overdone' when it was concerned with children. She then turned angrily on all the enemies of the idea in a speech of passionate advocacy (*Hansard*, 23 June 1942: 380, col. 1862).

It is possible to see Rathbone's advocacy of family allowances as an obsession which distracted her from the struggle for gender equality. Her own perspective was that the struggle was a complex one which needed to be understood from a variety of angles. She had learned, she wrote in 1934, that 'History is seldom . . . neat-fingered' (1934b: ix). One example of this appeared in *The Disinherited Family* where she pointed out that improvements in the position of women in the nineteenth century had also led to more subtle forms of oppression by men (1924: 342). For Rathbone there were always 'future tasks' to be undertaken by the women's movement (RP XIV, December 1936: 3.4). Her approach to these tasks was to trim her sails to the political wind:

> These periods of action and reaction are common to all great movements. The only way to meet them is to take full advantage of every favourable wind and tide in public opinion. When these are contrary, it is sometimes wisest to take shelter and sit tight, not attempting efforts which only stale the workers and exhaust their resources and may lead to being actually forced backward rather than forward. (1936: 56)

The personal struggle to obtain recognition for women in public life was always informed by this strong sense of continuing misogyny. Rathbone was aware of how the structures were used to disguise the resistance of Parliament to feminist influence. She asserted that MPs paid 'lip service' to legislative changes proposed by women, and she accused the Government of allowing Second Readings of Bills in the full knowledge that they would be defeated (*Hansard*, 28 November 1930: 245, col. 1751).

In the 1930s Rathbone's awareness of misogyny went together with an occasional observation on a more general incipient fascism. In a debate on police reforms in June 1933, five months after Hitler became Chancellor in Germany, she drew attention to the rise of fascism in both Germany and Italy, and asserted that working people in Britain had 'a very real and strongly-grounded apprehension' of a revolution from above. This was greeted with cries of 'Rubbish' and 'Nonsense', which she countered with a demand that this fear should not be fed by the terms of the proposed legislation (26 June 1933: 279, cols. 1192–6).

Conclusion

In the House of Commons Rathbone was one of a small number of women MPs among a very large number of men. On issues concerned with equality, she felt the need to speak for women, while at the same time she was only too well aware of the precarious nature of the women's place in the structures of power. The position of women MPs symbolised this precariousness. Theirs was a tiny number of voices speaking on behalf of very large numbers of women with diverse interests and they – or at least some women MPs – were well aware of this. Rathbone believed that she spoke for oppressed women, silent because of their unwillingness to complain of a system with which they were familiar, in which many of them felt secure. She was also aware of the contradictions inherent in the pressures on her as an MP; of the dangers of tokenism, but also, more crucially, of the tenacity of the male hold on power. Rathbone desperately needed to be effective, and strove to work alongside others, while at the same time she knew that what she had to say made her fellow MPs – including the women on occasion – uncomfortable and therefore defensive.

Rathbone claimed to represent women's interests, but her ideas on the operation of democracy were those of a liberal democrat, uneasily combining representation of interests with the personal conscience of the representative. She struggled to make sense of the process of communication between MP and constituent, between those with power and those who put them in power. Her position was sometimes contradictory and often ambiguous, perhaps inevitably because of the contested meanings of such words as 'representative', 'interests'. She felt particularly that working-class married women needed someone to speak for them because of the way they were viewed by those in power. Rathbone was an independent, middle-class woman, and she was unmarried. There were Labour women MPs who could claim with greater credibility that they represented the interests of working-class women, but Rathbone's observations as a suffragist of the problems of women's relationship to the power structures had shaped her view that women's interests were best served, precisely because of their weak position, by not being subsumed within party structures.

During the 16 full sessions for which she was a member, her speeches were concerned with a wide variety of issues, but there are distinctive themes which predominate: the demand for women to receive equal treatment with men; the call for those in power to recognise the reality of married women's lives; the desire to ameliorate poverty. Her determination to effect change led her increasingly to emphasise the needs of children rather than women. If there is one new focus which emerges in the mid-1930s it is the plight of the victims of Fascism which will be covered in Chapter 7. I see this as part of her intense identification with the victims of systems of oppression.

Note

1 Eva Hubback (1886–1949) was Parliamentary Secretary of the NUSEC until 1927 when she became Principal of Morley College, Lambeth. In the 1930s she continued working for feminism in the National Council for Equal Citizenship (through which the political activities of the NUSEC were maintained after the formation of the Townswomen's Guilds). For Mary Stocks see Chapter 3.

6

The Indian Minotaur, 1927–41

In the early years of her life as a Member of Parliament, Rathbone was deeply involved in the debates around the enfranchisement of Indian women. The impetus behind that involvement was her concern with child marriage in India. These two interconnected issues will be the focus of this chapter. There are four narratives of Rathbone's involvement in Indian affairs: her letters to and from Indian women; her correspondence with members of the British Establishment: her speeches in Parliament; and her book, *Child Marriage: The Indian Minotaur* (1934a). The differences between these narratives give us a vivid sense both of the intricacy of the issues and of the unstable nature of her response.

An imperialist framework

In the summer of 1927 Eleanor Rathbone read *Mother India* by the American journalist Katherine Mayo. The book attacked all India's institutions and religious practices on the basis of one visit, citing evidence from mainly European texts. This was Mayo's view of the Indian:

Inertia, helplessness, lack of initiative and originality, lack of staying power and of sustained loyalties, sterility of enthusiasm, weakness of life-vigour itself – all are traits that truly characterize the Indian not only of to-day, but of long-past history. (Mayo, 1927: 24)

Child marriage formed a starting point for her explanation of the Indian character:

Take a girl child twelve years old, a pitiful physical specimen in bone and blood, illiterate, ignorant, without any sort of training in habits of health. Force motherhood upon her at the earliest possible moment. Rear her weakling son in intensive vicious practices that drain his small vitality day by day. Give him no outlet in sports. Give him habits that make him, by the time he is thirty years of age, a decrepit and querulous old wreck – and will you ask what has sapped the energy of his manhood? (Mayo, 1927: 24–5)

And it was the passages on child marriage and on child birth in Mayo's book which moved Rathbone unbearably. After reading the chapter on 'conditions of confinement in the orthodox Hindu home', she 'slammed the book and pitched it away – resolved to bear no more' (1928–9: 203). Later she said that the information on child marriage in Mayo's book – which is scanty, in fact – was not totally new to her because she had been a representative of the International Women's Suffrage Association on the Child Welfare Committee of the League of Nations (*Hansard*, 9 July 1931: 254, col. 2369). But closer to the time of reading the book she asserted: 'to this American stranger, Katherine Mayo, many of us men and women over here owe our first coherent knowledge of the terrible facts' (1928–9: 213). She seems to have been unaware that child marriage in India had been the focus of campaigns by the National Vigilance Association in the years 1889–91 (Rubinstein, 1991: 101). She did learn soon to avoid referring to Mayo's book, and subsequently always cited eyewitness Indian reports of the effects of child marriage. She never openly adopted Mayo's views on sexuality, and concentrated her attacks not on the Indians but on the British Imperial administrators.

Antoinette Burton has argued that '"the Indian woman" served as an instrument of debate within suffrage circles, where she was used as empirical evidence of the need for votes for British women' (Burton, 1991: 56). Rathbone was not one of those who wrote about the protest of Indian women against their social and cultural oppression in *The Common Cause* before 1914 (Burton, 1991: 51–6, 63). The nature of Rathbone's entry into this discourse in the late 1920s suggests that she was unaware of these earlier debates. That she was not alone in her lack of awareness of the situation in India is clear from an article published in *Time & Tide* in August 1928 in which Dorothy Thurtle confessed that she had gone to India as 'an English feminist . . . expecting to find my India sisters down-trodden and oppressed' (*TT*, 24 August 1928: 792–3). Rathbone's reaction to the social tragedy which she had read about was from the beginning to involve Indian women in the solution, but it clearly did not occur to her that her own involvement might be seen as inappropriate or even harmful. The intricate connections between the issue to which she had responded with her customary fervour and the issue of Indian independence were much more complex and long-standing than she seems to have realised (Forbes, 1979a, 1979b). This blinkeredness may seem surprising, given her family connection with the early nineteenth century Indian independence movement (RP XIV, 1932: 3.4). It is possible that this very connection made her over-confident.

In her article in *Time & Tide* referred to above, Dorothy Thurtle had recognised that 'in India, as in this country, there are grave social problems to be faced and evils to be dealt with', but that 'these will not be properly tackled until India is a self-respecting, self-governing nation'. That Rathbone's framework, by contrast, was an imperialist one, was apparent in an early intercession in the debate in the House of Commons on a resolution to confirm the Labour government's commitment to 'native paramountcy' in its colonial policy in relation to 'coloured races' in December 1929. The Duchess of Atholl used this resolution to raise the issue of the practice of 'a pre-marriage rite among young girls, among many African tribes, a rite which is frequently referred to as 'the circumcision of girls' (11 December 1929: 233, 600). Atholl and Rathbone were both members of an unofficial all-party Committee for the Protection of Coloured Women in the Crown Colonies which had been examining the subject of clitoridectomy. Rathbone first intervened in the debate when Jimmy Maxton, an Independent Labour Party MP, had interrupted and was questioning the relevance of Atholl's speech. She shouted: 'Women do not count', and quelled him. She then moved an amendment – which was accepted – adding 'sex' to the final clause of the motion so that it read: 'Native self-government should be fostered; and franchise and legal rights should be based upon the principle of equality for all without regard to race, colour or sex.' Her speech was not focused on clitoridectomy but on the more general question of the relationship between men and women in 'many of these tribes', which she termed 'sheer slavery'. The argument of her speech gives a foretaste of the precarious position she was later to find herself in over Indian sexual politics. She professed to accept the importance of 'better relations between coloured men and white men', and acknowledged that 'The exploitation of coloured women by coloured men is no excuse for the exploitation of coloured men by white men.' However, her speech ended with what can be read as a powerful assertion of Western hegemony:

> Many of us will never be satisfied until the full hideous truth is disclosed and made known to the women of the world and everything that can be done is done to stamp out slavery of this kind, whether by legislation, by education, or by public opinion. Let them take this message to the men of the native races. There can be no equal citizenship between coloured men and white men till there is equal citizenship between coloured men and coloured women. (11 December 1929: 233, col. 608)

It is fair to Rathbone to place this statement in the context of the prevalent cultural discourse. The Governor of Kenya, Sir Edward Grigg, denied the implication that the relationships Rathbone was concerned about were slavery, but he concluded that: 'In general the status of women among the native tribes is such as might be expected among people emerging from a state of barbarism' (RP XIV: 2.1.38). Rathbone felt that she was challenging the view of those in power in criticising the attitude of 'European officials' who, 'being men themselves and chiefly in communication with men, take the man's view of men's rights' (RP XIV: 2.1.40). And she was praised in *Time & Tide* – not usually a source of support for her point of view – for the stand she took: 'Miss Rathbone is in good company in her recognition of the intimate connection between race equality and sex equality' (*TT*, 20 December 1929: 1526).

The House of Commons debate affords a brief glimpse into a complex controversy concerning the colonial administration in

Kenya of the new Labour Government. Susan Pedersen has described how the case revealed the 'difficulty of constructing feminist reforms across cultural lines and within an imperialist context' (Pedersen, 1991: 679). That Rathbone may have learned restraint from her increased exposure to a wide variety of witnesses to the Committee is suggested by a memorandum she co-authored in 1932 (RP XIV: 2.1.40). This paper may also reflect her sobering experience of intervention in Indian women's politics.

Speaking for Indian women

According to Stocks, Rathbone's first reaction after reading Mayo's book was to find out whether she had got her 'facts right' and to this end she exploited her position with the NUSEC to launch a survey of the condition of women in India. This was in itself an assumption of Western superiority; she was assuming that British feminists could and should play a leading role. She did not forget about the role which Indian women could play, however, and at the same time the NUSEC put pressure on the Simon Commission on Constitutional Reform which had been appointed in November 1927, to make use of women assessors and 'technical advisers' (*The Times*, 24 October 1929: 12a). However, her view of the use of publicity – she described it once in the Indian context as a 'healthy wind' (*Hansard*, 5 March 1935: 314, col. 1869) – and of the desirability of rousing public opinion, meant that she did not limit her approach to this type of restrained pressure on the holders of colonial power. She was later to write of the dangers of 'the use of emotional methods' in 'actually getting things done', but she also believed that 'very few reforms have been won by rational methods alone'. Her advice was to 'know when the time has come to allow your followers to let loose their emotions and become explosive' (1936: 73). In practice she was never that deliberate and contrived. What the narratives on India suggest is that where her emotions were deeply stirred, she was impetuous, manipulative and rash.

Friction between Rathbone and those whom she sought to represent came into the open in the autumn of 1929. The Indian political situation was particularly tense, and Indian women's organisations were becoming increasingly politically involved in support of the defiance by Congress of the British Government in India. Moreover, Rathbone's response to Mayo's book was especially offensive to women involved in the two main Indian women's organisations, the All India Women's Conference (AIWC) and the Women's Indian Association (WIA), who had been openly and actively opposed to child marriage since their inception (Forbes, 1981: 63; Basu and Ray, 1990: 41–6; Burton, 1991: 64–5). Dhanvanthi Rama Rau,[1] who was living in London while her husband assisted the Simon Commission with its report on the proposed Indian constitutional reforms, later recalled her experience of the conference called by NUSEC in October 1929:

> I asked for permission to speak, and was graciously allowed five minutes. I did not speak on any of the subjects on the agenda, but merely disputed the right of British women to arrange a conference on Indian social evils in London, when all the speakers were British and many of them had never even visited India. Not one of them had even asked if there were any Indian women's organizations that were dealing with the problems on the spot, the same problems that British women were exploring from the great and deceptive distance of fifteen thousand miles . . . We were already assuming the responsibility ourselves, and we were sure we could be more successful than any outsiders, especially those who were ignorant of the cultural patterns of our social groups and therefore could not be as effective as our own social reformers. (Ramusak, 1981: 15–16)

The conflict seethed below the surface at the conference and was kept there by Rathbone. A letter severely critical of the way the conference was called, and of Rathbone's behaviour there towards the Indian women, was signed by seven Indian and seven European women, among them Dhanvanthi Rama Rau. They asserted that the 'programme, agenda and resolutions' of the conferences had all been drawn up 'by two individuals', one of them Rathbone, and that she 'had forfeited Indian confidence by her close association with Miss Mayo'. The programme of the conference, they wrote, had been 'so arranged as to give undue prominence to comparatively minor efforts, overlooking . . . excellent work accomplished by voluntary movements in India'. There had been no consultation before the conference with 'London representatives of the women's movements in India' (*The Times*, 22, 24 October 1929: 12a).

That there were European signatories to this letter indicates that Rathbone could have chosen a different discourse. Ellen Wilkinson's response to a request from Rathbone to sign another letter contrasts with Rathbone's insensitivity on this issue:

> No-one could be more passionately anxious than I am to help the women of India, but knowing as I do from contact with a good many Indians how deep the feeling against the British is, I feel that a word from Gandhi could not only do a thousand times more good than any letter in *The Times*, but such a letter could be positively harmful in so far as it seems to press a reform upon them by an alien race. (FL Autograph Collection, n.d.: 92.3)

Rathbone did then withdraw personally from the NUSEC survey, but not from Indian politics. Her motivation for remaining active and her cultural perspective were expressed in a letter to Mabel, Lady Hartog, the wife of the former Vice-Chancellor of Dacca University who had just returned from India:

> I do feel rather distracted at the thought of all the wretched little brides who are likely to be sacrificed on the altar of India's political aspirations during the next few years . . .
> I suppose all one can do is to try to make the Indians see that they are being watched in this respect, so that racial pride will reinforce their desire for reform. (FL, 20 May 1930: 93.4)

Her first concern was thus for cultural practices and this put her in a precarious position in her correspondence with Indian suffragists. Her assumption was that Indian women – or at least the sort of Indian women she hoped would be involved in politics – also opposed these practices. They assured her that they did, but even those who shared her priorities had a different perspective. Rathbone was a representative of an Imperial power at the moment at which it was being forcefully challenged. In January 1930 all members of Congress declared their right to complete independence, and pledged themselves to prepare for it by civil disobedience if it was not granted. At the height of the campaign of civil disobedience which led to the imprisonment of thousands of members of Congress, including Gandhi, the Simon Commission published its report, advocating the enfranchisement of only 20 per cent of the population, with 33.5 per cent of those enfranchised being women (Pearson, 1989: 204). Even those Indian women activists whose main interest was social reform took a political stance in these circumstances. Dr Muthulakshmi Reddi, a founder member of the WIA, had argued that women should avoid becoming involved in politics until their status within society had improved. When Sarojini Naidu, a leading member of the AIWC and a passionate nationalist, was arrested, Reddi said, 'We women, however moderate and law-abiding cannot afford to be quiet at this juncture' (letter to Mrs Faridoonji, 23 May 1930, quoted in Forbes, 1981: 58). The urgency of the nationalist appeal was recognised by other feminists as the article in *Time & Tide* by Dorothy Thurtle indicated: she understood that the 'Nationalist appeal was irresistible' (*TT*, 24 August 1928: 792–3).

Rathbone presented herself as sympathetic to Indian independence, stating firmly in 1931 that Britain must 'recognise India's right to govern herself', but she immediately undercut this position by arguing that such a recognition should contain the 'necessary safeguards for all legitimate interests and minorities which might suffer wrong' (RP XIV: 3.3). Her primary concern was for the nature of the government of India rather than the nationality of those in power. In the debate in the House of Commons on India in December 1931 she pressed for extra spending by the Imperial government on social services in India, partly in order to counteract the 'forces of reaction' which wanted to restore and protect religious traditions (*Hansard*, 2 December 1931: 260, cols. 1183–90). This motive was also the force behind her advocacy of the enfranchisement of Indian women. The urgency of enfranchisement for her was driven by her concern for the issues which had drawn her towards India: child marriage and what she understood to be the linked questions of purdah and of maternal mortality. A speech to the House of Commons in March 1933 encapsulates her approach: she began with illiteracy among women, then moved to purdah, to 'the abominable injustice' of child marriage, and then maternal mortality as a prelude to her demand for a wider enfranchisement of women (28 March 1933: 276, cols. 940–50).

Rathbone's priorities and her distance from Indian women are reflected in her relationship with the Imperial power. Reading her correspondence with Indian women in parallel with her letters to the British male establishment reveals the contradictions of her approach: she attempted to wield influence by moral and political persuasion from inside the establishment, while presenting herself to others as an outsider. That her moral fervour *did* disturb her recipients is apparent in a letter from Lord Sankey, who found her criticisms so 'disparaging and disappointing' that he almost despaired 'of doing anything for India' (FL, 16 January 1931: 93.4).

As soon as she was elected, Rathbone began to bombard Wedgwood Benn, the secretary of state at the India Office, with letters, memoranda and questions in the House of Commons (FL, 92.2). In October 1929, four months after taking office, the Labour Government had declared its commitment to a process leading to dominion status for India and announced that it was calling a round table conference with British and Indian representatives. Constitutional issues and the response of Congress were dominating Benn's agenda and he staved Rathbone off, not even reading her first memorandum on child marriage. By the summer of 1930, she had become impatient, and wrote to Benn that 'apparently the only way of securing attention' for the issue was to be 'reckless in criticism . . . and as unguarded in generalisation as Miss Mayo' (FL, 8 July 1930: 92.2). He did then become more responsive, but his view was that the Sarda Act, which stipulated a minimum age for marriage of 18 for males and 14 for females, would be difficult to enforce at the best of times. Rathbone was not prepared to accept this position, and the enforcement and strengthening of the Act remained central to her activity, culminating in her lobbying behind the scenes for the Das Amendment Act which went through the Indian legislature in 1938. Rathbone's pressure was placed mainly on the British in India, but in a letter to Benn she expressed a view of Indian responsibility which was absent from her letters to Indian women:

it is only by stabbing Indians in their tender places by making them feel that public opinion in Western countries is alive to and shocked by the barbarity of their social customs as they affect women, that one can force them to really grapple with these evils. (RP XIV, 27 March 1931: 92.2)

Rathbone's first threat to use more militant methods to put pressure on the government came in this letter, where she wrote that her 'twenty years experience in the suffrage movement will suggest to me more blatant methods of getting the facts across the footlights'. Presumably in order to encourage Indian women to think along these lines, she sent a copy of Sylvia Pankhurst's book on the militant suffrage movement to one of her Indian correspondents (FL, 11 January 1934: 92.1). It was an empty threat: Indian women's militancy was directed towards the British government, and the British women who were acting with Rathbone were not those who had been militant suffragists.

Relating to Indian women

Rathbone's correspondence with Indian women is extensive, revealing and complex. She adapted her views to suit her understanding of the political position of her correspondent, and her approach shifted as the political context changed. She was buoyant at first and apparently confident that the evils of child marriage were amenable to amelioration, if not transformation, through a combination of political pressure and the increased involvement of women in politics in India. She wanted Indian women to add their voices to hers, assuring one sceptical correspondent that Indian women would be more likely to influence British statesmen than Englishwomen (FL, 9 January 1935: 93.12). This approach did not appeal to them, as is clear from a letter she received in 1932 after the Lothian Committee Report on Indian Franchise had proposed a reduction in the proportion of women voters from 1:2 to 1:4.5. The writer, Mrs Hamid Ali, stated that the report had 'disappointed and disgusted us all', and had led her to conclude that 'educated Indian women' could expect nothing from the British Government and must wait for independence. She rejected Rathbone's suggestion that they 'work from inside' as 'most degrading' (FL, 29 October 1932: 93.9). Rathbone defended her interference on the grounds that 'Englishwomen, who are fully enfranchised themselves, feel it their duty to do their utmost to help their sisters overseas' (FL, 8 March 1933: 92.1), and that 'it cannot be right that

British men should be able and expected to express views and exercise influence, while British women are asked to keep their hands off' (FL, 8 January 1932: 93.5). Still implicit in her thinking was the imperialist perspective: 'as long as British men have a large say in deciding the issue, British women feel that we must take our share of responsibility and do the best we can' (FL, 17 March 1933: 93.9.20).

These letters signal a shift in emphasis on to the question of women's franchise. In a House of Commons debate on India in January 1931, Rathbone asserted of Indian women that the 'only safeguard against their oppression' was 'to see that women are able to take their share in promoting and shaping their own destinies in the future government of India' (26 January 1931: 247, col. 714). She attributed her conversion to the view that 'women should be able to pull their full weight – or as much of it as possible – in the new constitution' to the writings of Dr Muthulakshmi Reddi (FL, 24 December 1932: 9.2). In March 1931 she was one of a group of British men and women which submitted a memorandum to the Round Table Conference on the future of India pressing for an increase in the franchise for women, and suggesting the possibility of reserved seats. The memorandum was similar to that drawn up by the Indian women delegates to the Round Table Conference. But at the next meeting of the All India Women's Conference in April 1931 under the presidentship of Sarojini Naidu, it was agreed to settle for nothing less than full adult franchise and a memorandum to that effect was drawn up. Mrs Subbarayan, who was a delegate to both the first and the second Round Table Conferences held on Indian constitutional issues, submitted a separate memorandum in which she argued that the majority of Indian women were still in a state of 'civic inertia' (Pearson, 1989: 207). Rathbone sympathised with Mrs Subbarayan – and patronised her:

> Don't be too depressed about it all. The mistakes the Indian ladies are falling into are not unnatural, considering their brief appearance in public affairs. We had much the same difficulties to encounter here from our own extremists. (FL, 15 May 1931: 93.5)

Moreover, her correspondence with Mrs Subbarayan at this time demonstrates her continued private obsession with the child marriage question: she suggested that 'the case is injured by the apparent apathy of the Indians themselves and even of the women's societies', which she accused of having become 'absorbed in the political struggle' (FL, 16 July 1931: 93.5). Mrs Subbarayan's attention was indeed absorbed in the political issues, and she was so distressed by criticism of her position as delegate that she eventually withdrew (FL, 17 February 1932: 93.5).

Rathbone had carried over to the Indian context her belief that admitting differences between women was a sign of strength rather than weakness:

> I feel that the worst thing that can happen is that our Parliament should receive the impression that Indian women are united and unanimous in rejecting the Lothian proposals. A split would be far preferable. It would reflect greater credit on the good sense of Indian women and would be a truer representation of facts. In every difficult question there are divergent opinions and a seeming unity deceives only those who want to be deceived. (FL, 24 January 1933: 93.10)

She was also prepared to confess – at least to Mrs Subbarayan, whose views on Indian women's franchise were close to her own – that 'the Englishwomen's societies which have interested themselves in India are just as much divided as Indian women themselves' (FL, 8 January 1932: 93.5). Rathbone assumed that the experience of suffragists in Britain would be an exemplar for the struggle of Indian women, and she drew untenable parallels between the political groupings in Britain and those in India. She did not at first fully comprehend how the specifity of Indian culture meant that for many Indian feminists the differences between British women and Indian women were more significant than those between Indian women. Although she entered Parliament in order to wield power for women, Rathbone still saw herself as a woman as an outsider, as not fully implicated. This was not how she was seen by Indian women, for whom there was not always a gender distinction to be drawn in the exercise of imperial power.

Nevertheless, this acceptance and tolerance of difference did enable Rathbone to have what seems to have been a very open and affectionate correspondence with some Indian women whom she described in the House of Commons as 'ardent excitable women' (*Hansard*, 28 March 1933: 276, col. 947). She was characteristically forceful, using the threat that 'public opinion' in Britain would

accept Katherine Mayo's prejudiced presentation of the Sarda Act –
which had made child marriage illegal – as 'a piece of window
dressing', if Indians did not themselves agitate for its more effective implementation (FL, 17 July 1931: 92.1). Her correspondence
at first mainly concerned efforts to put the Sarda Act into effect,
but the contested area soon became the franchise.

Sri Maya Devi had opened her correspondence with a letter of
congratulations on Rathbone's election to parliament, but then
went on to explain frankly why there was resentment among Indian
women at the efforts of Englishwomen to become involved in
Indian questions. She expressed her own views in favour of adult
suffrage forcefully, and in response Eleanor pressed her to 'look at
the matter realistically and practically' (FL, 7 September 1931:
93.4). Although her preparedness to settle for a political compromise was not shared by her Indian correspondents, the letters are
still characterised by mutual respect, especially after her visit to
India in January 1932, when she formed warm personal relationships with women whose views were strongly opposed to her own.

Rathbone went to India because she was persuaded by Lady
Hartog that she needed to meet Indian women on their own ground.
Rathbone explained her motive for going to Mrs Subbarayan in a
letter, which demonstrates her indomitable confidence but also
her awareness of the delicacy of her position:

> I am anxious to see things for myself . . . and feel that I may perhaps be
> able to do something to interest British officials and their wives quietly
> on our views about the franchise etc issue, while seeking to acquire
> information rather than impart it.
>
> I hope perhaps I may also be able to do something to dispel the sus-
> picion of me which I know exists among those Indian women whom I
> encounter. But I shall not force this anyway. (FL, 8 January 1932: 93.5)

Losing control

In the letters which Rathbone wrote in India for circulation among
her friends, she expressed her surprise at the physical appearance
of the country – 'the most beautiful . . . I've ever seen' – and she
thought that Mayo had exaggerated the 'unpleasantness' of India:
'As idolatory goes, river worship seems a rather natural and

touching form of it.' But she was 'depressed' by Indian politics: the priorities were not what she wanted them to be. She dined with Indians who were 'charming to me personally. But their conversation for 2½ hours was one long indictment of British rule, past, present and future' (RP XIV: 1.8.13). At the time of Rathbone's visit India was governed by emergency ordinances because of the policy of civil disobedience instituted by the Congress. She did learn something of the contemptuous treatment Indians received from British officials, of the 'unnecessary cruelty' of 'a too aloof and centralized administration acting through insufficiently trained and supervised staff' (RP XIV, 28 August 1941: 4.21). But her criticisms are of the way the system operated and are contained within a framework of acceptance of the Empire. Her visit had made her more sensitive to the interconnections between the independence movement and the issues which concerned her, and she bore witness in the House of Commons of the strength of the Congress movement and the significance of Gandhi's symbolic campaigns (*Hansard*, 27 June 1932: 267, cols. 1567–70). While she became aware of the significance and force of nationalism in the politics of India, she still feared the consequence of the British leaving 'control altogether out of our hands'. As she described the 'oligarchy' to whom 'we are handing over our trusteeship', her reiteration of the word 'control' in her speech in response to the establishment of a Joint Select Committee on the Indian constitution is striking (22 November 1933: 283, cols. 183–91).

After the collapse of the Labour Government in the autumn of 1931, Rathbone continued her correspondence with Ramsay MacDonald and began to correspond with both Benn's successor, R.A. Butler, and with Lord Lothian (FL: 92.2, 93.7). The attitude towards the Indian women which she expressed in the latter correspondence was patronising, suggesting that the AIWC statement in favour of adult franchise 'really only represented a very small body of opinion', and that Dr Reddi changed her mind on reserved seats 'out of loyalty to Mrs. Naidu' (FL, 9 April 1932: 93.7). Sarojini Naidu was the one Indian woman leader whom Rathbone clearly had no respect for at all, for reasons that are not entirely clear. She had earlier described Naidu as a 'poisonous woman' (FL, 16 April 1931: 92.2), whose 'policy of eyewash and shameless lying about the conditions of Indian women have been, apparently, completely successful' (FL, 29 November 1931: 93/7). She now argued that 'most of the women, even those active in education and social work, are only beginning to "think politically" and had not really thought the details out.' Opposition to the 'wife's vote and to co-option of women' was based on 'ill-thought-out grounds, from which I could easily have dislodged them if I had had more time' (FL, 9 April 1932: 93.7). It is perhaps not surprising that she suggested to Austen Chamberlain that she wanted to talk privately with him because 'there is much that one can say much better privately, without Indians present' (FL, 24 May 1933: 93.13).

Rathbone's premise on the franchise was still that it was best from the British angle to press for the largest number of women electors as possible, because of the greater value she placed on social as opposed to political reform. In a letter to her constituents she wrote that her efforts had been 'concentrated on endeavouring to secure for Indian women such a status in the new constitution, as voters, members of elected bodies and in administrations, as will enable them to work effectively for the removal of the grave social evils which oppress them' (RP XIV, March 1934: 3.4). Meanwhile the British Government's proposals were steadily reducing the number of women who would be enfranchised, and the situation was still further complicated by the inclusion of women's franchise in the controversy over 'communal awards' which separated the disposal of seats according to religion. In April 1933, Rathbone established a British Committee for Indian Women's Franchise, composed of representatives of women's organisations, in order to lobby for an improvement in the proposals. Members of the committee gave evidence to the Joint Select Committee which was established to consider the future government of India in April 1933. Ray Strachey[2] – a former colleague of Rathbone's in the NUSEC – was one of those who gave evidence, and her understanding of the situation was even more patronising. She made no mention of Indian women in describing the event to her mother, asserting that the government was 'being held back by Indian officials' and was encouraging the British feminist agitation. She wrote nostalgically that it was like 'sniffing the old suffrage agitation'

(Smith, H.W. mss., Lilly Library, Indiana University, Bloomington, IN: 28 July 1933).

Rathbone told her constituents that she had 'co-operated closely with the delegates from the Indian women's societies who came over to give evidence before the Joint Select Committee', and that the British committee mentioned above was designed to allow those Indian delegates 'all the support which it was the duty of the women's movement in this country to give them' (RP XIV, March 1934: 3.4). Her correspondence with Indian women at this time suggests warmer and closer involvement than this statement implies. Perhaps the warmest in her expressions of affection for Rathbone was the Raj Kumari Amrit Kaur, a staunch nationalist and admirer of Gandhi, who wrote that Indian women 'are indeed fortunate in having such an able and devoted advocate of our cause in you', while openly resisting the compromises which Rathbone urged her to make. Amrit Kaur's affection resulted from personal contact with her in the summer of 1933 when she came to London with Hamid Ali and Muthulakshmi Reddi to give evidence to the Joint Parliamentary Committee on Indian constitutional questions. Rathbone's view of Amrit Kaur before that summer was that she represented the 'extreme and idealistic view of that section of the All-India Women's Conference which objects to the wife's vote and will be content with nothing less than adult franchise' (FL, 9 March 1933: 93.9). After her arrival in England at the beginning of the summer Rathbone wrote to Lord Lothian – the chairman of the Indian Franchise Committee – that he should meet Raj Kumari Amrit Kaur because 'her attitude may be damaging', although 'she seems in a less extremist mood than I expected' (FL, 15 June 1933: 93.7). At the end of the summer, Amrit Kaur wrote that contact with Rathbone had led to her 'realize many things, most of all this that selfless workers like yourself are an inspiration to all of us'. For her, Rathbone's friendship was 'something very precious. It is such friendships that make life worth living' (FL, 14 September 1933: 93.12). It is perhaps, however, sensible if cynical to bear in mind that Amrit Kaur continued to believe that the influence of British women on their government was much weightier than that of Indian women, despite Rathbone's denial of this (FL, 9 January 1935: 93.12; 11 February 1935: 93.12). Rathbone seems to have been open in response, for instance expressing her hope that the Indian suffragists would be able to understand her need to address the British establishment in a language they would understand:

> I have a notion that bits of the argument in my Supplementary Memorandum may rather grate on you, eg the allusion to Parliament's belief in its 'trusteeship for the dumb millions of India.' I want to bring home to the Conservative section of the JSC [Joint Select Committee] that they cannot have it both ways. (FL, 14 October 1933: 93.12)

Raj Kumari Amrit Kaur placed value on the need to maintain contact with Rathbone both on personal grounds and in order to keep the channels of communication open between British and Indian feminists. Dr Reddi was another of Rathbone's correspondents who took a good deal of trouble in lengthy letters to explain her understanding of the political situation. Reddi was also prepared to communicate Rathbone's views before the women of the AIWC despite her knowledge of their reluctance 'to go on discussing and proposing alternatives' (FL, 24 February 1933: 92.1).

The tone of Rathbone's letters gradually became more hesitant – she apologised to the Begum Shah Nawaz for 'giving these hints which are the fruit of my long experience at home of the forms of propaganda which most effect our Parliament' (FL, 8 March 1933: 93.5) – but she was also becoming increasingly anxious as she realised that her belief in compromise was not shared by her correspondents and that they preferred to have a smaller number of women in India enfranchised than to have a method of enfranchisement of which they disapproved. The original demand of the Indian women leaders was for full adult franchise, but they were prepared to compromise to some degree, and accept adult franchise in urban areas. Rathbone felt that such a demand was unrealistic and pressed them to support the idea of enfranchising the wives of certain categories of male voters. It seemed to her preferable that at least some of the Indian women leaders be publicly willing to compromise. In a forceful letter to Reddi she suggested that the 'actual effect' of the demand of the AIWC for adult franchise would be 'to play into the hands of the worst reactionaries both in your country and in mine. They will laugh up their sleeves at the way they have tricked you and persuaded you to accept the shadow for the substance of equality.' She then went on to claim that British suffragists were given 'the wife's vote' and although 'we did not like it . . . we accepted it as the best we could get'. She then compounded this unusual construction of the 1918 Act, by adding:

> It worked well, and it led on in five years to complete adult franchise. There can be no doubt that it did much to improve the status of married women, by making it clear that the State regarded them as their husband's partners in citizenship. (FL, 9 February 1933: 92.1)

She asked Dr Reddi to 'forgive the frankness' with which she had pressed her view, excusing herself on the grounds that she was anxious 'to secure for women in India the fullest possible share in their own constitution'. Another interpretation is that she was unable to accept Indian women's judgement of the situation because of her own perspective that the value of enfranchisement lay in its relevance to social reform rather than political justice.

> Frankly, I felt very frightened lest my plain speaking hurt the feelings of many people and especially of Indian women themselves. But I am so old a campaigner in the women's movement that where the sufferings and injustices inflicted on women are concerned, I really cannot remember or bother about national distinctions. (FL, 28 February 1934: 93.14)

This reflection also suggests that she understood the interests of women to be outside or above the culture in which they occurred, and that she felt that she knew what was right for women in other cultures simply by virtue of being a feminist. This understanding was shared by other Western feminists, and expressed through the International Alliance of women suffragists (the International Woman Suffrage Alliance which became the International Alliance of Women for Suffrage and Equal Citizenship in 1926) where women of all races were depicted standing 'shoulder to shoulder, marching toward universal equality' (Alberti, 1989: Ch.8; Burton, 1991: 67). Travelling in Palestine later that same year, Rathbone declared: 'Though we may have difficulty in understanding each other's language, we shall find a language of the mind which we share in common' (RP XIV, n.d.: 2.5).

Exorcising a demon

By 1934 Rathbone seems to have become inured to the view that
the franchise reforms would 'in effect involve . . . the transfer of
power from a few Englishmen to a few Indians' (RP XIV, March
1934: 3.4). She continued to understand the British in India as a
potential source of progressive change (*Hansard*, 5 March 1935:
314, col. 1869), and she appeared to have little faith that the Indians
might either change themselves or see things differently (15 May
1935: 301, col. 1819). While she sometimes constructed Indian
men – or at least the leading politicians – as 'somewhat in advance
of British opinion' on the enfranchisement of women, she understood them to profit too much from the 'terrible social customs'
which she opposed (28 March 1933: 276, col. 948). She had learned
something of the complexity of women's politics in India by then,
but she had not abandoned her prior commitment to the 'gigantic
evil' which haunted her for seven years (1934a: 13). She wrote
Child Marriage: The Indian Minotaur (1934a) when she felt she
had done all she could by every other means to influence those in
power on the issues which it raised. As she wrote to the Begum
Shah Nawaz:

> I felt I had to write it, because the reply I got in December from Sir
> Samuel Hoare to the last of the thirteen questions amounted to this: that
> the Governments both Central and Local could do nothing in the matter,
> not even undertake the education of public opinion as to the provisions
> of the Act and the necessity for them.
>
> Frankly I cannot let it go at that. The unnecessary sufferings and
> deaths of these young wives and widows have become a continuous
> nightmare to me. (FL, 29 February 1934: 93.12)

In the preface she defied:

> anyone with a particle of imagination to read in full the documents from
> which I have so freely quoted without rising from the perusal with a
> mind steeped in gall. If I have tried to discharge some of this gall in the
> faces of the public, it is only after three years' fruitless trial of more lady-
> like ways of endeavouring to arouse a greater general sense of concern
> and responsibility for the 'great and corroding evil' . . . which is eating
> the vitals of the Indian peoples. (1934a: 9–10)

Part of her argument was that there was a link between the subject matter of her book and the question of the enfranchisement of

women. But the book can be read as an expiation or an attempt to exorcise the demon which had haunted her since she read Mayo's *Mother India* (1927). The use of the Minotaur as a symbol and the language which she used – although Elizabeth Macadam had 'insisted on modifying some of its acridities' – point to the intensity of her revulsion: she had clearly imagined the consequences of child marriage which she described as 'prolonged, agonizing and lonely deaths' (1934a: 9, 15). Using mainly Indian sources to support her case for the failure of the administration to put into effect the existing legal age limit for marriage, she advocated a campaign by Indian women modelled on the militant suffrage campaign in Britain. In her letters to her Indian correspondents about the book, she showed that she was aware that it was 'bound to annoy many people' because, although she accepted that 'an Englishwoman's responsibility is mainly limited to the actions of her own country- men and women', she nevertheless felt that 'in order to give a fair and balanced picture, it was necessary to speak out frankly about the Indian share of responsibility' (FL, 29 February 1934: 93.9). She presented the book as a 'plain recognition of painful facts' (FL, 29 February 1934: 93.4). Since this letter was written to a Muslim this may well be a reference to her description of purdah in the book as 'the imprisonment for life behind the bolts and bars of social custom' (1934a: 13). She asked forgiveness for giving pain to her friends and stated, somewhat hypocritically, given some of her statements in her letters to British politicians quoted above: 'Those are the truest friends of Indians who say to their faces what others only say behind their backs' (1934a: 114).

The response she received from Indian women was polite. Mrs Hamid Ali wrote that *Child Marriage* was 'extremely helpful', but that it failed to recognise the difficulties faced by Indian women who opposed the practice (FL, 9 August 1934: 93.8). In her response to the book Raj Kumari Amrit Kaur explained to Rathbone what had been done by the AIWC as a result of 'the prac- tical suggestions contained in your book'. But she firmly, if tactfully, rejected the offer of money: 'While we are most appreciative of your kind offer to raise money for an All-India Organisation to com- bat early marriage, we feel that we should and must do this work ourselves' (FL, 3 September 1934: 93.12).

In writing *Child Marriage* as a last desperate attempt to influence opinion, Rathbone's assumption was that this would be the last opportunity for about 15 years to have an affect on Indian women's franchise. The final stage of the process of their enfranchisement for Rathbone came with the publication of the report of the Joint Standing Committee which was used as a basis for the India Act passed in the summer of 1935. Rathbone knew that the AIWC would be so dissatisfied with the report that they would not press for changes in it, yet she still suggested possible ways of responding to it short of total rejection: 'we are so used to working to get what we can as we can and making it a basis for more, that we can only go on with that method and hope for the best' (FL, 9 January 1935: 93.12). This was the approach she took in the debate in 1935. She spoke forcefully in favour of reserved seats for women in the Provincial Councils and opposed the clauses requiring women to apply for the vote (*Hansard*, 5 March 1935: 298, cols. 1867–74). Although there was no scope for her participation any longer, and her energies were by then involved in other causes, Rathbone kept in touch with her Indian correspondents. The Begum wrote at length to explain about her decision to withdraw temporarily from the controversy over communal reserved seats. In 1936 she was still in touch, urging Rathbone to 'come out to India and study the condition of the women behind Purdah' (FL, 13 May 1936: 93.4).

India and patriotism: the final act

Rathbone intervened once again in Indian affairs during the Second World War in a way which exposed the limitations of her comprehension of her own cultural prejudices. The outbreak of war together with the build up to it intensified Rathbone's patriotism and it became her main discourse, one that contained internal contradictions about what precisely she was defending. These contradictions and contested meanings were brought sharply into focus in a correspondence with Jawaharlal Nehru, the Congress leader. The exchange of letters began after Rathbone had written 'An Open Letter to some Indian Friends' in May 1941 (RP XIV:

4.19). The political purpose of writing such a public letter is not at all clear; it seems likely that Rathbone was expressing a personal sense of outrage at the behaviour of Indian nationalists. After some attempt at compromise on both sides, Congress was by this time backing Gandhi's campaign of non-violent opposition to the war. Rathbone asserted that she intended deliberately to 'set down the case against the non-co-operators as I see it', for fear that non-co-operating Indians might think that 'all progressive-minded British people are with them in throwing the whole blame on the British authorities'. What she thought would be achieved by this was presumably greater clarity. Certainly its effect was to produce a long and detailed reply from one of those who received the letter, but Nehru's response did not penetrate the cultural perspective which her involvement in India had already exposed (RP XIV, 22 June 1941: 4.20).

It is a riveting yet discomforting correspondence to read because both writers use Western Liberal concepts – freedom, honour, progress – to reach different positions. Rathbone's view was that Nehru's perspective was arrogant and prejudiced: yet it was precisely those qualities which are most obvious in her two letters. She assumed that she could make judgements on the question of India and the war, despite her confessed lack of knowledge of Indian affairs. She asserted – an assertion which he in fact accepted – that Nehru must 'owe much to Western and especially to British teachers' (RP XIV, 28 August 1941: 4.21). She wrote of the refusal of Congress to support Britain in the war in the romanticised terms of betrayal, painting an image in Churchillian terms of the British 'walking, all of us, in the valley of the Shadow of Death', where 'Every day takes its toll of the young men, our best and finest.' She ended with the claim that Britain was bearing the main responsibility for a world cause, which, if lost, would mean that there would be 'no freedom or independence' (RP XIV May 1941: 4.19). The letters demonstrated how deeply the imperialist mentality was rooted in her thinking: it prevented her from understanding the overriding passion for national independence in those who had lived under imperialism. Her cultural complacency led her to assume that Indians must learn from the British. She skated over the history of British imperial control of India and commended the virtues of patience and gradualness which had been the 'method by which our own liberties have been gradually built up', a method 'which has worked well and saved us from many of the misfortunes which have befallen other peoples' (RP XIV 28 August 1941: 4.21).

She may have learned something from Nehru. After receiving his first letter, before she had replied to it and when pressing for the Government to attempt to find some compromise with Congress in India, she pointed out that: 'The Indians are a race who are influenced by an idealism as great as our own. Those of them who differ from us are passionate patriots in their own way as we are in ours' (*Hansard*, 1 August 1941: 373, col. 1739). But she was still clearly reluctant for Britain to lose control of the situation, 'to put the future of India entirely in the melting pot without a better indication of what result that would bring', opposing the policy of promising Dominion status without a corresponding commitment from Congress not to 'impede the war effort' (1 August 1941: 373, col. 1738; 30 July 1942: 382, col. 674).

Rathbone never doubted that Britain was a more advanced nation than India. The concept 'backwardness' was inextricably part of her language and her thinking. She wanted to change women's lives for the better, and 'early marriage, pre-marital circumcision, inadequate midwifery, nursing and medical services' were all aspects of women's lives which cramped their potential as human beings, and she used the concept 'backward' to describe this situation (RP XIV: 2.1.45). The irony is that in this she was in agreement with the Indian woman with whom she had least sympathy: Sarojini Naidu. Naidu – like the Begum Shah Nawaz – denied that she was a feminist and asserted that there was no need for feminism in India where there was a high degree of co-operation between men and women, but she declared in 1933 that 'The woman is the measure of civilization; her home is the centre of culture, civilization is the grace of life and beauty is the measure of civilization; woman alone can realize that beauty and make life civilized' (Pearson, 1989: 200, 217). Where Rathbone and Naidu differed was in whom they were prepared to entrust the future of India.

Conclusion

In the debate on Indian policy in December 1931, Rathbone said: 'To those who have that rare and uncomfortable faculty it often seems that a single line of vital statistics, an average or percentage, contains a tragedy, more substantial than all the tragedies of Shakespeare and Aeschylus' (*Hansard*, 2 December 1931: 260, col. 1183). Her aim was always to awaken the conscience of others, believing that if only people could be presented with the evidence of the suffering of others, they would support the policies she advocated. Armed with this moral fervour, she sailed confidently into the choppy seas of Indian politics, finding there a whole political agenda which she did not fully comprehend and could not influence in the way she had hoped. She advised the Indians to learn 'the inevitability of gradualness' from the example of Britain (1 August 1941: 373, col. 1738). There is a contradiction in this attitude which is central to an understanding of Rathbone's thinking on India. Her emphasis on the necessity, indeed the desirability of gradual political change conflicted with her sense of urgency about social reforms. She wanted to prevent the suffering of Indian women and children, and she saw this need as more urgent than political independence. She did not see that the political discourse from which she advocated reform undermined her own position. She claimed an imperial stake in Indian women's affairs: 'Whether we like it or not – whether it is destined to endure or not – the very fact that British rule *has been* constitutes a responsibility' (1928–9: 213, emphasis in original). This concept of responsibility constructed Indian women as 'dependent clients on whom to confer aid, comfort, and (hopefully) the status of having been saved' (Burton, 1990: 296). In her imagination Rathbone linked women's experiences at the hands of men across cultures and years. At the end of *Child Marriage* she described how she had walked in the Memorial Gardens of Cawnpore, and connected the women and children 'imprisoned and then butchered' during 'the Mutiny' with the much larger number of 'other women and children . . . who had suffered imprisonment less rigorous but so much more prolonged, leading as surely to a dark and terrible death' (1934a: 119–20).

Rathbone saw herself as both critic and goad of her own

Government, believing firmly in the need for campaigning, for bringing pressure to bear on those in power. Her confidence in this process varied, and the story of her involvement with India needs to be looked at in its domestic political context. She arrived in parliament in the full flush of feminist enthusiasm evoked by the final enfranchisement of British women and her own personal triumph in gaining a seat as an Independent. At the same time 13 other women were elected – the largest number yet – the majority of whom were committed to social change, as was the new Labour Government. Within two years the national and international scene was overshadowed by financial crisis and the rise of fascism. By the mid-1930s Labour had been heavily defeated twice at the polls and confidence in the possibilities of change had been eroded by events at home and in Europe. Under Rathbone's continued confident assertion of the possibilities of change there is a sense of desperation as the national and international political context became increasingly bleak.

Notes

1 Dhanvanthi Rama Rau (1893–   ) was one of the first women students at the University of Madras. Friendship with an Indian woman doctor led her to become an active campaigner against child marriage. She spent 10 years in London where she formed an Indian Women's Association to keep Indian women living there, and British women, in touch with events in India.

2 Ray Strachey (1887–1940) became a suffragist as a student at Cambridge. After the First World War she combined political activities with writing (including the classic, liberal study of the women's movement, *The Cause*, which was published in 1928). Her main focus as a feminist was on women's employment.

7

A Passionate Patriot
Fighting Fascism,
1930–45

When Rathbone wondered whether there might be a 'wave-length set up by human suffering to which the minds of women give a specially good reception', what mattered to her were the political results of such sensitivity (1929: 16; 1934a: 17; 1936: 75). These she hoped would be 'a changed attitude on the part of society towards human happiness and suffering, especially towards the happiness or suffering of less powerful and articulate members' (1936: 75–6). This was her approach to the social questions which formed the narrative of the previous chapters: it also informed her stance on international issues in the interwar period. In 1944 she told the following story in the House of Commons:

> I was talking only the other day to a school mistress who said that at her girls' school she spoke to her class about the sufferings of children in Europe. At the end one little girl said 'Well, I always thought that I could not eat turnips but after hearing what those poor children in Europe are suffering, I feel I ought to be glad to eat anything'. (25 January 1944: 396, col. 618)

The central focus of her concern in international affairs in the 1930s was the struggle against fascism. She responded to the suffering of victims – refugees in particular – believing that the Nazis practised 'methods in their sadistic cruelty [which] have hardly been paralleled in the history of the world' (26 July 1938: 338, col. 3015). She was also totally committed to the need for collective resistance to fascist aggression. In opposition to what she saw as an 'evil' – fascism – she constructed Britain as a site of democratic freedom. In opposing fascism on the international scene, and in criticising the government's policy of appeasement, she was again seeing herself as mediator between the voiceless and power. It was in this spirit that she wrote *War Can Be Averted* (1938), the article 'A Personal View of the Refugee Problem' (1939), and a pamphlet, *Falsehoods and Facts about the Jews* (1944). When war came she saw it as an opportunity for change for women, a mood which needed to be exploited as speedily as possible because of the likelihood of a postwar reaction.

'Honour and freedom and fidelity'

In her speech in 1930 on the Bill to allow women to retain their own nationality on marriage Rathbone said:

> We ask for something which satisfies the broad principle to which we cling, namely, that if a woman has a passionate sense of her own nationality, if she feels that she is British in blood and wants to remain British until she dies, she shall be able, of her own free choice, to gratify that sense of her passionate attachment to her own nationality. (*Hansard*, 28 November 1930: 245, col. 1753)

For Rathbone love of country was a good in itself: she described the 'appeal to patriotism, love of the Fatherland and religion' contained within 'Nazi and Fascist ideology' as 'good aspects' of German and Italian propaganda (16 February 1938: 331, col. 1966). However, her patriotism moved beyond the 'sense of nationality' to which she referred in the speech quoted above. Her speeches and writings on both foreign policy are expressed within a discourse of patriotism in which she constructed Britain as representing the ideals to which she subscribed. In 1937 she asserted that the British Government had 'smirched the honour of Great Britain in the eyes of the world', adding:

> I find that 'honour' has become an unpopular word with the younger
> generation, but after all, there is such a thing, and in the minds of many
> of us it is a thing without which, properly interpreted, life is not worth
> living, either for a nation or an individual. (19 July 1937: 326, col. 899)

As she was aware, the word honour belonged to a language already
anachronistic to those who shared the policy position Rathbone
was putting forward in this speech. She was condemning the
British Government for its policy of non-intervention in the Spanish
Civil War, and her view was that the government 'have never
shown courage or even impartiality. They have subordinated
everything to their desire to avoid provoking Germany and Italy.' In
February 1939, she spoke of the commitment to post-Munich
Czechoslovakia as 'a question of honour', and referred to the 'debt
which we owe not only to Czechoslovakia as a State but to every
one of her citizens who is now leading a shrunken life, with poorer
prospects of employment and poorer social services because of
the sacrifices which have been forced upon her' (7 February 1939:
342, col. 830). What she meant by honour is perhaps elucidated by
a speech she made during the war. She refuted the argument that
it was not Britain's responsibility to feed refugees on grounds of
personal morality: 'the fact that a fault has been committed by one
person does not relieve of secondary responsibility those who can
prevent suffering from arising if they are in a position to do so' (8
July 1943: 390, cols. 2368–9). Although Rathbone also put forward
arguments based on a more pragmatic understanding of the aims
of government policies, her patriotic discourse imagined 'the
nation' as a site of moral behaviour with the same ideals she held
up to individuals. She spoke of 'the nation' in personalised terms as
caring 'for honour and freedom and fidelity to its pledged word and
the security of smaller nations as well as for peace' (5 November
1936: 317, col. 336).

In one of her first speeches in the House of Commons Rathbone
had asserted that 'the greatest asset of this country is national character'. She said that she had 'been told by people who have been in
such places as the South American Republics that the word of an
Englishman is the very synonym of truthfulness' (13 November
1929: 231, col. 2098). She understood the British character to be
both 'natural' and the result of a long process of cultural develop-

ment: 'We British are by nature a relatively unexcitable and self-controlled people, upheld in troublous times by our consciousness of strong and friendly forces around us and with a sense of mutual responsibility bred in us by generations of self-government' (1944: 10). As a result of this process, British 'civilisation' was of a 'matured type' (*Hansard*, 16 February 1938: 331, cols. 1963–6). What Rathbone valued were the 'democratic institutions and liberties' which had been 'hammered out' in 'England' (RP XIV, May 1941: 4.19). Central to these was freedom of speech. She had opposed the Incitement to Disaffection Bill of 1934, co-operating with 'the Opposition Parties in fighting the Bill inch by inch in Committee and, with the aid of the campaign outside Parliament, we induced the Government to accept many drastic amendments' (RP XIV, February 1935: 3.4). The Bill, she declared, would 'tear a hole in British liberties through which an elephant may get through' (*Hansard*, 16 April 1934: 288, col. 826).

Her response to conflicting political ideologies was to maintain the principles of toleration and freedom of expression which she understood to be the basis of liberty. Her insistence that feminists should accept difference and tolerate its open expression is thus part of her ungendered understanding of liberal freedoms. However, she was also aware of the particular threat to women in the 1930s, 'when liberties all over the world are being seriously impaired' (*Hansard*, 16 April 1934: 288, col. 826). For her the only justification for 'the placing of legal limitations on the free expressions and circulation of opinions and ideas', was if such free expression 'either infringes the similar rights and privacy and freedom of action on the part of other people or inflicts some kind of injury upon others or upon the public generally'. Her view was that 'to give a man a leaflet does not compel him to read it, and, therefore, he is not intruding upon the liberty of thought and action' (2 November 1934: 293, col. 583).

Collective security

Rathbone's criticism of the Government on the related questions of foreign policy and refugees was expressed in terms of the ideals which she ascribed to Britain. The policy she consistently argued for was collective security, calling for 'the drawing together of the free democracies of the world in defence of something which is even a greater cause than the cause of peace, the cause of the liberties and freedom of the world' (6 February 1934: 285, cols. 1083–7). Her faith in British institutions was undermined by the failure of the government to support collective security, and she expressed it in personal and moral terms:

> The final abandonment of Abyssinia left many of us with a feeling that though the future might hold greater disasters, perhaps the fruit of that desertion, it was unlikely that anything could happen to make us feel more ashamed or more wounded in our racial pride than we did already. (1938: 49)

She compared a speech by the British Foreign Secretary which declared a commitment to collective security, to 'the removal of a tooth which had been aching for months' (1938: 41). Her shame for her own country was transformed after 1939 into a passionate moral pride, declaring that 'Britain has expiated her sin' (RP XIV, May 1941: 4.19).

Rathbone forecast German aggression in Poland and Czechoslovakia in a debate on foreign affairs in the summer of 1936 (*Hansard*, 31 July 1936: 314, col. 1935). She had quoted a biblical image in her introduction to *The Ethics and Economics of Family Endowment* (1927) which she now repeated to convey her sense of the interconnectedness of nations as well as people: 'we are all "members of one another"' (1938: 80). But there was nothing archaic about her analysis of the path to war – it was one that would eventually receive the widespread agreement of historians. As she noted in the House of Commons in the summer of 1938: 'After every fresh concession, the aggressive powers become more openly arrogant and insolent' (*Hansard*, 26 July 1938: 338, col. 3019). In 1937 she wrote *War Can Be Averted* (published 1938) in a desperate attempt to persuade 'intelligent and observant but non-expert enquirers in language they can understand and in a book they can afford to buy', that 'collective security could be achieved if Great Britain would put herself at the head of a group of States within the League', and 'that the obstacles to this are not lack of Power but lack of Faith and Will among ourselves' (1938: v). She argued that far from the League of Nations having failed, 'its pow-

ers were never tried, except in the Abyssinian case . . . with a deliberate neglect of all the conditions laid down by its founders and
interpreters as essential to success' (1938: 71).

Fear, faith and freedom of expression

Seeking for an explanation for the failure of Britain to live up to its
ideals, Rathbone found it in the personal fears and interests of the
members of the government, the 'property interests, class prejudices, fear of Communism and dislike of Russia' (1938: 86). She
was always sensitive to the class nature of the British political system, disliked titles, and suggested that members of the aristocracy
were not representative of 'the side of British life' which she cele-
brated for its free and democratic nature (*Hansard*, 18 February
1941: 331, col. 76). Her view was that the 'ordinary citizen' had a
false perception of foreign policy 'partly because the well-to-do
classes control by far the greater part of the press' (1938: 24).
Although she condemned Stalin as a dictator, she advocated an
alliance with the USSR, and she classed those countries which had
resisted fascism as 'proudly independent or proletarian', forecast-
ing that they would increasingly rely on Russia 'as their sure friend'
(1938: 76).

In her attack on British foreign policy she exonerated 'the people in general' whom she saw as 'slow to move, occupied with
relatively petty domestic issues, unimaginative, easily deluded,
dulled by repeated horrors into accepting horrors as inevitable'
(1938: 70). A government could 'usually secure acquiescence in its
foreign policy', and it was therefore 'not the nation's fear of war that
is holding it back. Is it their own?' (1938: 25). Her answer to this
question in the House of Commons was:

> The Government are doing their best to bring up the British people into
> the habit of sheer cowardice, and sooner or later they will pay for it,
> because when the time comes when they want the British people to fol-
> low them and stand up for what they think vital interests, they will find
> that the people have learned their lesson only too well. (*Hansard*, 23
> June 1938: 337, col. 1376)

Rathbone appealed to the courage of the British voters which she understood as being undermined by the Government – and by pacifists. She devoted two out of eight chapters of *War Can Be Averted* (1938) to developing her arguments against pacifism and the peace movement. Her standpoint was ungendered: she ignored, as she had in the First World War, those feminists who associated women with peace (Liddington, 1989). Central to this condemnation was the use of 'propaganda' to stimulate fear: 'They draw ghastly pictures of the horrors of the last war and of the greater horrors of wars present and to come. They expiate on the futility of anti-gas and anti-air-raid precautions. What is the object of that unless to stimulate fear?' Her view was that such fears would do nothing except 'cloud the brain and paralyse the will' (1938: 159). She told the same story in the House of Commons, referring to pacifism as 'that spirit, that dangerous movement' (*Hansard*, 26 October 1937: 328, col. 68). She wanted those who sought for peace to give 'guidance to a distracted public', and that guidance for her must be 'limitation of armaments by international agreement, under conditions which take into account the needs of national defence and the fulfilment of League obligation' (1938: 160). Her own advocacy of collective security, although she believed that this was the way to avert war, was based on preparedness to use force (1938: 74).

When the war began she did not lose sight of the possibility of using collective peaceful action to prevent it spreading, and was prepared to accept the offering of peace terms to Germany in the autumn of 1939: 'Is there one chance in a million that a peace by negotiation, which is honourable and secure, could be won by holding out a sort of ladder between ourselves and Germany?' (*Hansard*, 12 October 1939: 352, cols. 631–2). A negotiated peace and a statement of war aims were demands made by many left-wing politicians until May 1940 when the German armies moved west and a coalition Government was formed. Many on the left continued after this date to express their concern about the potential for the Government to abuse their power by the suppression of civil liberties. Rathbone was faced with a threat to her accustomed solidity of principle. She pressed for the declaration of 'war aims' in the early months of the war and again in October 1940:

To many of us, it seems almost a platitude to go on repeating that we have no Imperialist or aggressive aims, but I am not at all sure that, in view of the continuous and in many ways skilful propaganda of Germany and Italy, the idea that this is merely a combat between two groups of Imperialistic powers may not gain hold. From the point of view of foreign propaganda, it is extremely important that we should go on repeating, even ad nauseam, the ideals for which we stand. (15 October 1940: 365, cols. 660–3)

But she was also afraid that 'dissident minorities' might 'weaken the national effort by at any rate public expositions of their views as to the futility and the uselessness of the present war'. She confessed that she said this 'with great reluctance, because a little while ago I could not imagine supporting any kind of limitation upon freedom of speech' (22 May 1940: 361, col. 209). War had made Rathbone anxious about the possibility of 'public injury', and she expressed anxiety about the ability of 'dissident minorities to weaken the national effort' (22 May 1940: 361, col. 210). Her anxiety had been laid at rest by the end of 1940: she made a study of votes at by-elections for peace candidates which suggested to her that 'we can let the dogs bark, because the barking has not had much effect upon the war effort or the resolution of this country'. There is a contradiction here: her concern to 'be very careful of how much we impede the free expression of public opinion in this country, however much we disagree with it', was limited to the case where opinions she disagreed with – at least in wartime – were in a minority (3 December 1940: 367, col. 487). I read her view on the question of persuasion, of propaganda, as part of her discourse on progress. She believed that 'right' behaviour and thinking would emerge eventually. On her visits to Egypt, Palestine, Yugoslavia and Romania, she said she was struck by the 'subtlety and perseverance' of 'Nazi and Fascist propaganda' (16 February 1938: 335, cols. 640–4). She accused the British government of 'parsimony and lack of imagination' in their failure to 'enter into competition with Hitler and Mussolini on their own lines' (1938: 106). Her assumption was that fascist ideology could be defeated by the expression and example of Western democratic ideals.

The victims of fascism

For Rathbone Nazism was an 'evil spirit' which she condemned soon after the seizure of control of the German government by the Nazi party. She saw it from the first as a threat to 'the peace and freedom of the world', but the first threat was to the freedom of individuals within Germany. She laid stress at first on the persecution of Socialists and Pacifists rather than Jews, 'because less attention has been drawn to that aspect of the German persecution' (*Hansard*, 13 April 1933: 276, col. 2763). Then on 31 May 1933 she chaired a meeting of women's organisations called by the NUSEC, where a unanimous resolution was passed expressing 'dismay' at Nazi dismissals of women from government service, and pointing out that 'any injury done to the women of one nation must be deeply felt by the women of all nations' (*The Times*, 2 June 1933: 9a).

Rathbone's concern for civil liberties combined with her championship of the victim to inform her passionate advocacy of the cause of refugees from fascism. The first group of refugees she focused on were from Spain. Her perspective at first had been that of a critic of the Government's policy of non-intervention in the Spanish Civil War, and she tracked down and made lists of those MPs who seemed to her to be pro-Franco (RP XIV: 2.10). She visited Spain with Ellen Wilkinson and the Duchess of Atholl in April 1937, and that summer she was deeply involved in attempts to evacuate refugees from Santander (RP XIV: 2.11). She worked behind the scenes in her position as secretary to the Parliamentary Committee for Refugees, and regularly tried to stir the Government's conscience about refugees (RP XIV: 2.11, 12, 13, 14, 15; annotated Parliamentary speeches). It was in the language of conscience that Rathbone wrote an article in the *New Statesman and Nation*, published a month later:

> It is as though one stood hour after hour, day after day, with a small group of people outside bars behind which hordes of men, women and children were enduring every kind of deliberately inflicted physical and mental torture. We scrape at the bars with little files. A few victims are dragged painfully one by one through gaps. (1939: 568–9)

She wrote and spoke because of her sense that 'all the time we are conscious that streams of people are passing behind us unaware of or indifferent to what is happening, who could if they united either push down the bars and rescue the victims, or – much more dangerously – stop the torturers'. Her understanding of the concept of political responsibility was that it stretched beyond 'the evil' done by people or 'nations', to 'every bit of evil in the world which they or their nations – with which they identify themselves – fail to prevent'. Governments bore primary responsibility, but individuals should 'exert every means we possess of influencing Government to change its policy'. In the end Rathbone saw the war as the only way finally to 'stop the torturers' (1939: 568–9).

During the war she was deeply concerned with the fate of Jews. She had been fascinated by Jewish culture on her visit to Palestine, admiring the way they had 'during centuries of persecution . . . maintained their identity, their faith, the customs enjoined by their religion' (1944: 14). After the news of the holocaust which was taking place was broken to the House of Commons in December 1942, Rathbone pressed the Government with questions and requests for a debate, protesting again and again about the continued restrictions on the entry of refugees (for example, *Hansard*, 17 December 1942: 385, cols. 2076, 2086, 2089; 20 January 1943: 386, col. 446; 11 March 1943: 387, cols. 846–9). When the debate on the holocaust was finally held in December 1943, Rathbone made one of the most impassioned speeches of her time as an MP on a question which she thought about day and night, which was on her conscience all the time. She knew that it was not fervent words that were most needed, but action, and she also knew how little could be done, that 'the vast majority of the victims are outside our reach'. She was angry and frustrated at the way those who were working for refugees were manipulated by the government. Her aim was to pressurise the Government to encourage neutral countries to welcome all refugees with the promise that Britain would take responsibility for them. She declared that she was convinced that she was backed by 'British public opinion' with its 'keen sense of the practical', by 'every section of opinion in the country worth consideration', by a 'generous-hearted and humane' people (14 December 1943: 395, cols. 1467–74). After the end of the war she supported the establishment in Palestine of a 'Jewish State as part of the British Commonwealth of Nations' which she believed could be achieved 'with full justice to the real rights of the Arabs of Palestine' (20 August 1945: 413, col. 365).

When faced with the consequences of war on the civilian population of Europe Rathbone was in a dilemma. She accepted the necessity of an economic blockade intended to speed up the end of the war, but she wanted desperately to go to the assistance of the victims, refuting the arguments used against such a policy:

> The other argument which I venture to dispute is one which is always a dangerous argument, about the thin end of the wedge, that if we extended this scheme to Belgium, it would be said, 'If to Belgium, why not to Poland, perhaps, and the Channel Islands?' If we can do something to relieve suffering on a limited scale without doing greater harm in other areas, we have a perfect right to do it. (8 July 1943: 390, cols. 2368–71)

Her knowledge of the problems of wartime Europe may have shifted Rathbone's understanding of national feeling. She became aware of the problems looming in the postwar settlement of occupied territories in Europe where the nationality of the displaced person would be much less important than his or her relationship with the 'enemy nations' (25 January 1944: 396, col. 615).

The 'great eye-opener'

Although Rathbone knew that 'war encourages brutality', she also saw it as a 'great eye-opener' (1940: 105), and therefore as a time of opportunity for social change. This understanding of war fitted into the construction of the way change happens which she subscribed to for 40 years, the need to take 'full advantage of every favourable wind and tide in public opinion' (1936: 56). In the House of Commons in 1935, she had asked that the question of the representation of women on provincial Indian assemblies not be thought of as 'a question of feminism' – explicitly because of the danger of 'anti-feminist prejudice' – but rather as 'a question of life and death' (*Hansard*, 10 May 1935: 301, col. 1304). During the war she stated firmly that she was 'a feminist, a 100 per cent. feminist' (20 March, 1941: 370, col. 369). As a patriot and a feminist she demanded the registration and extensive use of women in the services as well as in industry. In 1941 she declared herself 'tremendously proud of the success women have achieved' in the army, and hoped that women 'would be used even more in the combatant units'. In her view 'There ought to be no test of the kind of service that a woman should be called to but what kind of service she is able to perform' (2 December 1941: 376, col. 1088). Rathbone's patriotism sat less comfortably with her feminism on the questions of equal pay. Her sense that men were making a greater sacrifice during the war by serving in the armed forces meant that she was reluctant to oppose union agreements about the relaxation of 'pre-war practices'. These – as they had in the First World War – embodied the principle that women were only replacing men on a temporary basis. But she was aware that assurances that women should be paid 'the rate for the job', were often undermined by the redefinition or regrading of work. She was ambivalent about the concept of 'men's jobs', and was determined that wartime practice should not stultify future change, and 'operate as a kind of stone wall, a stratification of the pre-war position of women in industry' (3 February 1942: 377, cols. 113–14). She was afraid of a repetition of the 'old story of welcoming women as heroines in war-time and then throwing them out afterwards', and demanded that women be consulted on postwar 'reconstruction' (5 March 1942: 378, col. 891).

In 1942 in a debate on government expenditure, Rathbone claimed that there was 'a growing sense of irritation among women of all parties and of no party in the country at what they conceive to be the regular Government game with women of: "Heads I win, tails you lose"'. She recalled an image used by Emmeline Pankhurst of having temporarily buried a bone she had to pick with a Minister, and threatened the Chancellor of the Exchequer with the growing 'number of bones all over the country which women have buried', asserting that 'we have not forgotten where we have buried them' (13 May 1942: 379, cols. 1879–80). Her largest bone was, of course, in the shape of a family allowance. Soon after the outbreak of war a memorandum written by Leo Amery MP was sent to the government on behalf of a group of MPs. They asked that a scheme of family allowances should be put rapidly into operation, citing five 'war-time purposes' for their proposal. Rathbone referred to these 'purposes', and made clear her own view of the relevance of war in her last book on the subject of family allowances:

> those of us who have been pondering these things in our hearts recognise that nearly all these purposes belong to peace-time as well as war. Malnutrition, low health, bad housing, smouldering discontent, a burning sense of the injustice of a system which gives so much to the few and so little to the many, the growing realisation by married people that they can escape poverty by avoiding parenthood or limiting their children to one or two – all these are not new factors. They have long existed. The only thing that is new is the awakening sense of what these evils mean to the whole community. (1940: 105–6)

A slow and uphill fight

The Case for Family Allowances (1940) was an abbreviated version of *The Ethics and Economics of Family Endowment* (1927), but there are significant differences. The wartime book repeated the arguments and much of the material of *The Disinherited Family* (1924) and *The Ethics and Economics of Family Endowment*, but the tone of the book is less passionate, less exigent. The explanation of this probably lies partly in the format of the 'Penguin Special' with its audience, the 'general reader', and partly in the fact that Rathbone's attention was not strongly on the issue at the time: suffering as the result of poverty had been replaced for her as a priority by suffering as the result of fascism and war. Her speeches in the House of Commons on the subject were as passionate as ever: and they were more strongly informed by her patriotism. She defended her proposal that any family allowance scheme should be extended to 'aliens' partly because 'they regard our national cause as their cause' (*Hansard*, 20 March 1941: 370, col. 374). And her arguments focused strongly on the trend in population:

> I beg the House to ask themselves this question: Is it really safe, with our far-flung responsibilities, that the proportion of the Anglo-Saxon race, compared with almost every other race, certainly every other white race, should continue to be a steadily diminishing proportion? (23 June 1942: 380, cols. 1865–6)

A year later she declared that Britain had a 'world mission', when again expressing her dismay about the decline of the birth rate (16 July 1943: 391, col. 354). Rathbone had addressed the population question throughout her campaign for allowances, but her comments in the 1920s had been dismissive of the arguments she later put forward:

> Public opinion in this country oscillates between the fear of a declining birth-rate and the fear of over-population. The motive of the former fear is usually political; those who feel it are either ambitious for the spread of Anglo-Saxon civilization over the earth or obsessed with the thought of jealous Continental neighbours and teeming Oriental millions. (1927: 107)

Yet these were precisely the views that she came close to expressing in the mid-1930s, when she declared that she found it 'alarming' that 'the eugenic results' of ill-health among women was 'attracting so little attention', and then added:

> I often think the day will come when the people of this country . . . will ask themselves whether a country with Imperial responsibilities such as ours can afford to look on and do nothing about the steady shrinkage of the white populations compared with the yellow, the brown and the black. (*Hansard*, 25 March 1935: 299, col. 1649)

These comments place Rathbone among those whom Anna Davin identifies as falling 'easy prey to the racist ideology of eugenics', when motherhood was a 'matter of imperial importance' in the period 1900–40 (Davin, 1978: 18, 14). My sense is that when writing for a non-eugenist audience in the 1920s when she was at her most confident and hopeful, Rathbone kept her distance from eugenic arguments (1924: 311–24). But she did write in terms of 'race-stock', and used metaphors of 'seed-time and harvest' for the birth-rate (1927: 114, 116). As Davin has pointed out, concerns about the deterioration of the 'national stock' were commonplace in political circles in the interwar years, and ideas of 'degeneracy' were part of the Victorian Social Darwinian heritage. Rathbone denied that professional people were better 'race-stock than artisans, or artisans than labourers', but she was a patriot and she wanted to encourage those to be parents who were 'fittest to recruit a nation with traditions and responsibilities such as ours' (1927: 114). Macnicol contends that she 'displayed a marked fondness for eugenic arguments' (1980: 88). He refers to a speech she made to the Eugenics Society in January 1925, which was published by the Family Endowment Society, and quotes from 'The Rumeration of Women's Services' of 1917. My reading is that Rathbone used arguments from eugenics to support her case when she felt that this would appeal to her audience, and that her patriotic discourse contained a eugenic perspective when Britain seemed to her to be shouldering international responsibilities in wartime and in the 1930s.

The framework of the argument for family allowances is the same in all three books in which Rathbone put forward her demand: the impossibility of achieving adequate financial support for families with children under existing practice; the inextricable linking of the idea of the 'living wage' with equal pay; the effect on wives and husbands of the existing system, in particular the way it propped up masculine complacency; the success of experiments with family allowances in other countries. The differences are in emphasis and structure, and they may say something about changes in her thinking. In *The Ethics and Economics of Family Endowment* (1927), she had begun by looking at the economic case for allowances, then moved on to the ethical case. The 1940 version reverses the order and its opening passages are different from the equivalent section of *Ethics*: the focus is on 'the family' as an institution. Her assessment uses the words of both her earlier constructions of it as the source 'of the strongest emotions, most enduring motives, most accessible sources of happiness' (1924: 123; 1927: 12; 1940: 14). In 1940 she repeated the assertion made in 1927, that the family was a bulwark against 'certain explosive and disrupting forces' (1927: 12; 1940: 14). The 'Family' was given its capital 'F' in 1927; its prominent early placing in 1940: in all three books she made wry comments about the dangers of sentimentalising it. And in all three she explained that she was concerned to examine 'the present method of providing for families' (1924: 123); a phrase which became 'whether Society at present makes to the Family quite a fair return for what it gets from it', in the later two versions where the emphasis is more on ethics than economics (1927: 12; 1940: 15).

By 1940 marriage had, it seemed, changed. Rathbone wrote that 'young couples about to marry as often as not assume that the wife will continue the work of her profession or industry . . . , and the man regards his mate as a partner rather than a dependant' (1940: 104). But, she added, 'subconscious instincts have a way of lasting like damp below the surface long after the weather has changed, until at last sun and air from the healthy outside world penetrate and gradually dry them up'. And 'the impediment to reform' was not only to be found in the 'wealthy capitalist classes', but among Labour MPs who spoke eloquently about their personal knowledge of poverty, but ignored the 'one simple and direct means of relieving that poverty' (1940: 104–5). She again attacked dilatory trade union attitudes in a debate in the House of Commons on the White Paper proposals for family allowances in June 1942 (*Hansard*, 23 June 1942: 380, col. 1862).

The long struggle for the introduction of allowances continued throughout the war (Land, 1979). When the Bill was eventually introduced into the House of Commons in March 1945, Rathbone welcomed the securing of the principle she had argued for for 25 years, but deplored both the amount – 5 shillings instead of the 8 shillings proposed by Beveridge – and most of all the proposal that the allowance be paid to men. She declared that she would not vote for the measure if that clause was not amended, 'because it treats the wife as a mere appendage, literally a hanger on, of her husband' (*Hansard*, 8 March 1945: 408, col. 2276). One of the reasons why Rathbone was prepared to accept compromise on the amount of the allowance in the 1945 Act, was that she feared the possibility of a reaction after the war such as had taken place after the First World War (23 June 1942: 380, col. 1863). Although she believed that the women's movement had given women an irreversible 'passion for freedom and self-determination', she never lost her sense that the 'fight for women's citizenship' was 'very slow and uphill', and she warned against the assumption that 'victory is completely won and that all is lovely in the garden' (1934b: vii; *Hansard*, 3 August 1943: 391, col. 2130). Nor did she lose her awareness of the misogyny which shadowed the increasing visibility of women in the political arena. She was the subject of this vicious comment by A. McLaren, the MP for Burslam: 'I see that she is not present now. What a pity. I wish that she had stayed. For

years she has wasted her life advocating family allowances. I suppose that is a good enough substitute for the absence of a family'
(*Hansard*, 23 June 1942: 380, col. 1876).

Although she became an adept parliamentarian and was thus
arguably co-opted into the patriarchy, Rathbone never lost her sensitivity to the belittling of women in the House of Commons: 'Is my
rt. hon. friend aware that if Parliament and the Press spent their
time discussing all the silly things which silly men say about
women, there would be little time for anything else?' (2 December
1942: 385, col. 1785). When Ernest Bevin said in answer to a question about regulations concerning the registration of women for
work that he could not 'be expected to clear up every difficulty in
a woman's mind', Rathbone interjected: 'Is that hon. gen. aware
that the embarrassment in the women's minds is not due to any
particular stupidity of women's minds but to the extraordinarily
imperfect information hitherto given to them by the entirely inad-
equately staffed employment exchanges?' (27 March 1941: 370,
col. 677).

While welcoming the increasing number of women on government committees, Rathbone complained that the government
'ought to be convinced by this time that women are capable of
actually chairing committees, yet there is a constant tendency to
put one or two capable women on a committee while behaving as
though it were quite necessary to have a man in the chair' (3
August 1943: 391, col. 2131). One of the reasons for this tendency
was the 'hesitation and timidity' with which Ministers approached
'the question of women' (2 December 1941: 376, col. 1087).
Another was the 'Turk Complex' which she had named in 1924, but
identified in her writing on women's wages. Made aware of the
problem of associating this psychology with 'our gallant Ally', she
referred to it now as the 'old Adam' and subsequently, not wishing
to do an injustice to Adam, as 'the old serpent'. This 'subtle and difficult enemy' lay behind the complaints against 'a former
stockbroker of 40 being supervised in carpet-sweeping by a
W.A.A.F. of 19'. 'Why not?' asked Rathbone, 'A W.A.A.F. of 19 would
almost certainly have more experience of carpet-sweeping than a
stockbroker' (3 August 1943: 391, col. 2130).

It was the older woman who was the subject of hostile

construction the following month in the debate on the possible
extension of the age of registration of women for war work. Dr
Thomas, MP for Southampton, argued that women of menopausal
age should not be registered, asserting that:

> the feminist movement is not anxious for this matter to be brought out,
> because in their work for equality of pay between men and women they
> are afraid it will weaken their case. Behind this movement are some
> women who have not perhaps fulfilled their natural functions in life and
> sometimes they behave somewhat viciously towards their sisters. (24
> September 1943: 392, cols. 607–8)

In her response, Rathbone did not challenge the concept of 'natural
function'; she accepted that there was 'a difficult period' in a
woman's life, and she implicitly accepted that women's function
was reproduction, naming the change as one from 'the productive
period to the non-productive period'. However, she challenged the
precise timing of the menopause to 'the years from 47 to 51', and
asserted that 'Very frequently . . . it does not have anything like the
serious repercussions which the hon. Member represented'. When
interrupted by Dr Thomas with a claim to his 'considerable experience in these matters', Rathbone retorted: 'And yet these women
who are in such an abnormal mental and physical condition invariably continue their work as teachers, as doctors, as nurses, as
factory workers and as hard-worked housewives' (24 September
1943: 392, cols. 607–9).

Rathbone's arguments for the recognition of the part which
older women could play was imbued with the patriotism which
informed all her wartime discourse. In a letter written the year
war broke out concerning the possibility of wartime restrictions on
welfare benefits, she advocated that those 'directed against mal-
nutrition should be extended as part of a drive for national fitness'
(RP XIV, 14 February 1939: 2.7.11). She emphasised the 'contribution towards the community which women made, both in the
production of material wealth and the production and rearing of
children' (*Hansard*, 5 March 1942: 378, col. 891). In her speeches
on family allowances during the war she emphasised the importance of ensuring that the proportion of the Anglo-Saxon race did
not diminish, and called for larger families so that the 'Empire' –
which she preferred to call 'a Commonwealth of Nations' – could

be sustained by younger sons and daughters. She denied that she was an Imperialist, but she did believe that 'this country has a world mission' (16 July 1943: 391, cols. 552–4). She believed that Britain's performance in the Second World War left it 'standing . . . higher in the estimate of the world than we ever did before'. She made this claim in one of the last speeches she gave, two months before her death. The context was a debate on postwar conditions in Europe, and she called for the British Government to 'show the maximum imagination, initiative, energy and courage . . . Moral courage', which she asserted was 'the quality for which the world is thirsting, and for the lack of which millions are threatened with death' (26 October 1945: 414, col. 2416).

Conclusion

Rathbone carried her moral fervour and her concern for the powerless and the inarticulate from the domestic to the international arena. Her hopes were rooted in her faith in British democracy which she seems to have accepted unreflectively was based on ideals of free expression and personal liberty. As individuals bore a responsibility for others, so as a nation she believed Britain bore a moral responsibility to both individuals and countries threatened internally or externally by Fascism. She did not lose her faith in either individual or collective action, believing that war could have been avoided by a collective stance against the threat from Germany, and that Government reluctance to stand firm was cowardice. She presented herself as both sharing in the responsibility for the behaviour of the British Government, and prepared to criticise it for failing to live up to the principles of the democracy it purported to uphold (1938: 17, 49). In the House of Commons she became marked as a Government critic. Although she had always tended to be in trouble from the Speaker for her determination to say what she wanted to say, whether it was according to parliamentary rules or not, attempts by the Speaker to curb her become more frequent and determined in foreign policy debates in the late 1930s (*Hansard*, 16 February 1938: 331, cols. 1965–6; 23 June 1938: 337, cols. 1375–7).

Rathbone's patriotism emerged strongly as war loomed. Her patriotic and urgent concern for the victims of fascism arguably distracted her from the feminist commitments which had led her to become an MP. She did not feel any the less a feminist for making the decision that her energy and effort needed to be put into international causes. When war came she saw it as an opportunity to take a stand as a representative of women on conscription, where she was vigilant and staunchly patriotic, and on the much delayed introduction of family allowances. The debates on these issues demonstrate both the continuing misogyny of British political structures, and Rathbone's undiminished awareness of the long struggle ahead of feminism.

Conclusion

The starting point for Eleanor Rathbone's life of thought and action was her reaction to '*such* a world with all its wrongs shouting in one's ears and every miserable face claiming kinship' (Stocks, 1949: 53, emphasis in original). She had no doubt that this response had a firm, general, ethical basis. She remained totally committed to the idea that suffering caused by material conditions was intolerable and that change was both possible and a moral imperative:

> by what authority and in virtue of what proven social expediency do any of us who lead comfortable lives dare to tell the mass of men and women, on whose labours we depend for every one of the necessities and amenities we judge essential for ourselves, that they must be contented with the bare and animal existence which the present system alone makes possible for them? (1927: 118)

Her understanding of human needs was thus firmly based in the material: she believed that one should remember 'that the economic factor is not the only, nor even the most important, factor, but that it does react on all others'. But needs went beyond the material to 'the good life' where each human being could 'attain the full measure of the stature – physical, mental, and moral – which nature intended for him or her' (1927: 38). She later extended this construction to include the concept of self-determination which, linked with independence, provided the bedrock of her personal and political objectives.

This was then a philosophy firmly based on recognition of the individual. But her individualism did not prevent Rathbone from thinking in terms of 'the body politic' (1927: 8). Individuals as members of that body had a responsibility for all others within it. The response of 'facile goodwill' was not enough, what was needed was 'hard thinking and study' (1927: 7). Rathbone moved from an assumption that individual action was enough to a commitment to political action. That commitment remained rooted in an ideal of individual responsibility, and of responsibility to the individual within society:

> to recognize each member of the body politic as having a claim on the whole body, not merely the claim of a beggar on an almsgiver, but a claim based on the truth that 'even those parts which seem to be feeble are necessary'; and again, that every human being, while in one sense a part of the organic whole, is in another sense an inevitably separate and even lonely individuality, to be counted as an end in itself and not merely as a means to the end of others. (1927: 8)

The intensity of her personal response to poverty is explained partly by her own wealth. Inherited wealth bolstered her sense of public responsibility and also rendered her totally independent. Valuing it for herself, she sought independence for other women whose circumstances were very different from hers. Her wealth and education also gave her a role working on behalf of other women: she saw herself as a leader and later in parliament as a representative both of her class and her gender. There was a contradiction implicit here since she particularly wanted to speak for working-class women – and once claimed to speak for 'the unhappily married woman' (*Hansard*, 3 August 1943: 291, col. 2133). She never developed a critical analysis of the system which made it possible for her to be financially independent, seeking always to redistribute rather than restructure.

Rathbone's feminism had its roots in the concept of human needs which entailed more than the material. She believed that women were prevented from being 'fully developed human beings' within the society which existed throughout her lifetime (1927: 113). She called for a 'new feminism' in the 1920s, whose 'formula' was 'not equality but self-determination' (1929: 33). The struggle for the franchise had revealed the extent of the restrictions which constrained women. She used the powerful image of a 'volcanic upheaval which breaks up the verdant surface of the earth and lays bare the barren tracts, the sharp rocks, the creeping ugliness that lie beneath' (1929: 39), to convey her understanding of how the struggle for the vote revealed and connected all the other objectives of the women's movement. She claimed to have given 'the best years of my life' (*Hansard*, 20 May 1931: 252, col. 2014) to the suffrage movement, and the achievement of the vote represented the placing of 'the keystone of the edifice' which feminists sought to build (*CC*, 15 February 1918: 373).

Beyond suffrage, the reforms demanded by feminists all stood for 'an effort to relieve a mass of human suffering, or to break away bonds which are cramping and thwarting the free development of human capacity' (1929: 9). As her understanding of feminism was rooted in her belief in the need for self-determination for all human beings, so for her there was no firm distinction between feminist and social reform (1929: 13). She wanted wives to have an income independent from their husbands in order that they could achieve full individuality within the family, but she proposed no structural change in the institution. Later she was to place more emphasis on the need to alleviate child poverty through family allowances, although it is clear that this was never for her the entire justification for them. Her willingness to compromise on this issue grew from her insistence that 'Political workers must never allow themselves to forget that every period of feeling and enthusiasm is liable to be followed by a period of apathy and rejection' (*CC*, 30 June 1916: 155). For Rathbone the political context was a variable, not a constant: she increasingly emphasised the slowness of political change and the 'necessity of infinite perseverance; also for a good deal of patience, but not too much' (1935: 11).

Rathbone's energy was primarily directed towards political change and her writings address the question of how women can achieve such change. She accepted that there were political differences between women: she wanted 'women to meet together to discuss both sides of contentious political questions, and to hammer out the truth for ourselves' (1929: 3). This was part of the method which she advocated for bringing change about. First, the situation as it was had to be faced, then every effort put into bringing about change (*CC*, 5 September 1912: 374). There was only one question which should be considered and that was 'which path, new or old, congenial or distasteful, is likely to lead us straightest to our goal' (n.d., *c.* 1913b). The method she adopted was the formation by speaking and writing of a 'moralised public opinion' (*CC*, 28 April 1916: 390). She had faith that 'the minds of British men and women, helped by their innate sense of justice and fair play, can be trusted "to get there in the end"' (1927: 106). Having helped to 'kindle the sluggish mass mind to enthusiasm' (1929: 33), then democratic pressure would influence those in power.

Before women gained the vote, Rathbone was optimistic that entry into the 'body politic' would lead to positive change both within the political structures and within the family. Afterwards, she insisted that 'the achievement of women's suffrage – was like the bursting open of a door which gave access to so much riches that there must be innumerable women still living who took part in the movement . . . who now, contrasting women's position as it is and as it was, are able to measure the immensity of the change' (1935: 1). Her perspective was a long-term one, and she ended that same lecture with the warning that the 'fulfilment' for the 'women's movement . . . will take a long time. I shall not live to see the end of it, nor perhaps will even the youngest member of my present audience' (1935: 18). The main obstacle was the power of the patriarchy. In 1923 she quoted a passage from an anonymous article published in *The Woman's Leader* (2 March 1923: 34) – '"From the dawn of history . . . women have been oppressed, exploited, sometimes flattered and pampered, but always dominated by men"' – as a reminder of how '"age-old and world-wide" are the conditions which the feminist programme seeks to change' (1929: 17). But she was perhaps not fully aware of the immensity of the task which she undertook when she aimed to give women status within the family.

Rathbone's consciousness of oppression led her to react to the threat of fascism at an early stage, and she was also sensitive to the particular threat which Nazism posed to women in Germany. Yet she seems to have been unaware that ideas which placed emphasis on domesticity and motherhood for women had the same roots as those of fascism. Moreover, her opposition to fascist ideas was rooted in and strengthened by a deep-seated faith in British political institutions. This faith was challenged but not broken in the early 1930s by her experience of the politics of Indian independence. Her attention was drawn away from that challenge by what she saw as the more crucial failure of the British government to resist fascist aggression in Europe. Her relief when war was declared was accompanied by a restoration of her faith in liberal democracy which made available to her a powerfully patriotic wartime discourse. Within this complex process she held on to her belief that the absence of women from the political process was part of the problem, and that their inclusion would lead to a more compassionate government.

Although she never accepted that women were essentially different from men, in the 1920s Rathbone began to use an image of women as especially attuned to suffering. She always expressed this idea tentatively. This construction may well have been part of her response to the persistence of the social evils against which she struggled. Her consistent view was that human institutions were malleable and that they moulded the characteristics of human beings: gender was for her socially constructed. This construction allowed her a flexibility which made it possible for her to operate in the political arena without any radical change in the formulation of her ideas. The changes which took place in her ideology were mainly those of emphasis, and were developed in response to her increasing awareness of the precarious nature of women's toe-hold in the political world. Citizenship was not as powerful a tool as she had hoped: women were still silenced by structures and by attitudes, not only among men, but among women: 'The cutting of women's bonds has not made all the difference it should, because women's limbs are still stiff from bondage' (1935: 9).

Rathbone's desire to liberate women from 'bondage' crossed national frontiers. In her draft for a speech to be used on her visit to Palestine in 1934, she declared that 'though we may have difficulty in understanding each other's language, we shall find a language of the mind which we share in common' (RP XIV: 2.5.44). We can applaud and empathise with this desire for women to communicate across cultures, but her concept of responsibility for Indian women, her cultural imperialism, is unacceptable.

The recognition of women as fully developed human beings was Rathbone's core feminist aim and she did not achieve it. But she pointed out that many of the steps necessary for such an achievement were both recognised and put into place in her lifetime. The achievement of the vote for women is the most obvious, but other legal reforms did shift perspectives on the public status of women. The belief expressed in her articles written before the war and in her speeches to the NUSEC, that women would need to play an active part in the political process through organisational structure and through local government before they could become a force in national political life, has been vindicated. Her sense of the precarious nature of women's place within the structures of government form a salutary background to the obvious failures of some of her political goals. Her emphasis on the persistence of misogynist attitudes which militated against the fulfilment of those goals is still relevant. Her life and ideas can provide us with insight into 'the ways in which politics construct gender and gender constructs politics' (Scott, 1988: 27).

The central political goal of her life, that women as mothers should receive an independent income through their children, was never achieved. Her optimism that the payment of separation allowances during the First World War marked a significant change of attitude among men in power was misjudged. Later she became increasingly aware that in order to achieve the level of independence that was necessary, the amount of family allowance would need to be more than any government was prepared to allow. She was thus caught in a vicious circle: women would only participate fully in politics once they had gained self-confidence through recognition of their work. Until they did so, they would be unable to press for the changes which would lead to such a recognition, because women were not sufficiently present within the political system.

The articulation of the New Feminism in which Rathbone's was the dominant voice drew attention to the way the political structures were designed by men and for men, and were thus suited to men. This is still true and still militates against women's participation. Feminists are unlikely to accept her assumption that maternity contains women within domesticity, an assumption that made it difficult for Rathbone to imagine that married women with children could take a dominant role in public life. But she was confident that women whose main role was domestic could participate actively in the political process at grass-roots level. Moreover, while she wanted women's status within the domestic sphere to be recognised, she did not associate all women with the domestic.

The emphasis on the power and durability of the family in political discourse, and Rathbone's sense that woman's status within marriage was vitally important to her public status, is still relevant. Rathbone understood that women were oppressed within the 'private' family, and her solution was to give them financial independence within that structure. This has never been achieved and her arguments for such a solution are still a stimulus to thinking about the unresolved issues round the family.

Rathbone's understanding of gender as socially constructed and her refusal to claim an essentialist case for women reads with total conviction in the 1990s. Her distinction between identity and equality was a subtle construction which allowed for discussion of difference, without abandoning the pressure for equality.

Eleanor Rathbone rarely acknowledged her own subjectivity, but it is clear that she was referring to herself when she spoke of 'those who have that rare and uncomfortable faculty', of finding that 'a single line of vital statistics, an average percentage, contains a tragedy' (*Hansard*, 2 December 1931: 260, col. 1183). This moral stance was part of her Victorian inheritance. Much of Rathbone's vocabulary is that of a Liberal in the mould of Harriet Taylor and John Stuart Mill. Her understanding of the 'body politic' and the state is both ungendered and arguably naive, as are her ideas on representation and on class. Yet her thinking and practice, in particular her speeches in parliament, wrestled with the difficult questions which still face feminists today: what are women in politics for and how should they behave?

Eleanor Rathbone did not rest on any comfortable liberal cushion. Her response to suffering was to claim personal responsibility – and to generalise and politicise that responsibility. Three months before she died, she asserted that:

everyone in the world is responsible for every calamity that happens in the world, if he or she has left undone anything he could have done, without neglecting greater responsibilities, to prevent or mitigate the calamity even one iota. (26 October 1945: 414, col. 2416)

This awareness of the interconnectedness of people throughout the world, and Rathbone's assertion of the personal moral responsibility which such connections imply, is a discourse still available to active political feminists today. Moreover, her moral certainty was accompanied by an intellectual openness, in particular about gender. She did not construct a utopian future in her writings, but concentrated on a critique of current political and social structures, and on demanding action to ameliorate suffering. She did not demand the impossible, but put all her efforts into achieving the possible. As we move into the future, her tireless determination and her faith in the contribution which women can make to society are a welcome antidote to the discourses of cynicism and despair.

Bibliography

1. Writings by Eleanor Rathbone

This is a list of Eleanor Rathbone's main writings and speeches. It is not comprehensive: there are some articles referred to in the main text which do not appear here. The list is arranged in chronological order of publication or, in the case of her Parliamentary speeches, of delivery. Her speeches as President of the National Union of Societies for Equal Citizenship which were made between 1920 and 1929 are entered under 1929 when they were published.

This section can therefore be used to give a sense of the context in which the ideas referred to in the main text arose. Readers may also wish to read through this section in order to gain an overall sense of the continuity and change in Rathbone's thinking. I have argued throughout that she was above all a political thinker, writing to persuade. This annotated list will, I hope, give readers a firmer sense of this – and it will allow you to challenge my contentions. The summaries of her writings and speeches are of necessity very brief. I hope that readers will be enticed into going to the originals which are always passionately engaging in their expression. Rathbone's voice comes through strongly in its confident conviction throughout her writing and speaking.

There are two main collections of Eleanor Rathbone's papers. The larger one is in the Liverpool University Library in the special collections: Rathbone Papers (RP) XIV. This collection is mainly of 'correspondence and papers relating to her public activities' – which were considerable and are thoroughly documented – with a few private letters.

The Fawcett Library (FL) holds her correspondence and papers relating to India in Boxes 92 and 93, and papers from the NUWSS and the NUSEC, including Executive Committee Minutes.

There are a few letters from Eleanor Rathbone to Catherine Marshall in the Marshall Papers (CMP) which are held at Cumbria Record Office, Carlisle.

Annotated texts

(1903) *Report on the Results of a Special Inquiry into the Conditions of Labour at the Liverpool Docks*. Copies of this report can be found in Liverpool University Library, RP XIV 3.2, and in the Central Library, St Peter's Square, Manchester M2 5PD, SJ 20283.

The research on which this report was based was begun at the behest of Eleanor's father. After strikes at the Docks in the early 1890s, he had attempted and failed to find out from the employers, more about the conditions of the Dockers and what improvements might be made. The research looked at methods of employment, hours and rates of pay and trade unionism. There are detailed tables of weekly earnings and overtime, of trade tonnage in each month of the year and the distribution of work into porterage and stevedorage. At the end she looked for explanations of the continuance of the unsatisfactory system of casual labour, and suggested these were the fear of the employers that decasualisation would lead to increased unionism, and the satisfaction of the workers in 'the sense of "being their own masters"'.

(1905) *William Rathbone: A Memoir*. London: Macmillan.

After her father died in 1902, Eleanor worked with her brothers to collect material for a life of her father intended for a 'limited circle' (p. 53). She believed that 'the only motive which would have reconciled him to the notion of his Life being written, however briefly, for publication', was 'the hope that it might encourage others, especially young men and women of his own city, to trace out for themselves more definitely, and to follow more boldly, a career of public usefulness' (p. 493). The biography therefore concentrates on his '"social service"' (p. 139) – his political and philanthropic activities.

Eleanor's father began his commitment to philanthropy as a visitor for a Provident Society, and his involvement in politics in local government. He was elected to parliament in 1869 as Member for Liverpool. His particular interests were education (he was the driving force and chief benefactor of the foundation of Liverpool University), and the development of district nursing. But Eleanor saw poverty as the root of all his political concerns:

> The problem of poverty had begun to weigh upon him as a youth, and his mind turned to it again and again. His uneasiness about it lay at the root of his anxiety for a better system of local government and taxation, for the spread of education, for workhouse and district nursing. All these were means of modifying the cause or of alleviating the effects of poverty. (p. 364)

(1909) *How the Casual Labourer Lives: Report of the Liverpool Joint Research Committee on the Domestic Condition and Expenditure of the Families of certain Liverpool Labourers.* Liverpool: Liverpool Women's Industrial Council.

The research for this report was initiated by a 'small joint-committee . . . composed of representatives of the following bodies: The Liverpool Branches of the Christian Social Union, of the Fabian Society and of the National Union of Women Workers; the Liverpool Economic and Statistical Society, the Liverpool Women's Industrial Council and the Victoria Settlement' (p. v). The research process is meticulously described in the introduction and the report consisted mainly of the statistical results: the budgets of 40 households where the man was a 'casual labourer'. The political purpose of the research was to demonstrate the 'evil effect on the standard of living and on the whole conditions of family life' of the 'violently fluctuating weekly income' of Liverpool dock-labourers.

The investigators – who went round weekly to look at the budget book – were instructed to 'say everything you can' to the 'budget-keeper . . . to prevent her from thinking that the enquiry is an impertinent violation of family privacy', and 'to abstain from criticism or censure on the facts revealed to you by the book' (p. viii). The restraint was not carried over to the report, which carries an overtly moral message, referring to 'unsatisfactory households', where it was pronounced 'practically impossible' to obtain budgets where the mother was 'either a confirmed drunkard, or really stupid, or an out-and-out muddler or slattern'. Those who succeeded were carrying on 'an orderly and self-respecting homelife', where there survived enough 'virtue . . . to smell sweet and blossom in the dust and wreckage of the casual labourer's life' (pp. xxvi–xxvii). Rathbone asserted that 'the misfortunes of the family are in part attributable directly or indirectly to some defect of character or mind or body in one or both parents', but she also condemned the system because it 'seems to foster the formation of bad habits and [does] nothing to encourage the formation of good ones' (p. xxvi).

(1911a) with Emma Mahler, *Payment of Seamen. The Present System. How the Wives Suffer*. First published in *The Liverpool Courier*, 23, 24 January 1911. Available in the Fawcett Library, *Collected Pamphlets*, Vol. 8 (v).

The report of an inquiry by the Liverpool Women's Industrial Council on the effects on their wives of the method of payment of seamen. Although they could allot their pay in absence to their wives, there was no compulsion, and the recommendation was for only half the pay to be so alloted. Moreover, there was no payment for a month after sailing. Rathbone and Mahler condemned this 'totally unnecessary method of payment' which drove 'an appalling proportion of wives' into the 'toils of the professional moneylender' (pp. 7, 6).

(1911b) *Women's Need of the Vote: A Practical Illustration*. No publisher and no date seems to be known for this pamphlet, but it can be read in the Fawcett Library where it is in box 344.012813875.

In this short pamphlet Rathbone referred to the system of payment described in *Payment of Seamen* (1911a) and argued that the problem was not addressed by politicians because their wives had no votes, and many seamen could not use their vote because they were at sea on election day.

The Common Cause (CC). Copies of this journal which was published by the National Union of Societies for Equal Citizenship, are to be found in the Fawcett Library. From February 1920 when the NUWSS became the National Union of Societies for Equal Citizenship, the name of the journal was changed to *The Woman's Leader and Common Cause (WL)*.

14 December 1911, *CC*: 629, 'The Enfranchisement of Married Women'. This article consisted of an appeal for suffragists to sink 'their individual preferences' and support the amendment to the Reform Bill in the House of Commons which would give the vote to women householders and the wives of householders. Rathbone sought support on the grounds that the amendment was a 'practically attainable end', and that it would – unintentionally – establish 'in our franchise laws the truth that the status of a married woman is in reality and in equity that of a joint-householder'.

4 January 1912, *CC*: 674–5, 'The Economic Position of Married Women'. This forceful article was written in support of an amendment to a government bill which would enfranchise women householders and the wives of householders. Her argument was intended to force her reader to see the situation of the married woman in economic and political terms. She argued that 'the status of a married woman is in reality and in equity . . . that of a joint-householder'.

8 February 1912, *CC*: 752, 'Political Associations and the Vote'. A

paragraph exhorting readers to put resolutions in favour of women's suffrage before the annual meetings of political parties.

30 May 1912, *CC*: 119–20, 'To Liberal Women: A New Plan of Campaign'. This article was written to exhort Liberal women to ensure that the Government should not be 'false to the most fundamental principles of their own creed, which teaches that "taxation and representation should go together"' (p. 119). At the end of the article she asserted that it had 'always been a great source of weakness to the Women's Suffrage movement that so large a proportion of its ablest and most devoted adherents have comparatively little influence because they stand outside party' (p. 120).

5 September 1912, *CC*: 373–4, 'Methods of Conciliation'. Here Rathbone urged her readers not to allow 'the smallest slackening in the steady everyday work to be done in the constituencies in forming public opinion and crystallising and making explicit the public opinion already formed'. She denied that the traditional methods of the NUWSS had failed, and pressed for more petitions, lobbying by pre-printed postcards, and the asking of persistent questions at meetings.

(1912a) *The Problem of Women's Wages*. Liverpool: Northern Publishing Co. Ltd.

Rathbone read this in 1902 as a paper to the Liverpool Economic and Statistical Society, and it was published 10 years later when the issue of women's wages was becoming a controversial one in the suffrage movement. It contained the seeds of her ideas on 'the endowment of motherhood', and on the role of the state. Her premise was that a basic level of material provision is required for a human being to develop and thrive: the standard of wages of women were 'too low to ensure physical health and the full development of mind and character' (p. 24). The focus of the paper was on women as members of families whose interests were 'in perpetual conflict with their interests as industrial workers' (p. 20). She refused to enter into a debate about physical or mental difference, and argued that women's low wages were the result of the expectation, both of the women themselves and of their employers, that they would marry. She condemned the wage structure for two reasons: women expected to get married with the result they had low expectations of paid work, and this had the effect of lowering the financial benefits of the wage-system for their self-supporting sisters. It also made it difficult for their men to support families. Differences in wages, according to Rathbone, were thus not the result of 'the unalterable circumstances of sex', but of the 'arrangement' which led to the 'male parent' being expected to bear 'the cost of raising future generations' (p. 23).

(1912b) *What the Anti-Suffragist Men really think about Women.* Liverpool: The Northern Publishing Co. Ltd.

This 'Commentary' was written in a combative style in response to the letter by Sir Almroth Wright to *The Times* on 28 March 1912. Rathbone wrote that suffragists owed Wright 'a debt of gratitude for his candour' because he had enabled 'women in general to realise the kind of opinions about women which underlie much of the Anti-Suffragist propaganda' (p. 2). Beneath the 'impersonal arguments such as "physical force" or vague non-committal phrases such as "Man is Man,"', lay a 'contemptuous estimate of the mental and moral calibre of women' (p. 2). Rathbone assumed that exposure of the ridiculousness of Wright's views was the best way to refute them: lengthy quotations from his letter are interspersed with some brief responses from his opponents and ironic comments from Rathbone.

(1913a) The report on the Liverpool Women's Industrial Council survey of *Widows under the Poor Law.* Liverpool: Liverpool Women's Industrial Council.

The object of the report was 'to summarise and show the application to Liverpool of the facts, opinions, and suggestions as to the treatment of widows with children to be found in the Reports of the Poor Law Commission' (p. 2). Her own motivation in the report was to move her readers. She wrote in a tone of approbation that the Report was compiled by those – including herself – who have been for many years in regular contact with 'widows and children on out-relief, and have felt very strongly as to their unsatisfactory condition' (p. 1).

At the end of the Report, figures on the assessed need and actual income of individual households demonstrate her view that a sufficient income had beneficial effects. Rathbone concluded that of those widows and children surveyed:

> about 888 of the women and 2,672 of the children are living under conditions of grinding poverty, incompatible with healthy and happy life and almost certain to lead to physical degeneration and industrial inefficiency.
>
> It cannot be expected that a body of women living under such conditions should be conspicuously successful as housewives, or that their children will grow up as capable or taking their place in the world. (pp. 16–17)

(n.d., *c.* 1913b) *The Gentle Art of Making Enemies: A Criticism of the proposed Anti-Government Policy of the National Union*. Privately printed and circulated. Fawcett Library NUWSS/B1/3.

This short paper contains a sustained critique of the policy advocated in the spring of 1913 by the executive of the NUWSS to oppose all government candidates in by-elections, unless the candidate was a 'tried friend'. Rathbone had no objection to the policy in principle, but argued that it would be counterproductive in that it would lead to 'irritation and hostility to the Suffrage movement on the part of the rank and file of Liberals, and among Cabinet Ministers'.

27 March 1914, *CC*: 997–8, 3 April 1914, *CC*: 1021–2, 'The Position of Widows Under the Poor Law'; These articles were based on *Widows under the Poor Law* (see above) and argue a punchy and political case for removing widows from Poor Law administration.

4 January 1915, *CC*: 631, 'In Case of Invasion'. This short article contained an ironic and angry attack on the government's failure to mention women in their instructions to civilians in case of invasion, other than as the objects of efforts to prevent panic.

22 January 1915, *CC*: 663, 'Pensions and Allowances'. Writing as a 'worker for the Soldiers' and Sailors' Family Association', Rathbone pressed for the use of women to assess 'allowances additional to the minimum scale' for pensions granted to widows and wives of disabled soldiers and sailors and their dependants.

11 June 1915, *CC*: 131–2, 'Women and National Service'. This article again pressed for more extensive employment of women in wartime, including positions where they were at physical risk. At the end, Rathbone asserted that: 'In peace-time the vote is the symbol of citizenship. In wartime it should be the right to serve' (p. 132).

25 February 1916, *CC*: 611–12; 17 March 1916, *CC*: 648–9, 'Separation Allowances'. In these two articles she sought first to demonstrate that the wartime system of allowances 'affords a priceless opportunity for studying some at least of the actual workings of State endowment of maternity' (p. 611), and then argued a case for endowment from the total inadequacy of the prevalent wage system: it bore 'cruelly hard' on the wives and children of selfish men, and on widows and their children, and it led to a clash of interests between men and women wage-earners.

28 April 1916, *CC*: 39, 'The Study of International Relations'. This short article provides a foretaste of Rathbone's later involvement in foreign policy questions. She encouraged members of the NUWSS to study 'international issues' in order to create 'the atmosphere and the backing of a steady, well-informed, moralised public opinion'.

30 June 1916, *CC*: 155–6, 'Women Citizens Associations'. This article contained a warning against the reaction which was likely to follow enfranchisement. To help to consolidate what had been gained, she advocated the setting up of WCAs whose structure and work she described.

18 August 1916, *CC*: 238–9, 'The Political Sacrifice of Women'. This is a staunchly patriotic article which calls for universal suffrage from the age of 25.

5 July 1917, *CC*: 163–4, 'Municipal Votes for the Married Women'. With the limited parliamentary franchise practically secure, Rathbone attacked suffragists whose concentration on that issue had made them complacent about the failure of the Bill to give married women the municipal vote. She described in detail conditions of poverty in towns and wrote that to 'supply the driving power that is lacking in these matters of social reform, I can think of no one change that would be a quarter so effective as the conferring of the municipal vote on married women' (p. 164).

(1917) 'The Remuneration of Women's Services' in Victor Gollancz, *The Making of Women: Oxford Essays in Feminism*. London: Allen & Unwin.

In this confident and forceful article Rathbone outlined her critique of the living wage and her argument for the continuation of the payment of state benefits to mothers similar to the wartime separation allowances. It was written at a time when Rathbone believed that wartime changes had given women greater confidence, and had put such payments within political reach.

(1918) The Family Endowment Committee, *Equal Pay and the Family*. London: Headley Bros.

Rathbone wrote this together with the other members of the committee: Kathleen Courtney, Maude Royden, Mary Stocks, H.N. Brailsford, Emile Burns and Elinor Burns. The argument presented is similar to that in Rathbone's 1917 essay. The authors specified their demands and boldly proposed that there should be a 'weekly allowance . . . paid direct to the mother for herself and for each of the children, throughout the period when the care of the children necessarily occupies her whole attention' (p. 13). This allowance would be given for each child under the age of five – 'as a first measure only – to be extended later until school leaving age' (p. 41). The amount per week advocated was 5s for the first child and 3s 6d for each subsequent child: the sum for the mother was 12s 6d. These were comparatively modest figures: in 1925 Rathbone reckoned that 6s would be needed to cover the cost of a child, and that a man and his wife required 43s 8d to cover basic needs (1925: 864).

15 February 1918, *CC*: 373, 'The Future of the National Union'. This important article defended the executive's proposal to enlarge the aims of the
union to include 'the attainment of a real equality of status, liberties, and
opportunities as between men and women'. She argued that 'equality' was
not synonymous with 'identity', nor was '"equality" . . . too narrow a thing
to aim at'. She then set out her thinking on how the National Union could
provide organisational continuity for suffragists and feminists while working together with the Women's Citizens Associations to educate new
voters.

1 March 1918, *CC*: 600, 'The Endowment of Motherhood'. This was
Rathbone's most confident – or at least most forceful – expression of her
case. She asserted that 'what is at stake is really nothing less than the freedom of the wage-earning woman to do the best work of which she is
capable in the trade or profession for which her natural capacities fit her'.
She concluded with this rhetorical question about women workers: 'Must
they . . . be again shut up in a sort of lepers' compound of trades so
unskilled, ill-paid, and monotonous that no man covets them?'

26 April 1918, *CC*: 15, 'Our Common Cause'. This is another patriotic
article intended to 'stimulate the zeal of women for national service'.

25 October 1918, *CC*: 322, 'Liberating the Wives'. Rathbone suggested
in this article that when the postwar election took place suffragists would
find 'that they accomplished even more than they foresaw when they won
political citizenship for women'. She then painted a rosy picture of the
new respect with which 'the great majority' of husbands would regard
their voting wives:

> all through the nation there will be a tremendous political awakening on
> the part of married women who at the same time will become aware
> that their position, even in the happiest of homes, has changed for the
> better.

22 November 1918, *CC*: 371, 'National Union Societies and the General
Election'. Here she offered advice on participation in the coming election,
and in particular ways of pressing for 'the feminist reforms' on the programme of the NUWSS.

7 February 1919, *CC*: 514–15; 14 February 1919, *CC*: 525–6; 21
February 1919, *CC*: 540–2, 'The Pauperisation of Widows, Fatherless
Children and Orphans'. In the first of these three articles Rathbone put
the case for widows' pensions by comparing their 'years of penury,
drudgery and humiliation', and the deprivation their children suffered,
with the 'violation of Belgium' at the beginning of the war. In the second
she used evidence from the Reports of the Poor Law Commission of

1909 – asserting that there was no reason to suppose that assistance given had since risen in real value – to demonstrate that incomes for widows could not cover even necessary household expenses. The third and last article attacked those who were 'so ready to attribute our high rate of infant mortality and low standard of physical health among children to the inefficiency of their mothers' for lack of imagination and inertia. She argued that women's enfranchisement had roused politician's zeal for social reform, and urged suffragists to 'be importunate' (p. 541) for the widow. The article finished by raising and answering questions of who should be able to claim pensions, how they should be administered, and what the scales should be.

21 May 1920, *WL*: 363, 'Women and National Production'. This article sympathises with the opposition of trade unions towards the entry of women into their trades because of the undercutting of pay. Rathbone asserted that the problem of securing free and fair competition was difficult and could not be solved by the 'parrot-like repetition of that question begging phrase "Equal Pay for equal work"'.

3 September 1920, *WL*: 677, 'Feminists and Free Discussion'. A description of the Ruskin Summer School which demonstrated, approvingly, the fact that there was division among feminists on family endowment, widows' pensions and equal pay.

(n.d., *c.* 1920) with Mary Stocks, *Why Women's Societies should work for Family Endowment*. Liverpool: Family Endowment Council.

This pamphlet listed seven succinct points to support the case contained in the title, emphasising the injustice of the existing system which was 'an infraction of the principle that every human being is an end in himself or herself' (p. 4).

18 February 1921, *WL*: 39–40, 'Equal Pay'. Here Rathbone discussed the problems of deciding on whether equal pay should be based on time rate or piece rate. She pointed out that women in the Labour Movement were under pressure to accept the former, and asked 'how far this subservience was to be carried?' (p. 40).

(1924, 1986) *The Disinherited Family*. Bristol: Falling Wall Press.

This is the longest version of Rathbone's case for family allowances and her subsequent presentation of that case did not depart from it in any significant way. The opening chapter of the book gives a perspective on the 'Growth of the Dependent Family', and demonstrates its historical specificity to the nineteenth century. The main emphasis is on the way such a construction of the family ignores the needs of women and children (pp. 127–37). This is followed by an extended and critical analysis of the 'Doctrine of a Uniform "Living Wage", identifying the Social Effects' (Ch. III). These are summarised in an image she created later in the book:

> Let those who think that family life is strengthened by the complete dependency of wives and children, put themselves in the place of the women whose legal and economic conditions were described in Chapter III. It isn't necessary to select the victims of idle or bad husbands. Take the case of a woman who has married in youth the man of her choice and has found in him a partner neither better nor worse than the average run of men – fairly industrious and efficient, affectionate, well-meaning, capable when the stimulus is strong enough of great heroism and self-sacrifice; but in ordinary life ordinarily self-centred and self-indulgent, a creature of the habits acquired in his care-free youth, slow-witted and unimaginative about needs and feelings he has never experienced. The finer and more sensitive such a woman is, the more proficient in womanly ways, the better the housekeeper, the more devoted and ambitious a mother, the more likely she is to be chafed and irked by her dependency and the consequences – the expanding family and unexpanding income, the ill-equipped, overcrowded home, the lack of privacy and space, the inability to provide her children with the things they need. In her sore mind there forms a little festering pool of bitterness against her husband. (p. 328)

Rathbone attacked the sentimentalisation of motherhood (p. 177), and called attention to 'the steadily increasing strain' on mothers 'caused by the rising standard of educational and social requirements'. These, she argued, had 'reduced the wife's chance of supplementing what her husband "turns up" by her own or her children's earnings' (p. 181).

Moving on in Chapter IV to examine the experience of the woman wage-earner, Rathbone repeated the argument of her 1902/12 paper on wages, adding a forceful assertion that the 'airy suggestion of "equal pay" ' was ill thought-out and would intensify the 'inequitable distribution of resources' (p. 219). She added that the 'assumption that it was only when a woman does precisely the same work as a man that she is entitled to the higher scale of pay' led to the wrong estimate of women's and men's skills:

> When women took up men's jobs during the war, it was amusing, but it was exasperating too, to hear the naive astonishment expressed by

men when they found that women could actually perform delicate manipulative processes in engineering; or that they had the physical endurance and good humour enough to do the work of a tramway conductor for nine hours a day; or that they were clever at handling live stock on a farm. (p. 252)

The second part of the book begins with a survey of experiments in family allowance schemes in Australia, France, Germany, Belgium, Holland, Austria, Czechoslovakia, Switzerland, Denmark, Sweden, Spain, New Zealand and Japan. She returned to her argument in Chapter VI with a detailed refutation of the case of opponents of allowances: those who feared 'overpopulation and malpopulation', and the 'weakening of parental responsibility'; those who were afraid that allowances would lower the wages and 'increase the burden on industry', and finally 'the hidden Turk in man'. 'A man has no right', she asserted, 'to want to keep half the world in purgatory, because he enjoys playing redeemer to his own wife and children' (p. 345).

Rathbone did not put forward precise proposals, but Chapter VII outlines the 'conditions of a practicable scheme'. She believed that 'in the long run' a state scheme would be best, but agreed that an 'occupational plan' involving a pooling of funds, would be 'better suited, at least as a first step, to a people so instinctively conservative as the British' (p. 347). The book finished with a calculation of what a national state scheme would cost. Depending on the rate and the age limit, the total was between £179 million and £243 million per annum (p. 375). 'These are vast sums', she admitted, but pointed out that 'the national expenditure on drink, tobacco and amusements' was well over £260 million.

(1925) *Royal Commission on the Coal Industry: Memorandum of Evidence by Miss Eleanor Rathbone, on behalf of the Family Endowment Society.* Official Publications DISO RC 68 & 69, pp. 862–79.

This memorandum consists of a succinct presentation of the case for family endowment, together with a demonstration in figures of the effect of introducing it into the Coal Industry without an alteration in the total wages bill. The figures demonstrated that the situation was that 32.9 per cent of households (including 66.5 per cent of the children) were 'below human needs level', and the effect of endowment would be 'to place every miner, miner's wife, and miner's child above mean level, which is itself over 33 per cent. above poverty level' (p. 865). Rathbone was then questioned by members of the Commission. In her robust answers she argued that 'the rearing of children concerns the whole community'; that one of the effects of the introduction of endowment would be industrial peace, and that raising the standard of living among the poor would lower the birth rate in that group (p. 866).

6 February 1925, *WL*: 2, 'Family Endowment: A reply to Dame Millicent Fawcett's objections'. Rathbone focused in this article on Fawcett's argument that endowment would 'relieve parents of their legal obligation of their maintaining their children', arguing that it was 'contrary to all we know of human nature to assume' that 'most men would make less effort to improve themselves, if they thought that in addition to their wages an allowance would be paid.' On the contrary, the 'present scheme . . . supplies the careless and neglectful parent with an ever ready excuse'.

12 March 1926, *TT*: 254. A letter protesting against the paper's failure to understand the New Feminism. She wrote: 'As I see it, the women's movement comprises a large number of reforms, all of which are "feminism", but only some of them are "equality"'.

11 February 1927, *WL*: 12, 'What Is Equality?' Here Rathbone objected to the assumption that men should always 'set the pace', so that what they found desirable was assumed to be good, and what men had not got was assumed to be bad, and therefore that it was 'not part of the business of the women's movement to ask for it'. She asserted that the 'physiological differences between men and women' and the 'ensuing differences in their activities' led to the conclusion that '"equal citizenship" means something more than a knocking down of barriers and the removal of disabilities'.

25 March 1927, *TT*: 292. This was a letter in defence of Rathbone's position in the debate in the NUSEC. Again she asserted that 'Real' equality was not the same as 'identity', nor was it synonymous with 'nominal' or 'judicial' equality. She added that the 'Object' of the NUSEC had been extended beyond equality so that the organisation could provide a central focus and support for politically active women concerned with a variety of issues.

(1927) *The Ethics and Economics of Family Endowment*. London: The Epworth Press.

This was a paper delivered to a Methodist audience and was couched in ethical language. In it Rathbone put forward a case for the redistribution of wealth, appealing above all to the consciences of her audience. Referring to the 'system of uniform wages', she wanted her audience to ask themselves:

Does it help or hinder 'the good life' – make it harder or easier for the man, his wife, and each of his children to attain the full measure of the stature – physical, mental, and moral – which Nature intended for him or her? (p. 38)

Rathbone then developed an argument based on the importance of social conditions, arguing that poverty 'does debase the minds and characters as well as the bodies of many of those men and women brought up in it' (p. 40). She professed to be unable to understand those who could not see beyond the comparative improvement of social conditions in the mid-1920s, and concerns with their own rates and taxes:

these comfortable people could not endure that their own children should live for a week under conditions even of a well-to-do artisan's family, to say nothing of the home of our typical unskilled labourer . . . even the most enthusiastic member of the Labour Party, himself of the professional classes, would probably hesitate to send his children to an ordinary Council school, especially in a poor neighbourhood. (pp. 48–9)

Welfare reforms had compelled 'even the most selfish parent to recognize that his child is not merely his own creature, but a human being with its own rights and its own value to the community' (pp. 50–1). Society's whole attitude towards mothers Rathbone asserted, was a 'monstrous injustice and criminal folly', and the reason why 'even the unmarried man' acquiesced in this attitude, was 'the fact that the economic dependence of mothers and children is the best and far far the greatest weapon of masculine dominance' (pp. 61–2). It was not that the husband wanted to oppress his wife, but that 'he craves, in this one relation of an otherwise perhaps obscure and non-potent existence, to see himself as a protector of the weak and a dispenser of good things to the needy' (p. 57).

Rathbone happily welcomed the implication that allowances would lead to the redistribution of a considerable slice of the nation's income, because she was 'utterly convinced that the rich are too rich and the poor too poor' (p. 101). She accepted that the difficulty of cost in her preferred scheme was 'formidable', and suggested a gradual approach (pp. 100–1).

She finished the paper with a powerful statement of her ethical position on the interconnectedness of all human beings.

(1928) *The Poor Law Proposals and Women Guardians*. London: The National Union of Societies for Equal Citizenship. Fawcett Library 362.50942.

Rathbone argued in this short paper that the transfer of the work of Boards of Guardians to the County or County Councils as proposed by the Government, would result in far fewer women being involved in work to which they were particularly suited, because of the more political nature of Council elections, and the greater distances they would be required to travel.

(1928–9) 'Has Katherine Mayo Slandered "Mother India"'?, *The Hibbert Journal*, October 1928 – July 1929: 193–214.

Writing a year after the publication of the American journalist Katherine Mayo's controversial condemnation of Indian culture, Rathbone acknowledged that 'no reasonable person can blame Indians for being angry with Miss Mayo', who had obviously 'conceived a violent dislike for the Hindu – the male Hindu at least' (p. 197). But she asked 'which is the more important – hurt feelings of the race-conscious educated, articulate Hindu, or the millions of tortured bodies and wasted lives upon whose secrets Miss Mayo's book has shed its ray?' (p. 197). She then used figures and quotations from British Government and League of Nations publications, from comments by Indians, including Gandhi, to demonstrate 'the mischief and suffering wrought by early marriage, the untrained dai (midwife), the purdah'. She recognised that Indian women were demanding better education and denouncing child-marriage, but asserted: 'Whether we like it or not – whether it is destined to endure or not – the very fact that British rule *has been* constitutes a responsibility' (p. 213, emphasis in original).

(1929) *Milestones: Presidential Addresses*. Liverpool: National Union of Societies for Equal Citizenship.

1920, 'Equal Citizenship' (pp. 3–5). This first speech was already sober in tone, and Rathbone spoke of those 'happy innocents' who 'thought when the vote was won (though only for some women) the need for sex solidarity was over and we might venture to behave as if we had already reached the place where "there are neither male nor female; neither bond nor free"'. The Pre-War Practices Act which legalised the removal of women from jobs required by men returning from the war had provided a 'rude awakening'. Rathbone then looked at the legislation which the NUSEC was working towards, and reflected on the impact of enfranchisement:

> We do not want the women's vote to be acceptable because it is possible to say of it that it has made no perceptible difference to politics, except to facilitate the removal of a few disabilities directly affecting

women. We hoped and we hope still, better things from it than that. We want the contribution of women to national life to be a very distinctive contribution and to make a very great difference.

1921, 'The Uses of Unpopularity' (pp. 6–10). After a 'depressing' year of 'no gains' in legislation advocated by the NUSEC, Rathbone was determined both to recognise the difficulties facing members, and to chivvy them into keeping the societies going for the sake of the reforms which were still desperately needed. She suggested that during the war 'women got accustomed to quick returns and much praise, and there is no doubt that the experience enervated and demoralised many of them, especially the younger ones'. A presage of the controversy within the NUSEC in the mid-1920s appears with her exhortation to 'remember that it is a *real* equality of status, liberties and opportunities that we are looking for, not the legal, technical equality that consists in mere freedom from restrictive laws and disabilities'. She accused middle-class women of having used the 'wrongs of the sweated woman worker, the unhappily married wife, and the Poor Law Widow' rather than the intolerable fact that their own gardeners and coachmen had votes but they 'themselves had none' when it suited them, but that they now seemed to have forgotten their 'pledge' to the young, working-class woman.

1922, 'Retrospect and Prospect' (pp. 11–14). Rathbone painted a picture of a politics dogged by 'trade depression and unemployment', and by the search for 'international peace', making it difficult to concentrate on feminist reforms. She argued that women had 'practical minds', and, condemning the failure of the League to help the millions starving in Russia, suggested that it was 'much less important that we should secure for women better salaries and better opportunities in industries and professions . . . than that we should succeed in making the vote and political influence of women felt in the community'.

1923, 'Patience and Impatience' (pp. 15–18). At the beginning of this address Rathbone made a forceful plea for the need to tolerate differences of opinion within the NUSEC. She admitted to being often in a minority in the executive, and asserted that there were 'two kinds of feminism, or rather two ways of interpreting sex-equality. There are those who interpret it in terms of identity with men, and those who interpret it in terms of difference.' She suggested that the former kind did not 'imagine the status achieved by man to be so ideal that all that woman needs is to climb up and stand by his side', but that they had recognised that 'one of the tricks, devices by which men have sought to lead women to acquiesce in their inferiority of status is by pretending that it is not really inferiority, but only a difference corresponding to a real difference of function'. She referred to the 'period of reaction following the tremendous wave of progressive feeling which swept away many barriers in 1918–1919, and urged members to be both patient in 'the sense of not letting ourselves be discouraged or induced to desist by slow progress', and 'impatient, in the sense of not complacently accepting that progress is inevitable' (p. 17).

1924, 'Put Not Your Trust in Parties' (pp. 19–24). This speech consisted largely in an attack on the failure of the Labour Government to live up to its 'principles and past professions and pledges' (p. 22), on equal franchise, equal guardianship and Widows Pensions.

1925, 'The Old and the New Feminism' (pp. 25–30). Confident that 'within the next few years three of the six reforms of our Immediate Programme will be accomplished' (p. 26), Rathbone asserted that an equal moral standard and equal pay and opportunities would be 'elusive and difficult' (p. 27). Arguing that a programme based on these objects would not attract members, she outlined the philosophy of a 'new' feminism. The path the NUSEC was treading, she said, had been 'trod in by others before us who have been pioneers in asserting the rights of self-determination for their own group or class . . . We, like they, have to learn that the achievement of freedom is a much bigger thing than the breaking off of shackles' (p. 30).

1926, 'Apologia Pro Vita Nostra' (pp. 31–3). The previous year had brought, as she prophesied, three of NUSEC's reforms (widows pensions, equal Guardianship and separation and maintenance orders) into legislation, although not 'quite in the form or the full extent we desired' (p. 31). These successes vindicated the organisation's 'Parliamentary methods' (p. 31). She then returned to her theme of the 'new feminism', whose 'formula' was 'not equality but self-determination', and repeated her argument that this was the direction in which women wanted to go.

1927, 'Labourers Unto the Harvest' (pp. 34–8). At a time when 'the public, with pre-occupied minds or empty pockets, have passed us by' (p. 34), Rathbone was forceful in her criticisms and commendations of the Societies of the NUSEC. She acknowledged that 'many of our results, like the results of the forces which are opposing us, are invisible and intangible', and paid tribute to those who kept 'the flame of the spirit . . . burning in your hearts by a lively imagination', ending with the appeal to 'bring more labourers unto the harvest' (p. 38).

1928, 'It was an Obstinate Hill to Climb' (pp. 39–43). In the year of the full enfranchisement of women, Rathbone reflected on the long struggle for the vote; assessed the achievements of the NUSEC and urged members to consider 'by what if any readjustments of aim, constitution, and methods can we best face the tasks of the future?' (p. 43).

1929, 'Victory – And After?' (pp. 44–9). In her last speech, Rathbone again referred to the achievements of the NUSEC and repeated her view that an equal moral standard and equal pay and opportunities, were not fully susceptible to legal change. The future tasks of the organisation were first to knock down the 'remaining barriers of sex exclusiveness' (p. 46); secondly to 'use its new tool of citizenship upon those parts of the social structure where improvements are most necessary to meet women's special needs – upon questions such as family allowances, birth control, housing, and social insurance' (p. 47), and thirdly – she suggested rather than claimed – to offer a 'specialised contribution' beyond 'those questions which specially concern women and their children' (p. 47).

(1929–45) *Parliamentary Speeches, Hansard.*

Rathbone spoke often in the House of Commons, and she addressed a number of issues. I have selected, listed and occasionally annotated below key speeches she made on her main areas of concern. They are listed in chronological order under general subject headings:

Colonial policy:
(1 December 1929: 233, cols. 600–9) 'Women and Slavery'. In a debate on Colonial Policy Rathbone moved the following amendment to a Labour Party motion favouring the gradual introduction of self-government to British colonies:

Native self-governing institutions should be fostered; and franchise and legal rights should be based upon the principle of equality for all without regard to race, colour, or sex.

In explanation of her motion, she asserted that 'the position of the native women' in many tribes in Africa was 'one of sheer slavery . . . and carried on practically without let or hindrance from the British authorities' (606). She said that she was not opposed to the motion, and believed that the 'exploitation of coloured women by coloured men is no excuse for the exploitation of coloured men by white men' (608), but her final statement (quoted in Chapter 5) suggested that she was not prepared to accept colonial self-government while women were, as she understood it, slaves within marriage.

(9 July 1931: 254, cols. 2366–71; 2 December 1931: 260, cols. 1183–90; 28 March 1933: 276, cols. 940–50; 10 May 1935: 301, cols. 1310–18). These were occasions when she made her main speeches on the conditions of marriage and childbirth for women in India.

(26 January 1931: 247, cols. 710–14; 28 March 1933: 276, cols. 940–50;

22 November 1933: 283, cols. 183–91; 10 May 1935: 301, cols. 1335–8). These were speeches in which she pressed for extension of the franchise for Indian women.

(20 February 1935: 298, cols. 311–15; 5, 6 March 1935: 298, cols. 1867–74, 1977–80; 15 May 1935: 301, cols. 1815–22; 1 August 1941: 373, cols. 1735–8). These were speeches which focused on Indian independence.

Redistribution of wealth:
(10 April 1930: 237, cols. 2984–90). This punchy, idealistic and humorous speech encapsulates Rathbone's ideas on the political possibilities of women's franchise and on the effects of wealth and poverty: 'The poor in this community do not get the chance to rise to the full stature nature intended for them, neither physically or mentally. The sons of the rich get that chance, but they throw it away, because life is too easy and too pleasant for them' (2989). She suggested that the political parties had not yet realised that there is a woman's vote as well as a man's and that they might effectively put a heavier tax than they do 'at present on certain luxuries and the women voters at least would rise up and call them blessed' (2987).

She regularly pointed out that the needs of poor families were often met neither by wages nor by unemployment benefit. She took an active part in debates on the Unemployment Insurance Bill between February and May 1934 and proposed an amendment to insert the following:

> Provided that the need to be taken into account in assessing the allowances made to the applicant shall include a reasonable amount for rent and shall also include the minimum requirements of healthy physical subsistence for himself and for the members of his household in respect of whom the allowances are made. (26 February 1934: 286, col. 767)

Representation:
(3 February 1931: 247, cols. 1715–25; 20 May 1931: 252, cols. 2012–18). Rathbone defended the existence of university seats when the Labour Government proposed to abolish them.

(17 January 1945: 407, cols. 306, 307; 23 January 1945: 407, cols. 713–15). She advocated Proportional Representation when the Representation of the People Bill was debated.

Family allowances:
(6 February 1931: 247, cols. 2310–16). Rathbone took an early opportunity with the Living Wage Bill, introduced by Jimmy Maxton of the

Independent Labour Party, to put her views on the living wage to the House, while welcoming the Bill itself: 'Will the minimum wage . . . be based on the needs of the worker, or on the needs of the worker and his family . . . What kind of family? What size of family?' (2311).

She advocated family allowances when unemployment insurance was under discussion (21 July 1931, 23 November 1931, 11 May 1932); when debating allowances for income tax payers (30 September 1931, 26 April 1934, 11 June 1934), and when there was a debate on price control early on in the Second World War. The same impetus lay behind her support for education maintenance allowances: 'Do children live on books? Do they sleep in school? Do not they have to be fed and clothed? Do these things cost nothing?' (12 February 1936: 309, col. 1003).

More frequent opportunities for her to raise the question were offered as soon as war broke out. In this period she advocated allowances from a variety of patriotic perspectives as well as her usual arguments (4 October 1939: 351, cols. 2027–9; 17 October 1939: 352, cols. 795–9; 8 February 1940: 357, cols. 507–10).

She pressed for a full debate on the question, and when the first of these took place made a powerful speech in which she asked:

> How many generations are to grow up with stunted bodies and minds, while political parties are letting 'I dare not' wait upon 'I would,' while trade union leaders are considering whether if they grant security to the children it will diminish by one per cent. their chance of using the children's needs as an argument for higher wages, and while employers and capitalists are considering just how cheaply they can buy off the workers?

She was afraid that what would be offered was a scheme in the 'soup kitchen tradition, giving just enough to soothe sensitive consciences by blunting the sharpest edge of poverty'. She wanted 'children and their mothers to be recognised not as de-pendants hung around the necks of their fathers and husbands but as human beings, with their own feet on the floor of God's earth and their head in the sunshine' (23 June 1942: 380, cols. 1862–70). In the following year she raised the subject again twice (19 January 1943: 386, col. 37; 4 May 1943: 389, col. 25), before a debate on the 'Trend of Population' allowed her to make a long and another wide-ranging speech in which she called for a radical change in 'outlook towards the family' (16 July 1943: 391, cols. 551–62). When the Bill was eventually introduced in the House of Commons in March 1945, her fears about the inadequacy of the measure were realised. What led to her threat not to vote for it was the proposal that the allowance be paid to the father, 'because it treats the wife as a mere appendage, literally a hanger on, of her husband'. She suspected that one reason this proposal was made was that the cabinet was entirely made up of men, and she warned that the retention of that proposal would lead to an era of 'sex antagonism' (8 March 1945: 408, cols. 2275–83). In the final debate on the Bill she spoke briefly. While welcoming the Bill because it 'lays down a great principle', she referred to it as 'the end of the first stage in this fight', because the share of 'the national income' which it gave 'the mother through her children' was only a very little share so far (11 June 1945: 411, cols. 1418–20).

Women and National Insurance Benefits:
(15 July 1931: 255, cols. 667–71). Rathbone proposed an amendment to delete the clauses in the Labour Government's Insurance Bill which would discount the contributions paid by women before they married. She claimed for such women 'a fair field and no favour', and criticised their treatment on grounds of both logic and justice. Although the claims of married women to transitional benefit (i.e. benefits paid to those who had not paid enough to qualify for standard benefit, or who had exhausted their 15 weeks of allowance) had increased, this was despite 'extremely stiff conditions', and their claims for standard benefit had actually decreased. These statistics suggested to Rathbone that the increase in married women's claims arose 'not from fraudulent claims, but from the depressed condition of industry, and that when industry is depressed women are the first to be dismissed' (27 November 1931: 260, cols. 699–703; 11 May 1932: 265, cols. 1973–8; 14 June 1932: 267, cols. 290–3).

Equal pay:
Two full debates on equal pay in the Civil Service took place in the House of Commons during the 1930s. Rathbone put forward very similar arguments in her speech on each occasion, but with more detailed elaboration in 1936 (7 June 1935: 302, cols. 2240–3; 1 April 1936: 310, cols. 2030–5). She began by pointing out that it was in the interests of men that women should receive equal pay because its effect would be to limit the entry of women. She professed sympathy with the demand for equal pay on the grounds of both injustice and the 'unfair undercutting of men's work by women', and then turned to the usual argument used in opposition to equal pay which was that 'men have families to keep'. She urged her listeners to face the fact that while this was not universally true, it was a fact that men bore 'the much greater burden of dependency' (7 June 1935: 302, col. 2241). In 1936 she produced statistics which demonstrated that dependent wives and children actually outnumbered the entire actually

occupied population of employed people, employers and self-employed put together'. The system of 'meeting that immense burden of family dependency through differentiation between the wages of men and women is unscientific and ridiculously inadequate' (1 April 1936: 310, col. 2031). She argued further that the knowledge that men had families to keep was preventing women being given promotion. The 'one way of meeting this difficulty was to give equal pay for equal work and 'supplementing it by a liberal system of family allowances' (1 April 1936: 310, col. 2032).

Foreign affairs:
Rathbone's concern with foreign policy had its genesis in her awareness of the threat of Fascism. This was forcibly expressed in a debate on Foreign Affairs six weeks after Hitler became Chancellor of Germany (13 April 1933: 276, cols. 2762–5). She believed that it was Britain's responsibility to resist 'Fascist aggression' by full support for a policy of collective security (22 October 1935: 305, cols. 127–30; 10 December 1935: 307, cols. 843–50; 5 November 1936: 317, cols. 331–7). Such resistance she understood as part of an honourable British democratic tradition (16 February 1938: 331, cols. 1963–8). She was especially incensed by British non-intervention policy in the Spanish Civil War (19 July 1937: 326, cols. 1896–1900; 23 June 1938: 337, cols. 1371–6; 26 July 1938: 338, cols. 3015–21).

Refugees from fascism:
Rathbone pressed the government to assist in the evacuation of refugees from Spain (9 March 1938: 332, cols. 1953–7), and to give financial assistance to aid refugees from the Sudetenland (21 December 1938: 342, col. 2905; 9 February 1939: 343, cols. 1200–1; 7 March 1939: 344, cols. 1989–90). After the German invasion of Czechoslovakia in March 1939, she pointed out that 'thousands of these refugees are now probably in the hands of the Gestapo' (22 March 1939: 345, cols. 1323–4). She was desperate to rouse in her fellow MPs the same urgency and compassion she felt:

> Is the right hon. Gentleman's conscience haunted by the thought of the children and mothers who might now be exulting in the sunshine and looking forward to the spring, but who are rotting in their graves, or whose constitutions are irreparably damaged because of what we did not do in Spain, or of the little assistance we gave? (7 March 1939: 344, col. 1989)

During the war she regularly raised the question of continued restrictions on the admission of refugees and pressed for a debate on the holocaust (17

December 1942: 385, col. 184; 20 January 1943: 386, col. 184; 11 February 1943: 387, col. 285; 25 February 1943: 387, cols. 846–9; 11 March 1943: 387, cols. 846–9; 7 April 1943: 388, col. 588; 8 April 1943: 388, col. 813; 21 April 1943: 388, col. 1695; 6 May 1943: 389, cols. 314, 315). She spoke in the debate when it eventually took place (19 May 1943: 389, cols. 1130–9), and then raised the question again in a debate on the war situation seven months later. In possibly the most impassioned speech of her career as an MP, she said that she was among many who thought of 'this terrible question day and night. It is on our consciences all the time. We are not satisfied that the utmost has been done for rescue.' She knew that it was action rather than words which were most needed, and she also knew how little could be done, that 'the vast majority of the victims are outside our reach', but she was angry and frustrated at the way those who were working for refugees were manipulated by the Government:

> if we say publicly all we know and clamour for all we want, we are told that we are informing the enemy and hampering efforts that might otherwise be planned. So we have kept silent for months and damped down public agitation. Then nothing happens or very little that is apparent happens. It really seems as though the authorities go to sleep. (14 December 1943: 395, cols. 1467–74)

Women and war.

In her articles in *The Common Cause* during the First World War, Rathbone had argued that war provided an opportunity of exposing and breaking down 'ingrained habits of mind and inveterate prejudices' against the employment of women (*CC*, 11 June 1915: 131). Recognising that the attainment of 'equality of citizenship between men and women' in theory was not reflected in practice, she renewed her demands for such equality in the Second World War (20 March 1941: 370, cols. 368–74). And again she presented her feminist case within a patriotic discourse of national service (*CC*, 11 June 1915: 131). In the debate on 'Woman-power' in 1941, she declared:

> On the question of compulsion, most members who have spoken to-day have begun by complaining that they were not feminists. I am a feminist, a 100 per cent. feminist, who has been working for the large part of my life in trying to secure equality of citizenship between men and women.

She demanded that neither class nor age should limit either women's duties or their opportunities (2 December 1941: 376, cols. 1086–91). She was infuriated by discrimination on the basis of class, and criticised the class-based nature of the system of allowances to naval wives (23 June 1943: 390, col. 1149; 3 August 1943: 391, col. 2134). She combined her demands for women to be used in all types of war work with pressure for day nurseries (1 May 1941: 371, col. 585; 5 February 1942: 377, col. 1289). And she continued to be vigilant on the issue of women's representation on public bodies:

> We had a curious instance the other day of the committee which has been appointed, and consists of only three members, whose task it is to go into the question of wages and conditions of women workers in hospitals. It is to consist of two men who are in very important positions and one woman. (3 August 1943: 690, col. 2131)

(1932) with the Duchess of Atholl and Col. Josiah Wedgwood, *On Slavery Within the Family*, Memorandum to the Committee for the Protection of Coloured Women, Rathbone Papers XIV.2.1(40).

The committee to which this memorandum was submitted had been formed in 1929 and had focused immediately on the subject of clitoridectomy in Kenya. But Rathbone's concerns were more general and this paper addressed the question of the position of wives in 'parts of Africa within the British Empire' (p. 1). The authors acknowledged that the subject was 'clearly a large and difficult one' (p. 1) and pointed to the 'better status of women . . . in matriarchal than in patriarchal communities'. They asserted that they did not wish to 'put forward in any dogmatic spirit a definite remedy or remedies of the evils complained of' (p. 6). They suggested possible remedies such as the legal limitation of 'bride-price', a minimum age for marriage, the establishment of a legal right to 'escape from an excessively cruel husband' (p. 8), and the spread of education among women.

(1934a) *Child Marriage: The Indian Minotaur: an object lesson from the past to the future*. London: George Allen & Unwin.

The purpose of this book was 'to promote more effective action against the giant evil of child marriage and to use its history as a warning of the frightful risks to which we are exposing Indian women if we give them in the new Constitution of India no better means of self-protection than they have had in the past, during the years of our dominion' (p. 13). To support her case she made extensive use of sources from Indian witnesses, especially from the Report of the Age of Consent Committee, 1929, referred to as the Joshi Report. She described the failure of the Sarda Act which had imposed penalties for illegal child marriages, but had, she argued, citing the Census report, resulted in a 'rush of anticipatory marriages' (p. 46).

She stated that she believed in 'the necessity for a constitutional advance on the scale contemplated by the Government', but feared that 'the Princes' and 'the mass of Indian men of the better-to-do classes, who will be the chief recipients of political power', were not those 'to whom we may safely entrust the future of the women of India' (pp. 86–7).

At the centre of her 'remedies' for the tragedy of child marriage was the provision of a 'constitutional means of protest' for the 'women of India' (p. 82), by which she meant a franchise where there was nothing less than the ratio of one woman to four and a half men proposed by the Lothian Committee (p. 85). However, bringing 'women in large numbers into the political arena' was not, she argued, enough (p. 96). While admitting that it was 'rash for an outsider to express any dogmatic opinions as to the methods that should be used' (p. 106), she then went on to do precisely that. Her suggested methods were consciously drawn from the early stages of the militant suffrage movement, methods which she admitted she had at first 'disliked and despised' (p. 111). She claimed that she had soon recognised the power they had to bring other women into the movement. She suggested that such sensational methods as 'pilgrimages, by caravan and on foot, through the villages, preaching their gospel through speech and song and drama and cinema' (p. 109), and 'peaceful picketing, of those known to have planned child marriage' (p. 110), were especially suited to the geography and sociology of India.

(1934b) Foreword to Erna Reiss, *The Rights and Duties of Englishwomen: a Study in Law and Opinion.* Manchester: Sheratt & Hughes, pp. vii–ix.

This provides a précis of Rathbone's two longer essays on the women's movement written in 1935 and 1936.

(1934c) *Memorandum on the Scale of Needs suitable for adoption by the Unemployment Assistance Board in Assessing Assistance to Applicants.* London: Children's Minimum Campaign Committee.

This pamphlet begins with a list of points based on statements made by the Minister of Labour in the House of Commons which 'foreshadow a bold, far-sighted and generous policy, which will revolutionize the standard of assistance to the unemployed in this country' (p. 4). Rathbone then used calculations by sociologists and medical researchers to back up the case for specifying to the Unemployment Board a 'scale of assistance to satisfy at least the minimum requirements of healthy subsistence' (p. 5).

(1935) *The Harvest of the Women's Movement* (The Fawcett Lecture given at Bedford College, 29 November 1935). London: W.H. Taylor.

This lecture was very similar to the chapter listed below and they are summarised together.

(1936) 'Changes in Public Life' in Ray Strachey (ed.), *Our Freedom and Its Results*. London: Hogarth.

These essays contain the same message and much of the same material; the later chapter is longer. First they each provide a historical survey of the women's movement, beginning with J.S. Mill, and emphasising both its success and the 'years of effort by indomitable men and women' (1935: 4) which its achievements entailed. The descriptions of the suffrage movement pay tribute to 'women as agitators', but argue that 'the increasing violence of the militants resulted in the hardening the hearts both of the public and of the Government' (1936: 24). 'Changes in Public Life' expands in detail the explanation offered in both essays for the 'trickle' (1935: 5) of women into the formal political structures. Rathbone pointed out that 'the older women with strong political aptitudes and interests were attached to non-party organisations such as the Women's Institutes and the Townswomen's Guilds (TWGs), and had never joined political parties. Younger women 'who would be their natural successors' had joined the professions, and had 'not yet reached the stage in their careers when they can afford the distractions and expenses of parliamentary candidature' (1936: 32). Using an analysis made by Majorie Green, secretary of the National Council for Equal Citizenship (successor, with the TWGs, to the NUSEC), she showed that women candidates were more than twice as likely to be given unwinnable seats. Reflecting on the 'contribution' of women to parliament, Rathbone made an estimate of what she considered would be the result of gender difference (quoted in Chapter 6). She identified the 'avenues of public work' which women had entered since 1918 (pp. 33–44), including the peace movement.

The surveys in both essays – given in more detail in 'Changes in Public Life' – claim an impact by women on legislation: 'whereas during the first eighteen years of this century only four Acts were passed relating specially to the position of women, during the nine years after their partial enfranchisement some twenty Acts were passed' (1935: 6). But she admitted that subsequently 'progress in women's reforms' was much slower, and found the explanation in the 'much greater difficulties' facing 'equality of pay and opportunities', and an 'equal moral standard' (1935: 7). In 'Changes in Public Life' Rathbone claimed the 'heaviest task and chief success' of the years since 1928 was the (very limited) enfranchisement of women under the Government of India Act (1935). Looking to the future, she advocated the methods of compromise, 'being early in the field' (1935:

10), perseverance and 'a great deal of patience, but not too much' (1935: 11).

At the end of both essays Rathbone expressed the hope that 'among the results of the new citizenship of women . . . will be a changed attitude on the part of society towards human happiness and suffering' (1935: 18; 1936: 76). The last sentence of *The Harvest of the Women's Movement* puts this hope into a long perspective: 'But its fulfilment will take a long time. I shall not live to see the end of it, nor perhaps will even the youngest member of my present audience' (1935: 18).

(1938) *War Can Be Averted*. London: Victor Gollancz.

Assuring her readers that she was not an expert, Rathbone declared that this was intended as a book to explain the international situation to ordinary people. This she proceeded to do in a clear, concise, humane and passionately convinced narrative. She sought to persuade them that Britain's foreign policy was vitally important and that all Britons were responsible for it. She declared defeatism to be a 'fatal ingredient' (p. 110), to which the postwar generation was particularly subject, and asserted that there was still hope that collective action, based on a pre-paredness to use force, would prevent further aggression by Germany, Italy and Japan without full-scale war. In order for this to be effective, ordinary men and women needed to be '"all lit up" by the flame of a great purpose', so that they would be 'capable of the kind of effort that is going to be necessary to stop aggression and prevent Fascism from overrunning the world' (p. 168). Rathbone followed this emotional appeal by a shrewd analysis of the political situation, and an assessment of the political groupings which could be consolidated in support of the policy she advocated.

(1939) 'A Personal View of the Refugee Problem', *The New Statesman and Nation*, 15 April : 568–9.

The Refugee problem was the most heartbreaking Rathbone had encountered, and she began with an image of scraping with little files at bars in an effort to release 'hordes of men, women and children enduring every kind of deliberately inflicted physical and mental torture', while 'streams of people are passing behind us unaware of or indifferent to what is happening' (p. 568). She blamed the Government for 'petty meanness' and for giving up on a task for which they did have responsibility. She asked for a 'reasonably generous admission' of those refugees 'known to be in serious danger . . . coupled with the speeding up of arrangements for large-scale settlement overseas, financed by an international or colonial development loan' (p. 569). She wished that the 'rather uninspiring personalities upon the Treasury Bench . . . had indeed a collective soul, which could be condemned to spend eternity in seeing and feeling the torments which their policy has caused others to continue enduring, while their individual souls reposed blissfully in some insipid Paradise, listening to music played upon antiquarian instruments' (p. 569).

(1940) *The Case for Family Allowances*. Middlesex: Penguin.

The argument of *The Disinherited Family* (1924) is here compressed into one hundred pages of text with a tighter structure and updated information. The ethical case with which the book begins makes use of Margery Spring-Rice's *Working-class Wives*, which had been published the previous year, to demonstrate the effect of the wage system on the mothers of families. The economic argument which follows refers to income surveys of families in poverty from the 1930s, and emphasises the nutritional needs of children. The third section, entitled 'Remedies', looks at the possible schemes of family allowances through contributory insurance, equalisation fund or state benefit: Rathbone found most merits in the third. The history of the campaigns for allowances and their practice in other countries is covered in the fourth chapter of the book. In the last chapter, Rathbone looked at 'the opposing forces', and found them in 'the natural conservatism of the British working man' (p. 100), and – using a long passage quoted from *The Disinherited Family* – the desire of men to be 'the Benefactor' with '"dependants" whose livelihood depends wholly on the labour of their hands or their brains' (p. 104).

(1944) *Falsehoods and Facts about the Jews*. London: Victor Gollancz.

A pamphlet intended to clear up misconceptions about the history and culture of the Jews, at a time when Rathbone's concern about British responsibilities in Palestine was sharpened by growing awareness of the extent of the holocaust.

2. Key texts

Alberti, Johanna (1989) *Beyond Suffrage: Feminists in War and Peace, 1914–1928*. Basingstoke and London: Macmillan.

This book traces the activities of 14 feminists who had been involved in the suffrage movement before the First World War. Some of them had been constitutional suffragists and others suffragettes, and each of them was linked through friendship networks with at least one other of the 14. They were all politically active in the 1920s: these activities varied according to their view of the significance of the vote.

Black, Naomi (1989) *Social Feminism*. Ithaca and London: Cornell University Press.

Black defines social feminism as 'a particular version of feminism whose important characteristic is a focus on value and experience identified with women' (p. 1). Her interest is in 'how social feminism served to establish a relationship between activist women and "normal" male politics', and the book presents detailed studies of three feminist organisations: the Women's Co-operative Guild in England, the Union Feminine Civique et Sociale and the American National League of Women Voters (p. 4).

Burton, Antoinette (1990) 'The White Woman's Burden: British Feminists and The Indian Woman, 1865–1915', *Women's Studies International Forum*, 13 (4): 295–308.

Burton demonstrates that Victorian and Edwardian feminist perceptions of Indian women were contained within an imperial ideology rooted in cultural superiority. Female reformers such as Josephine Butler saw themselves as moral redeemers and Indian women as victims and dependants. Most of the reformers never visited India but they claimed sisterhood with Indians 'whose half-glimpsed lives fascinated them' (p. 297). This was the source of Rathbone's discourse on India, and of the resistance of Indian women to a construction which reduced them to inferiority and powerlessness.

Davin, Anna (1978) 'Imperialism and Motherhood', *History Workshop*, 6 (Spring): 9–65.

This path-breaking article is still essential reading for anyone interested in women's history in the first half of the twentieth century. Davin looks at writings on empire from the early part of the period together with contemporary analyses of infant mortality and infant welfare. She places these beside welfare legislation and the increasing interference by 'professionals' in working-class family life. She convincingly establishes a eugenist preoccupation with infant mortality and an assumption among a wide variety of political bodies and thinkers, including the Fabian Society, that responsibility for it lay with the mother. In trying to establish connections, she comes to no definitive conclusions, but, in her own phrase, sketches out some possibilities.

Dyhouse, Carol (1989) *Feminism and the Family in England 1880–1939*. Oxford: Blackwell.

This book provides vital information about feminist debates on marriage, work and the family in the period in which Rathbone was active.

Fleming, Suzie (1986) 'Eleanor Rathbone: Spokeswoman for a Movement', introduction to *The Disinherited Family*. Bristol: Falling Wall Press.

Fleming confidently claims that Rathbone 'pressed mothers' priorities to the centre of the political stage, establishing the "great principle" of mothers' right to financial recognition for their work' (p. 96). Although I think this judgement overestimates Rathbone's achievement and expresses it in anachronistic terms, Fleming's linking of some of Rathbone's ideas with the demands of the 'second wave' of feminism is exhilarating to read.

Forbes, Geraldine (1981) 'The Indian Women's Movement: a Struggle for Women's Rights or National Liberation?', in G. Minault (ed.), *The Extended Family: Women and Political Participation in India and Pakistan*. Delhi: Chanakya.

The theme of this article is the relationship between the struggles for women's rights and for national independence in India. In the nineteenth century women's organisations were formed by men, and Indian nationalist leaders were sympathetic to women's issues, seeing the 'advancement' of women to be an indicator of social progress. This view was shared by the Women's Indian Association and the All-India Women's Conference, formed in 1917 and 1927 respectively. Nationalism was accepted as a priority, and the responsibility of patriarchal attitudes and institutions for women's oppression was not examined. Forbes argues that the confrontation likely to arise from such an analysis 'would have served little purpose in the midst of a nationalist struggle' (p. 76).

Freeden, Michael (1978) *The New Liberalism: an Ideology of Social Reform*. Oxford: Clarendon Press.

Writing from the persuasive assumption that ideology is 'action-oriented', despite the pervasive British myth of pragmatism, Freeden is concerned in this book with 'the ideological contribution of a group of individuals towards solving some of the burning social and political problems' of the period 1886–1914 (pp. 2, 247). One of those individuals was Eleanor Rathbone's political philosophy tutor at Oxford, D.G. Ritchie, who combined Idealist and Darwinist ideas to form an optimistic and ethically based model of social growth. The dependence of political action and social growth on ethical guidelines is one of the central themes which Freeden identifies in this 'resurgence of liberal thought' (p. 253).

Harris, Jose (1989) 'The Webbs, the Charity Organisation Society and the Ratan Tata Foundation: Social Policy from the Perspective of 1912', in M. Bulmer, J. Lewis and D. Piachaud (eds), *The Goals of Social Policy*. London: Unwin Hyman.

This article analyses a particular event – the foundation of the Social Science and Administration Department of the London School of Economics. Through her analysis Harris provides a perspective on late Victorian and Edwardian social policy debates which illuminates Eleanor Rathbone's intellectual heritage and environment.

Harrison, Brian (1986) 'Women in a Men's House: the Women M.P.s, 1919–1945', *Historical Journal*, 29 (3): 623–54.

This article examines the contribution of women MPs and identifies the continuing anti-feminism of the institution and its structures; the heavy workload of the few women – and invariably conscientious – members; their expressions and actions of solidarity; their 'distinct rhetorical space' (p. 634); and their challenges to the 'widely held idea . . . that men and women should occupy separate metaphysical space' (p. 636).

Harrison, Brian (1987) *Prudent Revolutionaries: Portraits of British Feminists between the Wars*. Oxford: Oxford University Press.

Harrison's chapter on Rathbone is entitled 'Constructive Crusader', and it summarises his view of her as a humanitarian reformer. He does not provide an analysis of her ideas, and his focus is consciously on the inter-war period. The original contribution of his material are the interviews which he conducted with some of her colleagues, and recordings of these interviews are now in the possession of the Fawcett Library.

Holton, Sandra (1986) *Feminism and Democracy: Women's Suffrage and Reform Politics, 1900–1918*. Cambridge: Cambridge University Press.

This book is essential reading for an understanding of the ideology of British suffragists. Sandra Holton argues that 'By and large the suffrage movement was ideologically homogeneous', and that most suffragists 'appeared unconscious of the potential contradictions' between an 'essentialist case for women's emancipation', and 'a more deliberately rationalistic, humanistic conception of feminism' (p. 28). Instead of abandoning the humanist perspective, late nineteenth and early-twentieth-century suffragists gave increasing emphasis to the argument that possession of the vote would become 'a tool with which women of all classes were to reconstruct society in accordance with female values and needs'. They asserted that the state could have a nurturing role in a reformed and 'feminised democracy' (p. 18). This perspective was based on an acceptance of sexual solidarity that crossed class divisions in theory, and attempted to cross them in political action. Holton convincingly demonstrates the significance of this current of 'democratic-suffragism' for a better understanding of Edwardian politics.

Kent, Susan K. (1993) *Making Peace: the Reconstruction of Gender in Interwar Britain*. Princeton: Princeton University Press.

This book continues the theme of *Sex and Suffrage* (Kent, 1987), focusing particularly on the war years and on the way 'gender was utilized to construct war, and of the way war, conceived in gender terms, then shaped understandings of gender' (p. 10). She identifies an 'insistence on sexual difference' in the postwar period which 'received its impetus' both from the separation of men and women during the war, and from the need 'to recreate a semblance of order and peace' (pp. 132–3).

Land, Hilary (1975) 'The Introduction of Family Allowances: an Act of Historical Justice?', in P. Hall, H. Land, R. Parker and A. Webb (eds), *Change, Choice and Conflict in Social Policy*. London: Heinemann.

This is a core article for understanding the context of the introduction of family allowances. Land looks at the sources of support for allowances in the period before the Second World War and then examines in detail the complex path which led to their introduction at the end of the war. She demonstrates that there was opposition to allowances on the Right because of their assumed weakening of work incentives, and on the Left because they would restrict trade union negotiating power. She points out that three years of war did more than 20 years of campaigning by the Family Endowment Society: the reasons for their introduction bore no relation to the feminist genesis of allowances.

Land, Hilary (1990) 'Eleanor Rathbone and the Economy of the Family', in H. Smith (ed.), *British Feminism in the Twentieth Century*. Aldershot, Hampshire: Edward Elgar.

In this article, Land places Eleanor Rathbone into her narrative of the introduction of family allowances, arguing that the passing of the Act 'was probably the most notable personal triumph in legislation since the Act which celebrates the Plimsoll line' (p. 104). While Rathbone was inflexible on the details of schemes, and focused on economic arguments, Land presents her advocacy of allowances as 'an important contribution to feminist theory' (p. 105).

Land, Hilary (1992) Introduction to *Gender & History*, 4 (3): 283–92.

The contributions in this volume of *Gender & History* examine 'the conditions under which women's claims on the state for support in cash and services were accepted and incorporated, at least in part, in actual social policies'. Land's lucid introduction provides us with an understanding of how, 'In doing so, they illuminate how the conception of the modern Western state was deeply gendered as well as imbued with national, ethnic and racial assumptions' (p. 284).

Lewis, Jane (1980) *The Politics of Motherhood: Child and Maternal Welfare in England, 1990–1939*. London: Croom Helm.

This is a meticulously documented study which brings together the variety of campaigns for maternal and child welfare services, including birth control. Lewis traces the way the demands from women's groups for economic assistance to mothers in cash or kind were resisted by successive governments which succeeded in avoiding the issue of poverty and its effects on health, placing the blame for infant mortality and poor nutrition on the mother.

Lewis, Jane (1983) 'Eleanor Rathbone and the Family', *New Society*, 27 January: 137–9.

This article is one in a series on 'pioneers of the welfare state', and it provides a very useful summary of Rathbone's life and ideas.

Lewis, Jane (1991a) *Women and Social Action in Victorian and Edwardian England*. Aldershot, Hampshire: Edward Elgar.

This is a vitally important book for an understanding of the Victorian Women's Movement. Lewis's analysis of the 'lived lives' of five notable Victorian women 'shows how their ideas about the proper relationships between the individual, family and the state were forged in relations both to their gendered (and often contested) concepts of duty and citizenship, and to their shared conviction that on the commitment to social action depended social progress' (p. 1). Although three of the five – Octavia Hill, Mary Ward and Violet Markham – were opposed to women's suffrage, Lewis has made clear that women who were personally committed to 'understanding the poor' did not necessarily reject the possibilities of a wider public role for women.

Lewis, Jane (1991b) 'Models of Equality for Women: the Case of State Support for Children in Twentieth-century Britain', in G. Bock and P. Thane (eds), *Maternity and Gender Policies: Women and the Rise of the European Welfare States, 1880s–1950s*. London and New York: Routledge.

Lewis's article places the debate over family allowances in the context of the 'assumptions of social investigators and policymakers about family relationships and the proper role of the state in relation to the family', and of the 'social reality of women's position in the family and the meaning women gave to it' (p. 73). The article gives an invaluable overview of the ideology of family allowances and the way in which the feminist demand for it was submerged in a wider humanitarianism.

Macnicol, John (1980) *The Movement for Family Allowances, 1918–45: A Study in Social Policy Development*. London: Heinemann.

This study places the launching of the Family Endowment Society in 1917 into its historical background, and then goes on to look at the arguments for allowances based on poverty and demography, the connections between allowances and policies on unemployment and the attitudes of the political parties.

Pedersen, Susan (1989) 'The Failure of Feminism in the Making of the British Welfare State', *Radical History Review*, 43: 86–110.

This is the first of three important articles in which Susan Pedersen has examined the failure of feminists in the 1920s to achieve their goals in the political sphere. Here she tells 'a cautionary tale about the dangers of the adoption of difference-based arguments in a world where women lack significant institutional or economic power' (p. 106). She focuses in particular on the demands for family endowment expressed most forcibly by Eleanor Rathbone in the early 1920s. She argues that 'by 1925, the feminist vision of state-guaranteed economic independence for mothers had almost completely evaporated' (p. 92).

Pedersen, Susan (1990) 'Gender, Welfare and Citizenship in Britain during the Great War', *American Historical Review*, 95 (4): 983–1006.

In this thought-provoking article, Pedersen argues that before the First World War, 'no particular model of family relations had received the unambiguous endorsement of the state' (p. 986). The commitment to the 'gendered system of welfare provision' grew 'almost inadvertently' out of the wartime system of separation allowances (p. 985). The claim of contemporary feminists that mothering was a 'citizenship "function" equivalent to that of soldiering' contained a 'rhetoric capable of sustaining demands for independent social rights for mothers'. However, in her view they 'also allowed a dangerous analogy between the national obligations of the soldier and that of the fertile woman'. In doing so they 'betrayed their naïvety about the malleability and disinterestedness of the British state' (p. 1004), and were left in the interwar period, 'mired in pro-family rhetoric, while looking vainly to the state to iron out domestic inequalities of wealth and power' (p. 1006).

Pedersen, Susan (1991) 'National Bodies, Unspeakable Acts: the Sexual Politics of Colonial Policy-making', *Journal of Modern History*, 63: 647–80.

The attempts by Rathbone and other British feminists to construct feminist reforms across cultural boundaries are starkly exposed in this analysis. They were constrained both by their reluctance to jeopardise the national interest, and their blindness to the degree to which 'fear and denial of female sexual response suffused British as well as Kenyan society' (p. 680).

Pedersen, Susan (1993) *Family, Dependence and the Origins of the Welfare State: Britain and France, 1914–1945*. Cambridge: Cambridge University Press.

This erudite book examines, in such a way as to give a lively sense of the personalities involved, proposals for and practice of welfare policies concerned with family maintenance in Britain and France. The comparison between the two countries is both illuminating and startling. Very different policies emerged which were both the result of and had consequences for the social and political cultures of the two countries. In Britain socialists and feminists pressed for a redistributive agenda based on state interference which ran counter to the ideology of those with power and influence; in particular civil servants and trade unionists. The ideal of the family wage was retained and with it the integrity of male wages throughout the period.

Pedersen, Susan (1994) 'Eleanor Rathbone: the Victorian Family under the Daughter's Eye', in S. Pedersen and P. Mandler (eds), *After the Victorians*. London: Routledge.

This essay encapsulates the Victorian influences on Rathbone and places them together with her own personal political development. Pedersen's aim – succinctly and engagingly achieved – is to show that 'the public and the private' in Rathbone's life were 'integrally connected' (p. 120). There was no disjunction between her philanthropic vision of a redistribution of wealth and her feminist scepticism about male values and structures. Pedersen detects Rathbone's strength and her limitations in 'the simplicity of her analysis' (pp. 120–1).

Ramusak, Barbara (1990) 'Cultural Missionaries, Maternal Imperialists, Feminist Allies: British Women Activists in India, 1865–1945', *Women's Studies Internal Forum*, 13 (4): 309–21.

This important article looks at the work of five British women (Mary Carpenter, Annette Akroyd Beveridge, Margaret Noble-Sister Nivedita, Margaret Cousins and Eleanor Rathbone) who were involved in Indian women's affairs from the 1860s until the 1930s. Her assessment is that all five women 'were able to cross the boundary of race as feminist allies when their skills most suited the needs of Indian women' (p. 9). Ramusak's argument that her five women 'preached a gospel of women's uplift based largely on models adapted from their own experience in Britain' neatly encapsulates the view I present of Rathbone's perspective in Chapter 5.

Stocks, Mary (1949) *Eleanor Rathbone: A Biography*. London: Victor Gollancz.

Until the final paragraph Stocks maintained that 'the story of Eleanor's life has been told with austere respect for factual truth' (p. 333). This sentence is revealing of the perspective of Stocks on the writing of biography. My version is that this biography was written soon after Eleanor's death and offers an extremely personal, affectionate and admiring narrative of her life which is shaped by the perspective of the period immediately following the Second World War. Stocks had access to personal letters which no longer seem to be available.

3. References and further reading

Alberti, Johanna (1989) *Beyond Suffrage: Feminists in War and Peace, 1914–1928*. Basingstoke and London: Macmillan.

Alberti, Johanna (1990) 'Elizabeth Haldane as a Women's Suffrage Survivor in the 1920s and 1930s', *Women's Studies International Forum*, 13 (1/2): 117–25.

Alberti, Johanna (1994a) 'British Feminists and Anti-Fascism in the 1930s', in Sybil Oldfield (ed.), *Women's Lives and Culture (s)*. London: Taylor & Francis.

Alberti, Johanna (1994b) 'Keeping the Candle Burning: Some British Feminists Between Two Wars', in Melanie Nolan and Caroline Daley (eds), *Suffrage and Beyond: International Feminist Perspectives*. Auckland, New Zealand: Auckland University Press and Australia: Pluto Press.

Alberti, Johanna (1994c) 'The Turn of the Tide: Sexuality and Politics, 1928–31', *Women's History Review*, 3 (2): 169–90.

Ayers, P. and Lambertz, J. (1986) 'Marriage Relations, Money, and Domestic Violence in Working-Class Liverpool, 1919–39', in J. Lewis (ed.), *Labour and Love*. Oxford: Blackwell.

Banks, Olive (1986) *Becoming a Feminist*. Brighton, Sussex: Wheatsheaf.

Basu, Aparna and Ray, Bharati (1990) *Women's Struggle: A History of the All India Women's Conference, 1927–1990*. New Delhi: Manohar.

Beddoe, Deirdre (1989) *Back to Home and Duty: Women Between the Wars, 1918–1939*. London: Pandora.

Black, Naomi (1989) *Social Feminism*. Ithaca and London: Cornell University Press.

Bland, Lucy (1985) 'In the name of Protection: the Policing of Women in the First World War', in J. Brophy and C. Smart (eds), *Women-in-Law*. London: Routledge.

Burton, Antoinette (1990) 'The White Woman's Burden: British Feminists and The Indian Woman, 1865–1915', *Women's Studies International Forum*, 13 (4): 295–308.

Burton, Antoinette (1991) 'The Feminist Quest for Identity: British Imperial Suffragism and "Global Sisterhood", 1990–1915', *Journal of Women's History*, 3 (2): 46–81.

Cass, B. (1983) 'Redistribution to Children and to Mothers: a history of Child Endowment and Family Allowances', in C. Baldock and B. Cass (eds), *Women, Social Welfare and the State*. Sydney: Allen and Unwin.

Cott, Nancy (1987) *The Grounding of Modern Feminism*. New Haven: Yale University Press.

Curthoys, Ann (1993) 'Feminism, Citizenship and National Identity', *Feminist Review*, 44: 19–38.

Davin, Anna (1978) 'Imperialism and Motherhood', *History Workshop*, 6 (Spring): 9–65.

Dyhouse, Carol (1989) *Feminism and the Family in England 1880–1939*. Oxford: Blackwell.

Fawcett, Millicent G. (1918) 'Equal Pay for Equal Work', *The Economic Journal*, March: 1–6.

Fleming, Suzie (1986) 'Eleanor Rathbone: Spokeswoman for a Movement', introduction to *The Disinherited Family*. Bristol: Falling Wall Press.

Fletcher, Sheila (1989) *Maude Royden: A Life*. Oxford: Blackwell.

Forbes, Geraldine (1979a) 'Women and Modernity: Child Marriage in India', *Women's Studies International Quarterly*, 2 (4): 407–19.

Forbes, Geraldine (1979b) 'Votes for Women: the Demand for Women's Franchise in India 1917–1937', in Vima Majumdar (ed.), *Symbols of Powers: Studies in the Political Status of Women in India*. Bombay: Allied Publishers.

Forbes, Geraldine (1981) 'The Indian Women's Movement: a Struggle for Women's Rights or National Liberation?', in G. Minault (ed.), *The Extended Family: Women and Political Participation in India and Pakistan*. Delhi: Chanakya.

Freeden, Michael (1978) *The New Liberalism: an Ideology of Social Reform*. Oxford: Clarendon Press.

Garner, Les (1984) *Stepping Stones to Women's Liberty: Feminist Ideas in the Women's Suffrage Movement, 1900–1918*. London: Heinemann.

Giles, Judy (1993) 'A Home of One's Own: Women and Domesticity in England 1918–1950', *Women's Studies International Forum*, 16 (3): 239–53.

Gittins, Diana (1982) *Fair Sex: Family Size and Structure 1900–1939*. London: Hutchinson.

Harris, Jose (1989) 'The Webbs, the Charity Organisation Society and the Ratan Tata Foundation: Social Policy from the Perspective of 1912', in M. Bulmer, J. Lewis and D. Piachaud (eds), *The Goals of Social Policy*. London: Unwin Hyman.

Harris, Jose (1994) *Private Lives, Public Spirit: Britain 1870–1914*. London: Penguin.

Harrison, Brian (1986) 'Women in a Men's House: the Women M.P.s, 1919–1945', *Historical Journal*, 29 (3): 623–54.

Harrison, Brian (1987) *Prudent Revolutionaries: Portraits of British Feminists between the Wars*. Oxford: Oxford University Press.

Hollis, Patricia (1987) *Ladies Elect: Women in English Local Government 1865–1914*. Oxford: Clarendon.

Holtby, Winifred (1934) *Women in a Changing Civilisation*. London: Bodley Head.

Holton, Sandra (1986) *Feminism and Democracy: Women's Suffrage and Reform Politics, 1900–1918*. Cambridge: Cambridge University Press.

Jeffreys, Sheila (1985) *The Spinster and Her Enemies: Feminism and Sexuality 1880–1930*. London: Pandora.

Kent, Susan K. (1987) *Sex and Suffrage in Britain, 1860–1914*. Princeton: Princeton University Press.

Kent, Susan K. (1993) *Making Peace: the Reconstruction of Gender in Interwar Britain*. Princeton: Princeton University Press.

Land, Hilary (1975) 'The Introduction of Family Allowances: an Act of Historical Justice?', in P. Hall, H. Land, R. Parker and A. Webb (eds), *Change, Choice and Conflict in Social Policy*. London: Heinemann.

Land, Hilary (1979) *The Family Wage* (Eleanor Rathbone Memorial Lecture). Liverpool: Liverpool University Press.

Land, Hilary (1990) 'Eleanor Rathbone and the Economy of the Family', in H. Smith (ed.), *British Feminism in the Twentieth Century*. Aldershot, Hampshire: Edward Elgar.

Land, Hilary (1992) Introduction to *Gender & History*, 4 (3): 283–92.

Levine, Philippa (1987) *Victorian Feminism, 1850–1900*. London: Hutchinson.

Levine, Philippa (1990) *Feminist Lives in Victorian England: Private Lives and Public Commitment*. Oxford: Blackwell.

Lewis, Jane (1975) 'Beyond Suffrage: English Feminism in the 1920s', *The Maryland Historian*, 6 (1): 1–17.

Lewis, Jane (1980) *The Politics of Motherhood: Child and Maternal Welfare in England, 1990–1939*. London: Croom Helm.

Lewis, Jane (1983) 'Eleanor Rathbone and the Family', *New Society*, 27 January: 137–9.

Lewis, Jane (1986) 'The Working-Class Wife and Mother and State Intervention, 1870–1918', in J. Lewis (ed.), *Labour and Love*. Oxford: Blackwell.

Lewis, Jane (1991a) *Women and Social Action in Victorian and Edwardian England*. Aldershot, Hampshire: Edward Elgar.

Lewis, Jane (1991b) 'Models of Equality for Women: the Case of State Support for Children in Twentieth-century Britain', in G. Bock and P. Thane (eds), *Maternity and Gender Policies: Women and the Rise of the European Welfare States, 1880s–1950s*. London and New York: Routledge.

Liddington, Jill (1989) *The Road to Greenham Common: Feminism and Anti-Militarism in Britain since 1820*. London: Virago.

Liddle, Joanna and Joshi, Rama (eds) (1986) *Daughters of Independence: Gender, Caste and Class in India*. London: Zed.

Light, Alison (1991) *Forever England: Femininity, Literature and Conservatism Between the Wars*. London and New York: Routledge.

Macadam, Elizabeth (1925) *The Equipment of the Social Worker*. London: Allen & Unwin.

Macadam, Elizabeth (1934) *The New Philanthropy*. London: Allen & Unwin.

Macnicol, John (1980) *The Movement for Family Allowances, 1918–45: A Study in Social Policy Development*. London: Heinemann.

McKibbin, R.I. (1977) 'Social Class and Social Observation in Edwardian England', *Transactions of the Royal Historical Society*, 5 (28): 175–99.

Manning, Leah (1970) *A Life for Education*. London: Gollancz.

Morgan, Maggie (1994) 'The Women's Institute Movement – the Acceptable Face of Feminism?', in Sybil Oldfield (ed.), *This Working-Day World: Women's Lives and Culture(s) in Britain 1914–1945*. London: Taylor & Francis.

Mayo, Katherine (1927) *Mother India*. London: Jonathan Cape.

Nair, Janaki (1990) 'Uncovering Zenana', *Journal of Women's History*, 2 (1): 14–25.

Pearson, Gail (1989) 'Reserved Seats – Women and the Vote in Bombay', in J. Krishnamurty (ed.), *Women in Colonial India*. Delhi: O.U.P.

Pedersen, Susan (1989) 'The Failure of Feminism in the Making of the British Welfare State', *Radical History Review*, 43: 86–110.

Pedersen, Susan (1990) 'Gender, Welfare and Citizenship in Britain during the Great War', *American Historical Review*, 95 (4): 983–1006.

Pedersen, Susan (1991) 'National Bodies, Unspeakable Acts: the Sexual Politics of Colonial Policy-making', *Journal of Modern History*, 63: 647–80.

Pedersen, Susan (1993) *Family, Dependence and the Origins of the Welfare State: Britain and France, 1914–1945*. Cambridge: Cambridge University Press.

Pedersen, Susan (1994) 'Eleanor Rathbone: the Victorian Family under the Daughter's Eye', in S. Pedersen and P. Mandler (eds), *After the Victorians*. London: Routledge.

Pugh, Martin (1992) *Women and the Women's Movement 1914–1959*. Basingstoke and London: Macmillan.

Pugh, Martin (1994) 'The Impact of Women's Enfranchisement in Britain', in C. Daley and M. Nolan (eds), *Suffrage and Beyond*. Auckland: Auckland University Press and London: Pluto Press.

Ramusak, Barbara (1981) 'Catalysts or Helpers? British Feminists, Indian Women's Rights, and Indian Independence', in G. Minault (ed.), *The Extended Family*. Delhi: Chanakya.

Ramusak, Barbara (1989) 'Embattled Advocates: The Debate over Birth Control in India, 1920–1940', *Journal of Women's History*, 1 (2): 34–63.

Ramusak, Barbara (1990) 'Cultural Missionaries, Maternal Imperialists, Feminist Allies: British Women Activists in India, 1865–1945', *Women's Studies Internal Forum*, 13 (4): 309–21.

Rendall, Jane (1993) 'Citizenship, Culture and Civilization: the Languages of British Suffragists, 1866–1874', in C. Daley and M. Nolan (eds), *Suffrage and Beyond*. Auckland: Auckland University Press and London: Pluto Press.

Riley, Denise (1988) *'Am I That Name?' Feminism and the Category of 'Women' in History*. London: Macmillan.

Roberts, Elizabeth (1985) *A Woman's Place: an Oral History of Working-class Women 1890–1940*. Oxford: Blackwell.

Rubinstein, David (1986) *Before the Suffragettes: Women's Emancipation in the 1890s*. Brighton: Harvester.

Rubinstein, David (1991) *A Different World for Women: the Life of Millicent Garrett Fawcett*. Hemel Hempstead: Harvester Wheatsheaf.

Scott, Joan (1988) *Gender and the Politics of History*. New York: Columbia University Press.

Semmel, Bernard (1960) *Imperialism and Social Reform*. London: Allen and Unwin.

Simey, T.S. (1964) *Social Purpose and Social Conscience* (Eleanor Rathbone Memorial Lecture). Liverpool: Liverpool University Press.

Smith, Harold (1981) 'The Problem of Equal Pay for Equal Work in Great Britain during World War II', *Journal of Modern History*, 53 (4): 652–72.

Smith, Harold (1984) 'Sex vs. Class: British Feminists and the Labour Movement, 1919–1929', *Historian*, 47 (4): 19–37.

Smith-Rosenberg, Carroll (1985) 'The New Woman as Androgyne: Social Disorder and Gender Crisis, 1870–1936', in *Disorderly Conduct: Visions of Gender in Victorian America*. New York and Oxford: Oxford University Press.

Spring-Rice, Margery (1939) *Working-class Wives*. Harmondsworth: Penguin.

Stanley, Liz (1992) *The Auto/biographical I*. Manchester: Manchester University Press.

Stoate, Deborah (1988) 'Raising the Curtain: Social Reform and Campaigns for Mothers 1900–1918', MA dissertation, University of Kent.

Stocks, Mary (1949) *Eleanor Rathbone: A Biography*. London: Victor Gollancz.

Strachey, Ray (ed.) (1936) *Our Freedom and Its Results*. London: Hogarth.

Summerskill, Edith (1967) *A Woman's World*. London: Heinemann.

Thane, Pat (1984) 'The Working Class and State "Welfare" in Britain, 1880–1914', *The Historical Journal*, 27 (4): 877–900.

Thane, Pat (1991) 'Visions of Gender in the making of the British Welfare State: the Case of Women in the British Labour Party and Social Policy, 1906–1945', in G. Bock and P. Thane (eds), *Maternity and Gender Policies*. London and New York: Routledge.

Thaper, Suruchi (1993) 'Women as Activists: Women as Symbols: A Study of the Indian Nationalist Movement', *Feminist Review*, 44 (Summer): 81–96.

Vellacott, Jo (1993) *From Liberal to Labour with Women's Suffrage: the Story of Catherine Marshall*. Montreal and Kingston, Canada: McGill-Queen's University Press.

Vicinus, Martha (1985) *Independent Women: Work and Community for Single Women 1950–1920*. London: Virago.

Ware, Vron (1992) *Beyond the Pale*. London: Verso.

Wiltsher, Anne (1985) *Most Dangerous Women: Feminist Campaigners of the Great War*. London: Pandora.

Yeo, Eileen (1992) 'Social Motherhood and the Sexual Communion of Labour in British Social Science, 1850–1950', *Women's History Review*, 1 (1): 63–87.

Index